*Examining Witnesses*

# MICHAEL E. TIGAR

JOSEPH D. JAMAIL CENTENNIAL CHAIR IN LAW

*University of Texas, Austin*

# Examining Witnesses

SECTION OF LITIGATION

*American Bar Association*

*This book is dedicated to my children.*

Library of Congress Catalog Card Number: 93-70127
ISBN: 0-89707-843-8

Discounts are available for books ordered in bulk. Special
consideration is given to state bars, CLE programs, and other
bar-related organizations. Inquire at Publications Planning &
Marketing, American Bar Association, 750 North Lake Shore Drive,
Chicago, Illinois 60611.

98          5  4  3  2

# Contents

# *Preface*

This book is by a trial lawyer for trial lawyers. I have been trying cases for more than twenty-five years and writing about trials for nearly that long. For thirty-five years, I have been soaking up as much trial lore as I could.

I continue to believe that "the great advocates of this and every other time in recorded history have been students of society and not carnival barkers." This statement covers a lot of territory. For purposes of this book, which deals with the art, science, and technique of advocacy, it means that to win trials, you have to understand how jurors and judges are persuaded by the drama of evidence and the rhetoric of lawyers.

In this book, I have tried to provide more than recipes. With a recipe, you can cook something. With theory, techniques, and skill—informed by experience—you can call yourself a cook.

I believe that good lawyering can be taught. We are talking about skill in this book. Mark Twain tells the story of a dozen men on trial for running a game of chance, to wit, "seven-up" or "old sledge." Their lawyer, old Jim Sturgis, brought witnesses to say that it was a game of skill, but deacons and dominies summoned by the prosecutor pronounced it a game of chance. So Sturgis convinced the judge to put four deacons and two dominies on the jury, along with six old gamblers, give them candles and a couple of decks of cards, and "just abide by the result." As the deliberations went on, various of the "chance" jurors sent word into court to borrow money from their friends. At dawn, the jury returned its unanimous verdict:

> We, the jury in the case of *Commonwealth of Kentucky vs. John Wheeler, et al.,* have carefully considered the points of the case, and tested the merits of the several theories advanced, and do hereby unanimously decide that the game commonly known as old sledge or seven-up is eminently a game of science and not of chance. In demonstration whereof it is hereby and herein stated, iterated, reiterated, set forth, and made manifest that, during the entire night, the "chance" men never won a game or turned a jack, although both feats were common and frequent to the opposition; and furthermore, in support of this our verdict, we call attention to the significant fact that the "chance" men are all busted, and the "science" men have got the money. It is the deliberate opinion of this jury, that the "chance" theory concerning seven-up is a pernicious doctrine, and calculated to inflict untold suffering and pecuniary loss upon any community that takes stock in it.

Good lawyering is not a game of chance, or luck, even though both of these may play a role. Day in and day out, in the tournament of trial, skill wins out.

Mostly, this book is about jury trials, civil and criminal. The American jury has taken a lot of criticism these past days; I think it is the best way to resolve the cases that can't be settled. You will find, however, that persuasive techniques are the same whether a judge or jury is deciding. Lawyers who think that they can present their case more "neutrally" to a judge will quickly learn from that mistake, though at their clients' expense.

Indeed, the theory and skill of persuasion may usefully be mastered by those in disciplines other than law practice. Historically, the study of rational and nonrational persuasion was the work of philosophers and dramatists before it became the province of lawyers. Today, as I show in Chapter One, social scientists and students of language contribute to our understanding of trials; representatives of these disciplines can usefully be retained to help prepare for specific cases.

Authors think they write clearly enough that nobody needs a road map through the thicket of their words. Editors, who fancy themselves advocates for readers, think otherwise. The editors usually win. Here is a road map.

This book is designed so that young lawyers and law students can read it from cover to cover and see how one moves from meeting your client, to seeing your case, to presenting your case. The chapter arrangement and internal headings permit all readers to find a discussion of a particular point even though they have not read the whole book. In addition, the Source Notes contain cross-references between chapters and citations to other material. There are no footnotes, but the Source Notes are keyed to the page on which relevant or cited material is discussed or to which the note material relates.

I hope everyone will read the first and last chapters, which contain my view—I hesitate to call it a theory—of the trial process and which put the remaining chapters in context. When you read these chapters, you will see why the book is called *Examining Witnesses* rather than *Trial Strategy*. In brief, the theory is that you cannot sum up on a case you have not tried nor open to the jury on a case you have not prepared.

Chapters Two, Three, Four, and Five deal with direct examination. Chapter Two contains the basic ideas on which all direct examination must be based and the basic techniques for presenting a witness—any witness. The remaining chapters identify types of witnesses you are likely to meet. As to each type, there is a discussion of the decision to put the witness on, witness preparation, and adaptations of the basic theory to that type of witness.

Chapter Six discusses demonstrative evidence and other illustrative materials. This chapter might have been put right after Chapter One because the methods I discuss will find a place at every phase of the trial, in your case and during cross-examination of the opponent's witnesses. I suggest that everyone read this chapter because it is based upon the theories of juror perception set out in Chapter One.

Chapter Seven deals with the discrete problem of adverse witnesses. It logically bridges the gap between direct and cross-examination, for the adverse witness is called in your case but is treated as if on cross-examination. The decisive difference in my view is that if the adverse witness bites you, the jurors are more likely to think it is your own fault than if a witness called by the other side does so.

Chapter Eight sets out basic rules about how to cross-examine, then immediately suggests that you need not always follow the rules. I have resisted suggestions to break this into two chapters. Learning the basic rules about cross-examination is rather like playing scales. You must start by mastering basic techniques. But you will not enjoy practicing scales unless you have a vision of one day playing a sonata, and you must have in mind that eventually your performance will have nuances of expression and technique that go beyond the basics. For me, the metaphorical connection between playing music and cross-examination is proved by what I term "the theory of minimal contradiction." Chapter Eight introduces and explains this theory and moves you from basic cross-examination techniques based on witness control to more advanced techniques based on likely juror responses.

Chapter Nine collects material on witnesses that pose particular difficulties and integrates each discussion into the theory set out in Chapter Eight.

Chapter Ten, on preparing witnesses to face the other side's cross-examination, is very detailed and intensely practical, even while overshadowed by the ethical considerations that govern you and your witnesses' conduct.

Chapters Eleven through Fourteen treat expert witnesses. The ABA Section of Litigation book *Expert Witnesses*, edited by Faust Rossi, so well and so completely covers this terrain that one may ask why I go on at such length. To begin with, I have not duplicated any of Professor Rossi's discussion of the legal principles governing expert testimony. Nor have I repeated much of the discussion in my chapter in that book.

These four chapters also permit me to integrate expert testimony into the overall themes of this book. Expert witnesses appear in almost every kind of lawsuit, and omitting discussion of them seemed unwise. Second, I have a particular theory about the varieties of expert testimony and think it useful to talk about "hard subjects" and "soft subjects." Third, I have a distinct point of view about selecting and presenting experts. Fourth, one chapter in the Rossi book was not enough space to air my ideas about cross-examining experts.

Chapter Fifteen is a kind of envoi, or leave-taking. It tries to weave the main strands of the book together.

# Acknowledgments

In this space, I would like to acknowledge what I have learned from others. Were I to do so completely, the list of debts would make this introduction a voluntary petition in intellectual bankruptcy.

My mentor in the law was Edward Bennett Williams; I owe him insights without number.

When I was eleven or twelve, I told my father that I wanted to be a lawyer. He went to his room and brought out a copy of Irving Stone's *Clarence Darrow for the Defense.* "Here," my dad said, "This is the kind of lawyer you should be. He fought for people's rights." I still have the books by and about Darrow I bought over the next several years. Darrow was a sound student of the traditions of our art; his example has taught me in many ways.

I also thank the jurors before whom I have appeared, even though some of their most instructive comments were the least flattering; wise judges for letting me try my cases; interfering judges for helping me figure out how to try my cases despite them; my opponents in similar vein; and law students and lawyers I have taught in trial advocacy programs for forcing me to rethink the reasons for approaching trials in a certain way.

I have stood side by side with many great trial lawyers—and listened and learned from them all. You know who you are. Samuel J. Buffone taught me a lot about being a trial lawyer and about all I know about being a law partner. The courage and skill of my South African comrades, Abdullah

Omar and Siraj Desai—who have labored all these years in defense of the African National Congress and other popular movements—have inspired me.

Thanks also to the clients who have let me help them defend their lives and their rights.

My wife, Amanda G. Birrell, has taught me some of the most important lessons. My children, Jon, Kate, and Elizabeth, have brought me the sense of joy that should suffuse the life of everyone who strives in our profession.

For friendship and help on this book, thanks also to my legal assistant Jim Patterson and to colleagues and friends John Koeltl, Charlie Wilson, and Pat Hazel.

In writing this book, I have borrowed here and there from my own articles and essays. I have also relied on the works of others from time to time and on reported cases. All the citations can be found in the Source Notes at the end of the book.

Whenever possible, I have illustrated points in this book with examples. Sometimes I have used trial transcripts or trial notes. These are nonprivileged materials. Sometimes I have wanted to capture the flavor of exchanges between myself and other lawyers, or with clients and witnesses, that are not part of any public record. The attorney-client and work product privileges prevent me from reporting most such exchanges verbatim. At other points, an actual transcript does not make the point clearly enough, so I have amalgamated several real experiences into a single series of questions and answers. When you see an exchange of that type reported in this book, it is a fictionalized account for illustrative purposes and is not meant to refer to any actual persons or events.

# Chapter One

## *The Theory of the Case: Dead Reckoning, Gestalt, and the Closing Argument*

If you would undertake a project, you should first envision it completed, then figure out what materials, tools, and techniques you must use to do it. If you want to build a house, you will first see it completed in your mind's eye, then perhaps sketch it.

If you are going to try a lawsuit, you must first think about the trial as a whole and then consider what materials (witnesses, evidence), tools (arguments, questions), and techniques (leading questions, styles of discourse) you will use. More broadly, if you are going to make a profession of trying cases, you must first understand the trial process and then analyze what your role in it will be.

This book lays out the tools you will need. It suggests the proper ways to use them. This chapter introduces the structure and approach that I have adopted.

Robert F. Hanley counseled lawyers to study the great works on rhetoric, paying particular attention to Aristotle's *Rhetoric* and Quintilian's *Institutio oratoria*. Aristotle, who wrote in the fourth century B.C., diagrammed the structure of persuasive discourse, and argued for needed reform. Quintilian's work, thought tedious by some, put the study of rhetoric at the center of any enlightened system of education. The formal study of rhetoric, it is said, began in Sicily to train pleaders who appeared before the courts to claim lands seized by a tyrannical government.

Edward Bennett Williams wisely likened trials to dramatic presentations, in which the lawyer is producer, director, actor, and stage manager, but all within the quite demanding constraints of the evidence and the law. If we take Williams seriously—and we should—we will study the role of drama in history. For our ancestors, the Greeks, drama is a principal means by which moral and political lessons are taught. The drama of a trial is a search for justice in a public forum.

Both rhetoric and drama are essential to the trial lawyer. This is true for three reasons. First, when we try lawsuits, we are doing something that has been done before, and for centuries past. Those who first wrote down and taught the techniques we still use believed that this craft was knowable and teachable. Some have said that it is not because they wish this power to influence events to be controlled by a few for the benefit of a very few. Others simply believe that trying cases is an art form, so that innate talent will always trump study and practice. I do not believe that.

Therefore, returning to our traditional roots reminds us that there are principles of presentation and argument that have been validated through experience. Gaining this experience vicariously does not require one to wade through Aristotle, although you would find him a lot easier to master than Quintilian. You can glean the point by reading accounts of old trials. If you choose this ostensibly easier path, you will probably be reading the words of lawyers who did study the ancient art and science of rhetoric.

Second, it is always easier to act yourself into right thought than to think yourself into right action. Training to be a trial lawyer involves doing things the right way until you acquire the habit. I found that to do this efficiently, I needed names for particular devices and techniques so that I could classify what I had done. For example, I want to learn how to use metaphor effectively. I want to know when to ask rhetorical questions. I want to advance from an accepted principle through a series of steps to the result I advocate. In each of these cases, I am using a device of classical rhetoric. Why trouble to invent new categories for what I am doing when the old ones lie ready at hand?

Third, by placing ourselves within a professional tradition, we reaffirm that we have a role in achieving justice. We are not simply hired speakers.

Rhetoric became formulaic and arid well before the Middle Ages. In the early history of the United States, the very term was used to denote a system of rules for stilted speech. Even today, the word may be coupled with "mere" to mean artificial elegance or empty phrasing. Happily, there has been a modern revival of rhetorical insight into communication and persuasion.

Rhetoric and its kindred discipline semiotics are not concerned solely with speech making. They deal with the use of language in persuasion, including the language that witnesses use to describe events. In my view, there has been too much emphasis on lawyer argument and not enough on how witnesses spell the difference between victory and defeat.

Ed Williams told of a motion argument he made as a young lawyer. He staggered into the old District of Columbia Court of General Sessions with two books under each arm. (This was before the days of photocopiers, when law books had to be carted to court.) A courthouse habitué, a lawyer whose office was no doubt the telephone booth in the courthouse hall, looked at him disdainfully and intoned, "Throw away those books, boy. Get yourself a witness."

Almost all legal education in one way or another deals with rhetoric in the narrow sense, that is, with the form of arguments. A brilliant and provocative modern literature exists on this subject. For us, it is enough to understand this characteristic of legal education. Most of the advocacy writing and speaking that law students do is purely legal argumentation to a hypothetical tribunal. Until the late 1980s, appellate advocacy competitions stressed debate skills to the exclusion of the students' ability to parse a factual record and restate factual contentions persuasively.

In law practice, young lawyers spend less time now than formerly with witnesses and more time with law books.

Then comes preparation to try the big case. Depositions and discovery responses have mounted up. A trial consultant is hired. The trial consultant begins—and sometimes ends—by working with the lawyers to develop an expanded opening statement. This statement is exhibited live or by video to one or more focus groups selected from the community where the case will be tried. In these exercises, the emphasis is on the persuasiveness of lawyer speech, not so much on evidence and witnesses.

Yet witnesses are far more important in trials now than two or three hundred years ago. When Andrew Hamilton addressed the jurors in the case of John Peter Zenger, the colonial newspaper editor, he told them they were summoned from the vicinage because they had "the best knowledge of the facts that are to be tried." Today, jurors with personal knowledge of the disputed facts may be disqualified. Indeed, Hamilton was probably guilty of hyperbole. Juror personal knowledge was not much of a factor in trials after the sixteenth century.

For the past hundred years, the rules disqualifying classes of witnesses have been struck down one by one. Parties, accomplices, married women—their alleged implied bias becomes simply one more fact for the jurors to consider in evaluating their testimony.

Yet judges, jurors, and experienced advocates report that lawyer performance when examining witnesses is lamentable. To avoid such a judgment of your own performance, this book moves from three important major premises into a series of chapters that contain insights into the witness examination problems you will encounter in trial. The three premises are:

1. Deciders perceive whole stories.
2. The way you tell it makes all the difference.
3. You always navigate by dead reckoning.

I discuss these in turn.

## DECIDERS PERCEIVE
## WHOLE STORIES

Harry Kalven and Hans Zeisel, in their pathbreaking work *The American Jury*, developed a way to measure the different attitudes of judges and juries in particular kinds of cases. The book, and the research since then, repays study.

People, including judges and jurors, understand and restate events in terms of stories. They take the available evidence and weave it into a coherent whole. If pieces are missing, they will fill in the gaps based on intuition, probability, or prejudgment about "what must have happened," or "how somebody like that would have acted." This process of filling in is called "confabulation" by some writers.

A lawsuit is a contest between two different stories. Jurors hear the judge's initial instructions and the opening statements and begin to build a possible story that tells them how the case should come out. As they receive evidence, they fit it into their story. It is harder to put across evidence that challenges a juror's tentative story than evidence that supports it.

What shapes a story? We have spoken of juror attitudes, the judge's instructions, and lawyer rhetoric.

Every trial lawyer knows that jurors' attitudes vitally affect the kind of story they will make from a given set of facts. Some lawyers hire jury researchers and *voir dire* consultants to help them identify people likely to be favorable. Other lawyers use only their experience in and of the community and their accumulated trial skills. For our purposes, we can ignore those preferences.

For example, assume that many people believe large corporations conspire with one another against the public welfare by fixing prices, evading environmental controls, or selling unsafe products. In some communities, a majority believes at least some of this.

It is obvious that if you are a plaintiff in an antitrust conspiracy case, you would put the conspiracy theory out front. That is an insight, but not much of one. The more important insight is that jurors who believe the conspiracy theory more readily infer conspiratorial behavior from concerted or parallel conduct. Your order of witnesses, presentation of documents, and points stressed with witnesses will emphasize that theme.

Now turn to the other side of the case. What will be the defendant's (or defendants') response? Unadorned denial is a possible stance, but it is almost always inadequate. There is no story to a denial and therefore no coherent alternative to the plaintiff's story. I say "almost always" because, in some criminal cases, a defense based entirely on reasonable doubt—a form of denial made possible only by the burden of proof and the trial judge's repeated insistence on it—may be tenable.

The defense story may be that the plaintiff signed a fair contract at a fair price and is trying to weasel out by invoking the antitrust laws. The story may be that the plaintiff got knocked around in honest competition.

Stories like these fulfill the three requirements of which we have been speaking. They appeal to jurors, they are consistent with the substantive legal rules about antitrust and the procedural rules about what may be proved in an antitrust trial, and they can be told by a lawyer in an opening statement and closing argument.

What is the evidence for saying that jurors view evidence in this way? Theoretical works, all based to some extent on Gestalt theory, support my view. For me, however, the most persuasive evidence has been given by jurors in their verdicts, reinforced by mock jury studies conducted by first-rate trial consultants. Jury studies even provide the opportunity to listen to deliberations; in a real case, you have to rely on the jurors' recollections of deliberation, if indeed the local rules permit you to talk to jurors at all.

If you agree that there must be a story, how will you choose it, and how will you tell it? Choosing the story is a necessary predicate to identifying witnesses and planning the trial. I often tell young lawyers to write the closing argument in a case right away, recognizing that some parts of the story will necessarily be incomplete and contingent.

Consider an example. A widow and her children come to you. Their husband and father has been killed. The death is a traumatic event. How will you, hired to be their champion, tell that story?

You are going to be limited by the substantive and procedural law, and you may need to do some legal research before you actually make choices. Who was killed? A diplomat in exile from his country. How was the death caused? By a bomb placed under his car. Who placed the bomb? We don't know yet, but we think the killing was politically motivated and carried out under orders from officials of a foreign government. What kind of political motivation do you mean? The present regime wants to silence its critics in exile.

Our story begins to become clear: What is, at minimum, a wrongful death case becomes a murder carried out for political purposes with the connivance of a foreign government. The dead man was killed for his laudable principles. The theories of liability multiply to include killing an internationally protected person (a diplomat) and violating customary international law. The problems mount, too, because making a foreign state and its officers parties and obtaining evidence of their conduct will be difficult.

As I reconstruct the facts more completely, I see legal rules that add to the power of the story. As I consider new legal rules, I am guided in looking for new factual insights. You may well decide that the most effective telling of your story requires you to argue for a change or extension of existing law; if so, well and good.

On the factual side, you are limited ethically and practically by the truth. As we shall see, truth can be elusive. Perceptions of events differ and recollections are debatable; rules of evidence may limit admissibility; you may not be able to find a witness. But truth is not so contingent that you are ever justified in disregarding it. Being careless with truth invites disaster in our adversary system, which encourages your opponent to take advantage of your heedlessness. To this practical concern, add the ethical rules under which we all function, obedience to which defines us as members of this profession.

For the defense, you will usually be presented with the opponent's complaint or indictment, and you can guess at the story behind the formulaic allegations. Too many times, I have come to a case to represent the defense and found this basic work not yet begun. Sometimes the defense team has not tried to "game out" the plaintiff's or the prosecutor's story. More often, it has focused only on disproof and denial rather than structuring a story of its own.

The story is more important than technique. If you respect the jurors, they will probably forgive your technical faults. But if you forget the story, you will lose. This book is entitled *Examining Witnesses*, but the following fourteen chapters are worth little unless you know that the whole of a trial is different from the sum of its parts. That, too, is a Gestalt insight.

In a criminal case, the jury convicted a developer of bank fraud. The defense lawyer had tenaciously battled every prosecution witness. The defense case even showed the logic of all the "deals." The jury convicted because the jurors agreed with the prosecution's story. "Nobody could make this much money honestly. There had to be a conspiracy."

Jury work tells us that most people in the developer's community are ready to believe that those in business conspire against the public good. But most people in that community also believe that it is possible and not necessarily bad for somebody to make a lot of money quickly by shrewd investing and taking risks. If the defendant is personally admirable to the jurors, this story has an even chance. But unless this positive story becomes the theme of defense, no amount of competent cross-examination can succeed in winning the jurors over.

It is not enough to show that the prosecution witnesses are thieves or that they are singing for lenient treatment. The defense story of the case is that this defendant profited in the same way that many others have lawfully done—by recognizing and seizing opportunity, and attendant risk, in a volatile market.

In an antitrust case, the plaintiffs' theory was that the corporate defendants had conspired to depress the prices paid for crude oil under a long-term contract with the plaintiffs, who owned an oil field. Faced with such an accusation, the quick answer is, "We deny the allegations, and we despise the allegators." But jurors are usually not content to disbelieve or reject a story put forward by one side. They want to see how and why people act, including the plaintiffs who bring lawsuits.

The defense story began by observing that there was a contract between the plaintiffs and the defendants. It was negotiated among experienced people on both sides of the bargain. A deal's a deal, and the claim of collusion was arguably just a means to jettison the agreed price.

In addition, the defendants were not making supernormal profits refining the crude oil. Indeed, because the crude they were buying was of such low quality, they were compelled to spend millions of dollars on sophisticated refining techniques to get value out of it.

The advocate cannot begin to see such a story unless she delves deeply into the client's life and lore. It empowers jurors to walk with them through the background and history of the issues they are to decide. From this survey emerges, in the well-planned case, principles on which jurors will agree, such as "a deal's a deal," and "the person who takes investment risk to make a useful product is entitled to a fair, competitive return."

In another case, an attending physician ordered a nurse to inject a patient with a drug. The physician was negligent, for the reference materials cautioned against using the drug except in life-threatening situations. The physician settled. In a trial involving the nurse, what is the story? Professional principles dictate that a nurse should not unhesitatingly follow orders to give dangerous medications. She should exercise independent judgment. In addition, the dose was allegedly administered contrary to the directions in the reference manual.

Once the professional rules are proved, the story might be that this is just another case of somebody following orders and denying responsibility. Don't we say to our kids, "Just because the older children do it, that is no reason for you to follow along"? Don't we hope that if we take our car to a garage, the mechanic will exercise independent judgment when the owner tells him to perform a dangerous and expensive repair that the mechanic's training and skill tell him should not be done?

Put another way, there is no such thing as worthwhile technique for its own sake. Technique must be in the service of a claim for justice, a story with a moral. Choosing a story is an exercise in seeing the whole case while keeping an open mind as new facts and legal theories appear.

Now to the job of telling the story. If it's a good story, you should be able, before your preparation is far along, to summarize it persuasively in a few sentences. From these sentences come the key words and concepts that you will stress with every witness. The unifying theme of this book is that every witness's testimony must be related, while that witness is on the stand, to the story you are telling.

Impossible, you say. Do that with a custodian of documents. I'm glad you asked. My client was charged with an attempt to evade income taxes, allegedly by understating his personal income by about $7 million over four years. He did report several hundred thousand dollars of income each year. We would not stipulate to the admissibility of the original tax returns from the IRS Service Center.

Part of our defense story was that our client was not in charge of the financial side of the partnership. He reported income on the basis of what he knew he had received. His manner of living did not bespeak greater income than he reported.

On cross-examination, we took the Service Center witness over the tax returns, noting that the income reported was very high—in the top bracket—and that our client paid a hefty amount of tax. We noted that our client had not taken questionable deductions or gone in for tax shelters or anything like that. We noted the various stamps on the forms, showing they had been checked for accuracy by IRS personnel. By the time this first witness left the stand, the jury had already begun to see that witnesses would bear out the story that we told in the opening statement.

Each of the remaining chapters contains signposts and directions for the remaining journey. For the plaintiff, who must go first and bear the burden of proof, telling the story means organizing witness testimony, deposition evidence, and exhibits. Ideally, all exhibits should have been premarked and as many as possible admitted by agreement or in a motion *in limine* process. In the ordinary case, the exhibit list is appended to the pretrial order.

All noncontroversial exhibit rulings should, by one means or another, be obtained before trial. Each party, the plaintiff and the defendant, must consider how many exhibit admissibility rulings to try and defer until trial. There are some evidentiary issues, such as the balance between probative value and time-wasting, that cannot be made in the abstract and must usually be deferred.

An advocate who is well prepared and skilled in argument is benefited by deferring evidence rulings until trial, on the theory that she will win more contested trial rulings than the opponent. One risk is that you are not as persuasive as you think you are. However, a party whose case rests to any great extent on uncertain evidentiary, procedural, or substantive law premises will want more certainty about what will be admissible. That advocate will make maximum use of the *in limine* motion and pretrial evidence ruling process, simply to have the ability to plan how the story should be told.

I have learned this lesson painfully. I had prepared a fairly complex affirmative defense to a criminal case and had brought witnesses great distances to support it. The defense was that the defendant had changed his name to avoid unjust prosecution and that the injustice he faced was provable. This was a form of "necessity" defense. The proposed jury instructions were drafted, waiting for the charge conference. Just before *voir dire* began, the prosecutor rose and made an oral *in limine* motion to exclude a theory of defense that sounded like the one I had planned to use. The judge listened, pretended to hear my response, and granted the motion.

Since I believe in a full opening statement when the defense is going to put on evidence, I had very little time to reconsider the story we were going to tell. This was federal court, and *voir dire* wouldn't take long. The moral of this: Find out what will be allowed, or at least be prepared to make changes. The obvious corollary is that pretrial rulings on evidence and issues help ensure that your opening statement does not make promises the judge is going to prevent you from keeping.

In that case, we were able to shorten our story and still have it make sense, and we won. The jury acquitted on two counts, and the court of appeals reversed the third count with directions to acquit. In retrospect, the judge may have helped us by forcing us to try a leaner, cleaner case.

We did not retreat to bare denial. Rather, we decided, first, that we would not put on a defense at all. The prosecutor would be left with a case of somebody who had two different names that he used at different times. The prosecutor was not much freer to attribute a motive to the defendant's use of another name than we were.

The case then became one about what harm could possibly have been done. What was all the fuss about? Roy Rogers was born Leonard Sly, John Wayne started out as Marion Morrison, and Gary Hart (then a political contender) was once Gary Hartpence.

Pretrial clarity on evidence matters saves time and keeps you from doing time-wasting exercises that detract from your story—and indeed from your image as storyteller. "Were these records made and kept in the regular course of business?" "Was it in the regular course of business to make and keep such records?" "And were the entries . . . ?" And so on. Formulas such as this are part of our lawyer lore, but when we exhibit them in court we disempower the jurors and reinforce bad stereotypes of lawyers. Cicero was a brilliant lawyer. Yet when he wished, in argument, to mock a lawyer on the other side, he did so by acting out the formalist incantations of Roman civil procedure. These he contrasted with the work of one who practiced a useful art, like defense of the Roman Republic. You adulterate the story by ornamenting it with useless ritual.

Those who try cases with me grow tired of my repeating, "Go to court every day and say your case." I intend this sentence to describe what we have been discussing. Know the story of your case. Be able to evoke that story in few words. With every witness, every exhibit, every objection, every gesture, consider how to underline some part of your story. Repeating the sentence helps to guard against regarding some witnesses as simply routine or some tasks as unrelated to victory. Your opponent, the judge, your client, busy witnesses, and your own sloth may nudge you toward changing a sensible order of proof. Don't fall for it.

## THE WAY YOU TELL IT MAKES
## ALL THE DIFFERENCE

I could hunt among the ancient treatises on rhetoric to illustrate this point, but I prefer a more modern example. Here is Professor Jack Balkin, talking about a torts case that we probably all studied in law school.

> Every torts professor has a favorite hypothetical about causal responsibility—some wildly improbable and outrageous chain of events triggered by the defendant that somehow leads inexorably to the plaintiff's injury. I have always been partial to the facts of United Novelty Co. v. Daniels. In Daniels the defendant negligently set the nineteen-year-old decedent to work cleaning a coin-operated machine with gasoline; the decedent worked in a small room warmed by a gas heater with an open flame. The gasoline vapors surrounding the machine ignited when a rat ran from the machine into the flame, caught fire, and then ran back toward the machine, causing an explosion that killed the decedent. Naturally, the defendant company argued that it was not causally responsible for the freak accident. Nevertheless, the court upheld a jury verdict against the company because it could have foreseen that setting the decedent to work in the room under these conditions was unduly dangerous.
>
> The opinion in Daniels takes up barely a page in the reporters, but within this miniature one can find many of the most common structures of argument about human moral responsibility that occur in legal discourse. Consider, for example, the arguments that the defendant company might make (and probably did make) on its behalf:
>
> (1) The explosion was caused by the unpredictable movement of a rat, not by the defendant's negligence.
>
> (2) When the decedent began cleaning the machine with gasoline, it was completely unforeseeable that a

rat would jump out of the machine, run headlong toward an open flame, catch fire, and then run back precisely where it could do the most damage.

(3) Decedent was at fault for cleaning the machine with gasoline in the first place. The decedent must have known of the danger when the decedent voluntarily began to work.

Next consider the plaintiff's likely responses:

(1) Although the rat was the immediate cause of the explosion, the real cause was the defendant's ordering the decedent to work under unsafe conditions.

(2) It is completely foreseeable that if you set someone to work in a small room filled with gas vapors and an open flame, there is an unacceptable risk of an explosion.

(3) The decedent cannot be held responsible for the explosion, because the decedent was following the orders of the defendant employer and was a minor.

As one would expect, the defendant's arguments are designed to minimize the defendant's causal, legal, and moral responsibility, while the plaintiff's arguments are designed to enhance them. More importantly, however, each side recharacterizes the facts to support its position, emphasizing some details, minimizing or even omitting others—creating a coherent portrait of the situation from the raw materials of experience. Like all pictures, these characterizations are selective, for to record experience is always also to re-order and even to suppress it. In the second argument presented above, for example, the defendant describes the situation in minute detail, while the plaintiff speaks in more general, abstract terms. In this way each side can make plausible its claim about the foreseeability or unforeseeability of the decedent's injuries.

Balkin uses the terms "picture" and "portrait" instead of "story," but he is talking about lawyers and the trial process in the same way that we have been. "Story" is more descriptive of the rhetorician/dramatist/troubadour. "Picture" is metaphorical, but also helpful. Manuals on photography tell you to decide what will be the main subject of your picture and tell you to choose a point of view that will emphasize that subject.

When a witness describes a scene, you want to use enough detail to make the jurors have a mental picture. When proving how the accident happened, plaintiff's counsel will ask the witnesses to start by talking about the workplace and the boss's control of people's schedules and duties. By the time the decedent gets into that room, the plaintiff wants the jury to picture acts being directed and controlled by others.

There are two aspects to "how you tell it." The first is the rhetorical exercise of structuring the argument to lay the facts in a certain order and pattern. The second is understanding how principles of proof serve or disserve the advocate's effort to present the pattern.

## STRUCTURE AND ORDER

In the incendiary rat case, both sides begin with accepted principles of personal injury litigation. The defense stresses that we are all responsible for our own actions. We all ought to feel good about having such a sense of responsibility and about expecting others to have it. Therefore, we will not hesitate to treat the plaintiff's decedent as we would want to be treated—as someone who freely chose a certain course of action—even when the consequences are uncompensated injury.

The plaintiff will stress the employers' superior knowledge and control of the situation—its power to affect events, including the power to put the decedent in a place of danger. We should, as community representatives, want to have and enforce rules about the exercise of such power.

Professor Balkin's article, however, is not about rat and gasoline cases. He shows how the basic positions I have just described, which he calls "individualist" versus "communalist," take a very similar form throughout the law of torts. Similar sets of ideologically based pairings can be found in contracts, property, or criminal law—indeed, every field of law that is shaped by the adversary system.

A litigator faced with two persuasive ways to describe the same facts may have a sense of insecurity or unease. If either formulation may be validated by the verdict of a jury, how will the jurors choose? The answer will lie in the ability of the lawyers on both sides and on the choices made by judges who preside at trials and review the results of trials.

Being able to render issues in these opposing, mutually exclusive pairings does not mean that legal rules are indeterminate or without principle. The statement of issues is paradigmatic, simply a structure to be filled in each case with particular factual content. When the content has been added, then juries and judges must exercise judgments based on their perceptions and, inevitably, their own sense of rightness.

In our daily lives, we often say, "that's just a value judgment," or "that's just your opinion," meaning that all such judgments or opinions are unverifiable and therefore arbitrary. Yet, as lawyers, we must constantly embrace value judgments about such things as responsibility, "just desserts," and rights. We must exhibit evidence to jurors and make arguments to build images of reality and validate the opinions and judgments that we want the jury to use in deciding.

Nor, as we shall see, will there always be a bright line between appeals to principle and arguments about facts. The line that Aristotle tried to draw, separating ethical, logical, and emotional arguments from one another, has long since proven impossible to maintain. Similarly, the Aristotelian distinction between matters merely probable and those demonstrable has evaporated, at least in litigation, and probably in the sciences as well.

Whether we like it or not, jurors bring all their faculties to bear in making sense of a case: intuition, feeling, and attitude, as well as the ostensibly rational processes of inductive and deductive reasoning. Therefore, persuasion through evidence must reach all of these faculties. To return to the Hanley and Williams counsels, we are seeing the unity of rhetoric and theater.

## PROOF OF FACTS

I once wrote,

> Facts are mutable because we never see them in litigation. We see instead their remnants, traces, evidences, fossils—their shadows on the courthouse wall. The witnesses recount: They have perceived, do now remember, can express and want to tell the truth, more or less. Things—paper, hair, bones, pictures, bullets—parade by, each attached to a testifier who alone can give them meaning. At proceeding's end, the advocate will try to impose some order on all of this, and convince the trier that it makes a certain kind of picture.

This passage summarizes the rules of evidence. A witness is more or less valuable based on perception, memory, expression, and veracity. It is an article of adversary system faith that every witness should be tested on these four elements in the presence of the trier of fact. Departures from this rule are justified only as permitted by exceptions to the hearsay rule or by showing that the rule does not apply because an utterance is "not offered for its truth."

With respect to objects, the passage recalls familiar lore: an object must be sponsored by a witness who shows that it is something that the jury should consider. The defendant's fingerprint on a gun is dramatic but irrelevant unless a witness connects the gun, and the defendant's chance to touch it, with the homicide.

In our daily lives, we make decisions based on what we have seen *and* heard. In trials, we must make sure that every out-of-court statement that is repeated satisfies a rule. Is it offered for the truth of it? If so, is it nonhearsay because of Rule 801? If not, can it come in under Rules 803 or 804? Have we remembered to satisfy the personal knowledge requirement, which applies to hearsay declarants as well as to witnesses on the stand? To be a trial lawyer, you must so internalize rules, including the hearsay rule, that moving through a foundational showing becomes second nature.

The main point, however, is that it is misleading to talk about "the facts" as constituting some objective reality to be "discovered" in past time. The "facts" will be "found" by jurors putting together the tales of witnesses. In this process, the jurors will be guided by their internal attitudes as well as attitudes imposed by the court's instructions.

We can see this in another way. Suzuki, a writer on Zen, drew a series of pictures of an ox and a man, each picture framed by a circle. The last circle was empty and was titled "The Ox and the Man Have Departed." By the time we get into a lawsuit, the ox and the man are gone. We start with a blank circle—and must fill it with the evidence that we find.

Let us see how this works in the incendiary rat case. For our purposes, Balkin is wrong in saying that "the defendant describes the situation in minute detail, while the plaintiff speaks in more general, abstract terms." That may be the form of utterance in an appellate argument, but at trial the plaintiff has as much interest in factual precision and detail as the defendant.

In deciding the order of proof, along come the familiar concepts of primacy and recency. Start strong, because people remember beginnings. End strong, because people remember things that happened more recently. In the structure of a trial, first events and last events of a particular phase—such as the plaintiff's case-in-chief—hold jurors' attention.

To begin, we want an image of this room—and of its dangers. Jurors cannot accept a story unless they can envision it. The plaintiff's evidence assembles the locations and objects and then introduces the events. The events will seem to be a foreseeable consequence of the arrangement of the objects, for which the defendant is responsible.

The defendant's evidence will focus upon the decedent's choices and decisions. After focusing on these choices, the proof introduces the objects as logically placed to avoid foreseeable dangers. Note that I have put Balkin's third defense contention—contributory negligence—first. I would do this even in a jurisdiction that has abolished or limited contributory negligence. Stories are about "just desserts," and the defendant must, in order to win, displace responsibility onto the decedent for his own death. "I was careful enough" is not only defensive, but it invites the plaintiff to embark on the risk/cost/benefit calculus that paints the defendant into a corner.

We repeatedly play out the adversary process by example. Let us pause now to see it in this case. The defendant employer takes the stand and testifies about the room where the death occurred. What is the most important point for cross-examination? Without waiting to see how, or whether, the witness trips up, you should be able to choose. The most important point will be raised first, for primacy's sake. Moreover, the jurors expect that when you rise to cross-examine your opponent, you will inflict some damage.

The most important point must be one that you can make by cross-examination, without useless arguing with the witness. It must not be the sort of point that is better left to final argument. It must, in short, be nearly foolproof. It must be a point that tells *your* story rather than one that deflects or denies the other side's. In the suicidal arsonist rat case, the plaintiff's point is that the defendant set the scene. He will not likely deny it. Your strong opening on cross takes the defendant through the charts, pictures, and objects with which you began your own case, getting agreement along the way.

One can imagine key elements of the cross-examination of the owner:

Q. You own United Novelty?
A. My family and I do.
Q. You run the business on a day-to-day basis?
A. I guess you could say that.
Q. No. Please tell me. Who runs the business?
A. I do.
Q. You hired Mr. Daniels?
A. Yes.
Q. You hired all the people who work at the company headquarters?
A. All except the accountant.
Q. He comes in only once a week, and your wife chose him, right?
A. Right.
Q. If you see a machine that needs cleaning, you decide who will clean it and when?
A. Yes.
Q. You have the power to say where machines are put on the company premises?
A. I guess that's right.
Q. Don't guess. Do you have the power?
A. Sure.
Q. You are the man in charge?
A. Yes.
Q. You can fire people who won't take directions?
A. I have done that.
Q. You tell people what to use to clean dirty machines?

You could think up dozens more questions, each of which shows a way in which this witness is in charge. The witness wants to tell you these things because he likes to think of himself as a person in charge. As long as you pitch the questions to that desire to be seen as important, you will probably get the answers you want. You can plot out this line of cross-examination before trial, taking care not to prolong it unduly.

But that is obvious, you say. Not so, say I. We make notes on a pad of paper as the witness testifies on direct. Usually, we draw a vertical line on each page—one side for notes of the testimony, the other side to make notes of points for cross. When the direct is over, we jump up and try to spear the witness on something in the direct that jumps up at us off of our notes. We forget our careful game plan. I have seen this done too often, and confess to having done it myself.

Hew to your planned cross. Use the surefire stuff. Then take a few "opportunity shots," and end strong. Remember recency.

Economy of motion is matched by parsimony of expression. The poet Stevie Smith wrote:

> It is the privilege of the rich
> To waste the time of the poor.

Lawyers think their privilege is to waste the jurors' time. The jurors will get even.


## ARE YOU SURE?

One evening in Umtata, South Africa, my friend Ken Frazier began teaching the trial advocacy program for students at the University of the Transkei. He started by asking each one to introduce himself or herself and to say a few words. Then he strode to the lectern of the classroom and said something like:

"Listen to you. I got here only today. I am just a black trial lawyer from Philadelphia, but I can't help noticing that most of you introduce yourselves timidly, tentatively. Maybe it is the atmosphere we have created here without meaning to do it. Maybe it is a part of the political system here in South Africa. But let me ask you something. You are going down the road and you need directions, and you ask somebody and they say, kind of hesitantly, 'Well, I guess it's maybe, well, about a mile and then I think you turn right.' Then, you ask the next person you come to, and they say with great conviction, 'Go down this road one mile. At the BP station, turn right and go one-half mile. It's on the left. You can't miss it.' Which one of those two people are you going to trust? I'll tell you. You are going to trust the person who looks like they know what they are talking about and believes what they are saying."

I think that makes the point.

## YOU ALWAYS NAVIGATE
## BY DEAD RECKONING

Sailors use a method called "dead reckoning." You know where the voyage began. You know your course and speed, and you have some idea about the current. You can plot an approximate, dead-reckoning fix. But you cannot be sure where you are until you sight land or a fixed object on the sea, such as a navigational buoy.

In trial, you have a similar experience. You can't know for sure what the jurors are thinking about your presentation until they come in at the end and give you their verdict. You look for clues, but the available clues are notoriously unreliable. In the first criminal trial in which I was involved for the defense, I was seated on the back row behind my mentor, Edward Bennett Williams. One of the jurors seemed to be "with us." He smiled at all the "right" times, he followed the significant points we were making. He nodded affably to us in the halls. When deliberations began, the other jurors elected him foreman, and he led the jury to guilty verdicts on eight out of seven possible counts.

Given the limitations on dead-reckoning navigation, what must you do?

First, keep to the trial plan you began to develop when you got the case; hasty change is bound to be based on inadequate data.

Second, have markers for yourself and the jury that predict your progress and then permit you to go back and refer to points along the way. Everything is leading to the closing argument, when you will try to bring the elements of the story together. Put your story, and its elements, clearly at the first opportunity, in the opening statement, and in *voir dire*. Tell the story and outline the evidence.

Third, use demonstrative evidence to underscore key themes in your story.

You have the best chance of predicting how the jurors will vote if you understand and identify with them and their life experiences.

It matters to jurors who is speaking, and who they are. If you are a prosperous-looking white male, an urban black female juror will probably approach the story you tell with caution, perhaps even suspicion. If you think to navigate past this obstacle by overcorrecting your course and focusing undue attention on that juror, you will make the problem worse because you are going to be viewed as condescending.

Your task is to step outside of your own education and upbringing and try to see the world from all the different perspectives that jurors will bring to bear. In argument, all trial lawyers use analogies from everyday life. Your analogies are worth nothing if they describe an everyday life that might be yours but is foreign to the jurors. You live in a law firm. You might hang out with people who make, or think they make, broad-gauge economic and social decisions, weighing and sifting and deciding at a distance. Most jurors deal with the consequences of those decisions—they buy the products, breathe the air, pay the prices, try to get along. Brecht asked,

In the evening when the Chinese Wall was finished
Where did the masons go?

In twenty-five years of lawyering, I have found nothing
so striking about my profession as its members' cultivated
ignorance of what people think of them and their clients.
That sort of arrogance is costly. Good jury researchers can
help us overcome it. Their work need not be unbearably
costly. In fairly large cases, a couple of good jury studies
will be helpful—I am not talking about full-blown dress
rehearsals, but more modest efforts designed to make sure
you are on the right track. Of course, in the "big" case, the
client may be able to pay for the full treatment. In *pro bono*
cases, some of the brilliant jury consultation firms will
volunteer their time. You can get the same sort of help from
political consultants, whose help I have found invaluable
in cases where we had no money for formal research.

If you are going to use this kind of expertise to help you
navigate, get it early. Lawyers tend to wait until the case
approaches trial before retaining a consultant. It would be
better to get help as soon as you have your story in some
tentative form, to help you make sure you are not making
early and significant errors.

The jurors are going to size you up. They will look as
well as listen. They will watch how you treat the lawyers
you work with and the paralegals who help you, the court
personnel, and the witnesses.

If I am going to navigate, I like local knowledge. Read
all the papers in town. Listen to all the radio stations. Think
about what churches people attend, who their political
leaders are, what the issues that concern their daily lives
are. Even in your own town, it is so easy to live apart from
the people around you.

I used to have a favorite saying about this, but I ruined
it. I was arguing in front of Judge James Leff in the New
York Supreme Court, Criminal Part, and urging him to take
a kindly view of my clients' political views. I dragged out

my saying, "And avert thine eyes from the lore of the wise, that have honor in proud men's sight. The simple, nameless herd of humanity hath deeds and faith enough for me."

"That's from Euripides," I added, smugly, I guess.

My opponent, a redoubtable chunky Assistant DA from Homicide with a heavy Brooklyn accent, rose to respond.

"Your Honor, I don't know about these Greek poets. I know when I take my pants to the tailor, he says, 'Euripides?' And I says 'Yeah, Eumenides.' "

In sum, understanding the voices and aspirations of jurors helps you to understand whether the course you think you are steering is the same one the jurors are following.

You are going to find your own voice through experience. It had better be your own, and not a borrowed one, because none of us is good enough to maintain pretense through a long trial. Jurors are quick to know who is being a phony and who is not. In mock jury survey work, trial consultant Hale Starr asks the panel whether they think the presentations were being made by an actor playing a lawyer or by a real lawyer. It's a good question. You want the jurors to think you are a real lawyer, with a real client who will really hurt if this case comes out the wrong way. Everybody knows that television actors' "clients" don't really win or lose.

As you navigate, remember also that you are trying to reach all of the jurors, to bring their collective judgment to bear. A good jury is a good cross-section, and you want their different life experiences, backgrounds, knowledge, and recollection to come together in the jury room.

When you make your closing argument, you will tell the jurors where you think the voyage has taken you. The clearest way to trace the voyage is by the markers you have passed along the way. The closing evokes the witnesses and exhibits in a coherent pattern that fits the story. That pattern cannot be made anew. Its elements must be found objects, gathered up from the signals you have sent in examining witnesses. That is, your witness examinations must have been properly crafted to leave your most persuasive points ready to revisit. The exhibits you have used now reappear in logical order.

Dead reckoning takes us past markers familiar to us, if only in our minds. We should have made this journey many times before. I have seen so many lawyers who take their cases one witness, or one day, or even one week at a time. They have not put together in mind's eye all the testimony and all the exhibits to have a firm sense of the whole voyage. This is wrong.

In federal criminal cases you are entitled to a "theory of the case" instruction. Regardless of forum or case, you should always draft and request such an instruction. Having the judge tell the jurors your theory—and note that you are entitled to a verdict if the evidence supports it—does more than help put your story across. The judge's involvement may cause jurors to examine your story more seriously than they otherwise would, as a plausible alternative to the view they had been inclined to take.

None of these suggestions means that you should continually turn to the jury like a one-person Greek chorus to draw the appropriate lesson from some bit of testimony or try to provide a voice-over as in a B movie. Usually, you must wait till closing argument to bring it all together.

"Members of the jury, do you remember when I spent about a half-hour reading Mr. Smith all the things he said before, and making sure he said them, and that he was under an oath when he did? I guess some of you must have said, 'What is that lawyer doing, wasting time with that?' I want to suggest I was doing something very important. I was giving Mr. Smith a chance to deny he swore to those things, and he didn't deny it. I didn't want anybody in this courtroom to say we didn't give him a chance. Because make no mistake, the evidence that you heard shows something pretty serious. This fellow Smith tells two different stories under oath. He is a person who would lie under oath, and he admits that. You have got to decide whether he lied here in your faces, and whether what he told when it was all fresh and before the prosecutors put pressure on him wasn't the real story. In order to decide that, you would need Mr. Smith to admit that he said those things, and that's what I was asking him to do."

In this example, you are calling to mind markers left along the way and suggesting to jurors a way of analyzing the case for themselves. This is not a new insight. Here is what Dan O'Connell, the great Irish advocate, said about it:

> You all know how to argue to a group of people who are set against your basic beliefs. You never get them by showing them that you have got the matter all worked out, in a set speech like the catechism—or whatever might be the Protestant equivalent of the catechism.
>
> We can't drag the jurors along with us. Make them imagine that their movements are directed by themselves. Pay their capacities the compliment of not making things too clear. Rather than elaborate reasonings, throw off mere fragments, or seeds of thought. These will take root and shoot up into precisely the conclusions we want.

To use the metaphor with which I began, your closing argument is a detailed plan of the house you have built by your examination of witnesses.

# Chapter Two

## *Direct Examination:*
## *Friendly Folks*

### WHY DIRECT EXAMINATION
### IS DIFFICULT

Direct examination of a friendly witness is the most difficult part in the trial lawyer's repertoire. You have understood the story of the case. The witness understands it, too. Yet the witness is forbidden by the rules of evidence and procedure from telling the story.

Why "forbidden"? The witness may not narrate but must respond to your questions one at a time. How often do friends sitting around swapping stories interrogate one another in this way? Not often, although some forms of discourse are more clearly interactive than an exchange of narratives.

The witness must speak from personal knowledge. This is a bedrock requirement of evidence law and a counsel of procedure. Yet, in daily speech, our narratives are a blend of observation, intuition, surmise, and speculation. In court, the witness who strays from the observable "facts" courts a double danger: the opponent's objection will be sustained, and the opponent gains fuel for cross-examination.

In daily conversation, a person usually speaks colloquially, even elliptically, leaving out ideas and events that are mutually understood among the conversants. So, the question becomes, How should the witness be when testifying? How should she show respect for the jurors and self-confidence in what is being told? How can she be ready with enough detail so the story makes sense to those who have never heard it before?

29

In addition, the witness must do the unfamiliar task of testifying in a courtroom, more or less isolated from those who are to evaluate the testimony. The questioner will be in one place, the intended audience in another, perhaps within two entirely different lines of sight.

All of this summarizes the *witness's* difficulties, which the lawyer must help her to surmount. The lawyer's problem does not end there, however. Direct examination is difficult because, as lawyers, we get relatively little practice at it. When our clients or other "friendly" witnesses are being deposed, we "defend" the deposition rather than directly examining them on our own. The deposition to preserve trial testimony is relatively rare. When we take depositions, the rules of relevance are relaxed and, most of the time, we are permitted to examine using leading questions. Here, again, we are not practicing the skills of courtroom direct examination.

These skills involve both positive and negative aspects. We must adopt a persuasive manner and help the witness and jurors. We must avoid setting up the witness for needless objections and cross-examination. In both aspects, we are doing anticipatory deconstruction, breaking down the witness's story into testimonial elements while at the same time critically examining each piece of it to determine how it fits with our whole story and how it can be made persuasive and attack-proof.

I have labeled this chapter "Friendly Folks" and the next one "Neutral Fact Witnesses" to describe important differences in witnesses' attitudes. The friendly witness wants to help. The neutral witness wants to get it right. Both goals are naive, and the direct examiner must help any witness avoid being frustrated by the limits that a trial process puts on the natural desire to tell a whole story coherently and be done with it.

So we have two major tasks. First, we must make the witness comfortable with what he is to do. Second, we must prepare ourselves to serve as an intermediary between the witness and the trier of fact.

## PREPARING THE
## FRIENDLY WITNESS

You and the witness are in your office. It is days or weeks before the witness will testify. Here are some things you might say. Edit the narrative as needed, because procedures vary. In real life, it will not be one-sided. The witness will want to interrupt with questions. Make sure someone else from your office, or connected with the case in a way not to disrupt the lawyer-client privilege, is sitting in. Think about whether notes you take are discoverable.

"Hello. Have a seat. Can I get you some coffee, or a soft drink or water?"

Do not order somebody else to do this.

"I wanted to get a chance to talk about the trial and answer your questions. This should take a couple of hours, but I think you set aside the time so we can really do a good job.

"Have you ever been a witness in court before? Tell me about that. . . . Well, just for myself, I'd like to go through it all with you, but I'll cut it short if I am talking about something you already know. Every case is different. Every judge, jury, and courtroom are different.

"Here is a diagram of the courtroom we are going to be in. It might not be just like this one, because there can always be changes. But this is basically it. You will be out here in the witness room until we call you. They have this rule that you can't sit in and listen to the testimony of any other witness. Now, when you are done testifying, we can ask the judge to let you stay for the rest of the trial, and usually she'll grant that.

"When you are called, the bailiff will walk with you into the courtroom. I'll make sure that Mr. Wilson from my office is there, too. I know you'll be a little nervous, but just walk right in. You'll walk up to this desk here, where a woman is sitting, just in front of the judge's bench. She should stand up, if she's paying attention. She'll say, 'Raise your right hand.' Do that, and she'll ask you to swear that you'll tell the truth. Do you have a religious objection to swearing the oath—I mean, would you rather affirm that you will tell the truth?"

Always ask this, and if the answer is "yes," work it out beforehand with the clerk.

"Then, you take your seat right here in the witness chair. Put your hands in your lap, sit up straight, and look at me. I'll be standing right here.

"Now comes the hard part. You know more about what you saw than anybody else in the world. More than I do, more than [the client], certainly more than the other side. The lawyer on the other side knows you know what you're talking about, and he might try to make some objections or interrupt us to keep you from telling what you know in the most effective way possible.

"I need a big favor from you. I need you to trust me on this. I am the lawyer for [the client]. It's my job to make sure that if the lawyer on the other side makes some objection or interruption, that gets handled.

"Another thing. There are all these rules in court. They don't let you just come in and tell your story like you know it. Maybe some of what you know is based on what you heard from other people. Or the jury can understand it better if we show them some pictures of the scene. For a lot of reasons, the way we do this is that I ask questions and you answer to the jury.

"In a few minutes, we will go over all the things you know. I have some pictures here, and I will be making sure they show the intersection the way it was. Everything you have to do in court can be summed up like this: Listen to every question, no matter if I ask it, the other side's lawyer asks it, or the judge asks it. Listen to it. Then take a second or two to make sure you've got the question in mind. Then answer that question straight and true. If the question is not clear, just say, 'I'm sorry, I don't understand what you're asking.' "

At this point, you might have a chart with the rules on it.

1. Listen to the question.
2. Take a second or two.
3. If the question isn't clear, say so.
4. If the question is clear, answer that question.

"If you remember these principles, you'll do fine. Now, maybe you're thinking, 'Who is this bozo telling me I'll do fine? What if I get confused and flustered in there and he asks me a question and I forget what I'm supposed to say?' Or maybe you watched some lawyer program on television and you're thinking, 'What do I do when the other side's lawyer puts his face about a foot from mine and hollers cross-examination at me?'

"For what it's worth, I think those are great questions. The answer to both of them is the same. Do just what's on the chart. Let's go through it.

"I ask a question. I don't know as much about the case as you do, so the question doesn't seem to make sense. You pause and say, 'I don't understand.' Or suppose I ask you, 'Did the red Ford stop here at the stop sign?' And you know it did, but then it started right up again and went on through, even though Stacy Wilson was in the crosswalk.

"All I'm asking is, please, you've got to trust me to know the case, trust me to know that you know all the important facts, and I want the jury to hear all you know. So just answer the question I asked, and then I will ask the next question that brings out more of the story. Also, there are all these rules about the form of questions I can ask, and the way things have to be done. If you let me ask the questions, then I can try to make sure we let the jury know the truth, and do that in the way the rules require.

"There's a whole other reason for listening, pausing, and just answering the question. That's the way we're going to control the lawyer on the other side. Because you are going to treat him the same way you treat me. Listen to his question. Then pause. In that pause, I get a chance to do my job. If the question is improper, or if he is being abusive and in your face, I can stand up and object. If the judge sustains the objection, good. If she overrules it and says 'Answer the question,' you have had a few more seconds to focus on rules 3 and 4, so you do the next right thing."

We interrupt this catechism because the next portion would deal with preparing for cross-examination; we resume that dialogue in Chapter Ten.

"Now suppose my question is clear, but you just plain forgot the answer for a moment. That happens to everybody, especially sitting up there in the witness chair. Maybe it'll happen today on something and we can practice. If you forget, smile and say something like 'I know that, but it just escapes me at the moment.' Then I get to ask, 'Is your memory exhausted on this right now?' And you say, 'Yes.' Then I can remind you of that fact, and we go ahead.

"You probably wonder who you should look at when you are answering. Half of that is easy. When I, or the other lawyer, or the judge is asking you a question, look at whoever is asking."

We have to step out of the narrative here because courtrooms and judges are so different. Do you examine from a seated position at the counsel table, from behind a lectern, standing at your table, or from wherever you like? How is the courtroom laid out? How far are you from the witness; that is, does the witness have to pan the courtroom with her eyes to look from the jury to you and back again?

Will you be in one of those small, almost intimate, courtrooms of the modern type where counsel, parties, jurors, witnesses, and spectators are seated in a kind of circle, so that it really looks like anybody can talk to everybody?

Whatever the rule and whatever the interior design, you want your witnesses to be comfortable. You do not want them jerking their heads back and forth and looking agitated. I operate on several key assumptions born of experience. The courtroom is an unfamiliar place for most witnesses. Jurors may not forgive the normal signs of nervousness, which may seem to betoken insincerity. You must be in charge, and every witness on your side needs to be reminded. You assert your control by preparation and by adopting techniques of examination that preserve your options.

You and the witness may benefit from videotaping a part of the proposed examination. Beware any requirement that you turn the tape over to your opponent, and make sure your witness is able to answer cross-examination questions about the process. I prefer to videotape only a few questions and answers so that the witness can truthfully say, "They just wanted me to see how I looked to other people, so they videotaped about a dozen questions and answers."

Your relationship with a friendly witness, particularly one who will testify at length or on an important subject, will say a great deal to the jury. The respect you and the witness show one another and to the other trial participants is vital. You are the only person who can help the novice witness know how to "relate" to the jury. Once, Lady Bird Johnson was a character witness for a defendant I represented. She came in over the weekend to be prepared to testify, accompanied by a Secret Service agent and our mutual friend Bob Strauss.

The questions one asks a character witness, and the answers she is permitted to give, are well confined. I was surprised that Mrs. Johnson worried about the basic matters of how to look, act, and present herself to the jurors. I made the mistake of thinking that with all those years in public life, this cameo role as a witness would not concern her. She was concerned, not only because the experience was novel. She is so gracious and accomplished that she wanted her testimony to be effective. She cared in the same way that most friendly witnesses care.

I described the courtroom. Then I said something like, "Mrs. Johnson, when I first came to Washington, D.C., in 1966, we lived on Capitol Hill. Your husband was president. And I still remember how you would dedicate those 'vest-pocket parks' and other green spaces. The children in the neighborhood and their parents would come to hear you. Those jurors are the mothers and fathers you were so effective at talking with. They are concerned about the same issues, and they have the same common sense they always did."

That explanation, Mrs. Johnson said, and Bob Strauss told me later, worked because it tied the experience of being a witness to other events in Mrs. Johnson's life. Every witness you will ever meet has—sometime, somewhere—explained something to somebody. That may be a good place to start.

How did this episode come out? Mrs. Johnson was asked, and answered, the standard character witness questions. The last one was, "Do you have an opinion about his integrity and honesty?" She said, "Yes. He has integrity, and he is honest." And then she turned to the jurors, looked them in the eyes, and said in tones redolent of those speeches in the parks, "You know, there's many people who don't *like* John, but nobody ever said he wasn't honest."

Almost every witness has special qualities that can make their testimony real. The nurse can say, "I checked the blood pressure," or, "I checked the blood pressure, just as I was trained to do." The second answer dignifies the witness in the jurors' eyes and lets the witness exhibit a quality of which she is proud. An experienced employee, well-briefed on antitrust risks, is better able to know if anything improper happened at a meeting than someone with less experience. A bank teller may have been trained to observe the characteristics of those at his workstation. A court official will have been trained to notice whether certain procedures were or were not followed. Learn your witness's special qualities, and integrate them into the direct examination.

How you say it is important. Barry Stevens, in *Don't Push the River*, gives an example. Compare these statements: "He's new at the job, but he's doing fine," and "He's new at the job, and he's doing fine."

In addition to making your witness comfortable with the job of testifying, you must make her aware of the various tools you, as the lawyer, have: refreshing recollection, making objections, showing pictures to the jury, filling in gaps on redirect examination. You tell the witness of these tools in order to instill confidence and to help the witness to focus on one, and only one, task: Do your best at answering the questions.

## BEGINNING STRONG

The scene moves from your office to the courtroom. The witness has a story. As Pat Hazel reminds us, the story must have a beginning, a middle, and an end. He is also right that you have choices about where to begin.

Usually, you will begin by introducing the witness. Sometimes the court clerk or reporter will ask the witness's name and perhaps even his address. We begin with the witness sitting in the chair, looking at you. You are as much in a line of sight between the witness and jurors as you are permitted to be. If you can move the obligatory lectern, do so. There are courtrooms in which there is a fold-down tray on the front edge of the jury box on which to put your papers. That's a good spot.

Even in a jurisdiction that requires you to examine from a seated position at the counsel table, there is probably nothing wrong with your having stood while the witness is being seated and sworn, and remaining standing for your first, introductory question. Later chapters talk about extending the time you are on your feet.

How should you introduce the witness? Well, certainly in a way that identifies and dignifies him. You want to let the jury know why this witness's testimony is going to be believable and important.

"Good morning. Will you tell the jury your name?" This question reminds the witness to speak to the jurors.

"Do you live here in Austin?" Or, if not, "What city and state do you live in?" You don't need to get more than the city and state unless the address is important to the story.

Remember, and be cautioned by, the story of a Texas lawyer who asked the witness, "Where do you reside, ma'am?"

"Tyler," she answered.

"Have you lived there all your life?"

"Not yet."

Your next question can be, "What do you do for work?" You can leave this out or defer it if it doesn't help the narrative. Notice that, borrowing from Tony Axam of Atlanta, we don't ask the ponderous, "What is your business or occupation?" We want an answer in which the witness shares his vocation.

Now, end the suspense, and tell the jury what you're doing. "Do you know why you're here?"

"Yes," should be the answer, and no more.

"Why?"

"Because I saw the train run into Mr. Thompson's car." Or, "Because I was the company engineer at those meetings in 1975."

Next, consider asking a question or two that sum up what the witness is going to say. "Was the railroad crossing gate shut or open when the train ran into Mr. Thompson's car?" Or, "When you were at those meetings, did you hear anybody discuss the price at which crude oil should be sold?"

These three inquiries—What work? Why are you here? What did you see?—may seem simple. If you think so, go to court and listen to the stilted introductions of witnesses—in language that neither the witness nor the jurors would ever use. Then comes a labored trudge through preliminary details. By the time the lawyer has dragged the witness to the place where something important happened, the journey has already exhausted the jurors' patience.

## DIRECT EXAMINATION
## ORGANIZATION

Omit needless words, unless forced by your opponent and the court to use them, and only then after making it clear that you would rather do without them. The following is a partial list of phrases that must be stricken from your vocabulary. If you find yourself using them, even in practice sessions, stop and think. These are only examples; they could be multiplied at will.

"Directing your attention to," followed by a place or time. Use a transition or a loop, having used a prologue to set up the action.

"Did there come a time when . . . ?" Use a transition or a loop.

"What, if anything, happened next?" This device is used so you don't lead the witness by suggesting the answer. Nonsense. *Something* happened next, the laws of physics say. It's probably a dumb question in any case. If you want to find out what happened next that was relevant, use a loop or a transition.

What are these "loops," "prologues," and "transitions"? A loop is a repetition of a part of a previous answer to underscore the answer and to help guide the witness to the next event. A prologue sets out themes in advance. A transition is a statement or question that signals a change in subject matter. All three devices can be used in direct and cross-examination—and with any type of witness.

## LOOPS

Here are some examples, from a mock trial based on a war crimes case:

Q. On that day, did you go to a village called My Lai?

A. Yes, sir.

Q. What time did you get to the village of My Lai?

A. About 1:30.

Q. Did you see Lt. William Calley on that day, sir?

A. Yes.

Q. Where did you first run into Lt. Calley?

A. In the village, sir, along a road that ran east and west.

Q. Did he say anything to you?

A. He told me to round up the people in the village.

Q. Who did you "round up" in response to Lt. Calley's order to you, sir?

A. About four or five women and kids.

Q. Were they all women and children, or were there any men?

A. Well, when we got back to the trail, we got back with Lt. Calley, and there were about thirty or forty Vietnamese there. I remember one old man; the rest were all women and children.

Q. Did Lt. Calley give you another order, later?

A. Yes, sir.

Q. What did he tell you to do?

A. He told us to take care of those people, and then he left. He came back a half-hour later, and we still had the people under guard. He said, "I thought I told you to take care of those people." And we said, "We are." And he said, "I mean kill them."

Q. When Lt. Calley said "Kill them," did he say anything else?

The loops in this example restate key points—the name of the village, the identity of the accused, the words spoken, information about the victims. Loops keep the story and the witness on track. Overused, they will draw an objection. Worse, overuse will cause the parts of the case you want emphasized to recede into a background of emphasis, like an actor's soliloquy delivered all in the same stentorian tones.

## PROLOGUES AND TRANSITIONS

Your direct examination must be divided into main themes. Perhaps the witness saw only a part of the action, so there is only one theme. The witness testifies and is off the stand; your "Why are you here?" is all the transition you need.

However, most witnesses will cover more than one subject. Usually, the witness's background and experience require separate emphasis, for they tell us why her views are important. The relevant action may have happened in separable episodes, each of which you have decided to make into a theme. A transition takes the witness—and the jurors—from one theme to another, without excess words and old verbal formulas.

An introduction is a collection of transitions, given at the beginning of the direct examination. It tells the jurors where you and the witness are going to go. To continue the metaphor, the transition tells them where you are now, and the loop reminds them where you have been.

You have introduced the witness and asked the summary question. Now announce your purpose, and how you will achieve it. "Ms. Jones, I am going to ask you first to tell us about yourself, then to show us where you were standing at the intersection on December 4, 1990, and, finally, to tell us just what happened." That is not a question. It is perhaps technically objectionable. Few opponents will be foolish enough to object to it. If you get an objection, stop using prologues in this form. Use transitions coupled with a quick question: "Before you tell us just what happened that day, tell us about yourself; do you live here in Tucson?"

A transition is an introduction to a subject of examination, so the jurors can shift mental gears. "Now, I'd like you to show us where you were," followed by a question. "Finally, I want you to explain for us just how X Company set crude oil prices in Alaska in 1965," followed by the first question in that series.

A transition can be punctuated by putting a new piece of demonstrative evidence, as discussed in Chapter Six, in front of the witness and the jurors.


## DEMEANOR, TONE, AND MOVEMENT

The rules of evidence that require you to move the story along one question at a time are second nature to you. You know where to sit or stand. Your demeanor must be respectful and not condescending. You must show genuine interest in the witness's story, though you have heard it a dozen times.

You must be ready to weave exhibits into the examination effortlessly, easily, and without causing interruption. The pace and timing of exhibits should help to unshackle you from your seated position or the lectern—and even from the accustomed place you have chosen if permitted to do so. Do not talk and walk at the same time, throwing away your words in the bustle of movement. You can make an exception where the action is suited to the words: "I am going to show you this letter . . . " as you move to the witness stand to do just that.

In some courts, be warned, the judge will prevent you from even this amount of visual drama. You will be compelled to hand the exhibit to the bailiff, who will then hand it to the witness. You can sometimes break this system by having exhibits, such as the kind described in Chapter Six, that can best be explained by the witness stepping down in front of the jury. Try to do that.

The witness, remember, is likely to be nervous in court. You bear the burden of preparing for both of you. For some, the choreography comes almost naturally. For others, it is more difficult. Rehearse enough to learn it. Learn not to turn your back on the jury—or anybody else—unless you mean to. Learn to move—backpedaling if necessary—

to keep attention focused on the witness and the exhibits. Use your words to guide the witness and the jurors. "Please look at the screen, where I have just put up this letter, in evidence as Plaintiff's 1034. You sent that letter?" "Your Honor, may Ms. Jones step down to the exhibit? Ms. Jones, please take this pointer and show us where you were standing."

## DECONSTRUCTION
## (WITHOUT A YELLOW PAD)

The witness is introduced, the story has a prologue, the transitions are set. Your outline of the direct examination takes shape. You mark the places where you will use an exhibit. You are ready for the next step, which is to fill in the details.

First, however, you must remember that doing it "by the numbers" is deadly. Most of us have seen lawyers who write out on a yellow pad the questions they will ask, or they create complex and detailed notebooks or checklists. Some of us have even seen the most compulsive example of such behavior, the lawyer who asks each question from the list, gets the answer, grunts "Uh-huh," and obviously crosses out the answered question. Avoid the chronological recitation that begins so far before the action that the jurors are asleep when the punch line arrives.

All such behavior is the enemy of communication. Don't do it. Make your lists if you must. Then get free of them, so that you frame your questions in the context of what is going on and taking account of the answer just received. Your notes can be on cards or sheets of paper, in large enough letters so you can glance quickly at them. An examination conducted with head down, gazing at the yellow pad, shows disrespect and disinterest, and makes it appear that you, and not the witness, are in charge. You will look like you are going through the motions of replaying what is on your yellow pad.

Lawyers march out of law schools accustomed to taking notes. They go to law firms where they attend meetings and take notes. The yellow pad comes to occupy too large a place. Get away from it.

Demeanor aside, you will fill in your outline by a method that works best for you. I agree with the expert advice, by Jim McElhaney for example, to think in paragraphs. This is obviously an artificial concept because the proper length of a written paragraph can vary depending on many arbitrary stylistic choices. By "thinking in paragraphs," I mean doing so in the way my eighth grade teacher taught me. A paragraph has a topic sentence, usually the first one. It contains one idea, and ends. The next paragraph tells the reader to take a breath and start a new idea.

In direct examination, each "paragraph" consists of several questions that, taken together, present one idea. In your notes, that one idea should be reducible to one or two key words. You ask your questions, develop that idea, and move on to the next one.

A paragraph is a smaller unit than a theme. Introduce each theme with a transition. Then move idea by idea, paragraph by paragraph, until you have exhausted that theme.

By thinking in terms of paragraphs, you should remember to have a topic question for each paragraph and to use loops when appropriate to tie the ideas together.

Transition: "Now, Mr. Wilson, I want to ask you about the bank holdup."

First paragraph, topic question: "Did you get a look at the robber's face?"

More questions, using loops: "How long a time did you look at the robber's face?" "How far was the robber standing from you?" "Do you see the robber here in court today?"

Second paragraph, topic question: "Did you give the police a description of the robber when they talked to you?"

More questions, using loops: "How long after the robbery did you talk to the police officer?" "When you talked to the officer a half hour after the robbery, did you tell him what the robber looked like?"

You might decide to vary the order of paragraphs. In this hypothetical, I chose in-court identification as the dramatic starting point for this theme and put that idea first. In a car crash case, you might open a descriptive theme by having the witness step to a map or diagram. Then you can ask for a description of the cars involved. The next idea might be the crash itself.

If you use an outline form for your direct that fills up themes with paragraph-ideas, you will free yourself to have a natural conversation with the witness that is purposeful and organized. Objections and interruptions will be less likely to throw you off.

## LEADING QUESTIONS AND AVOIDING NARRATIVE

The rules of evidence tell you that the witnesses' answers must be material, relevant, nonhearsay or admissible hearsay, and that exhibits must be admissible, as discussed in Chapter Six.

The most difficult problem in direct examination is to divide the action into a series of nonleading questions that do not call for uninterrupted narrative. The secret of doing this is to imagine each paragraph as a picture that you want to convey to the jurors. Then divide the picture into as many aspects or items of information as necessary to avoid narrative. Each aspect or item becomes a separate question. You control how much information the witness is supposed to provide by the breadth of the question you ask. The breadth of the question is determined by the importance of the information (more important items should be broken down into more parts) and how much help the witness needs.

Remember at all costs to avoid unnecessary repetition. Jurors often complain that the lawyers do not respect their ability to retain information and needlessly repeat the same information over and over. Some repetition is obviously effective. There is no hard-and-fast rule; one must simply be aware of juror impatience. Indeed, lawyer consciousness that the jurors are jealous of their time and critical of those who waste it is the principal reason that jury trials usually take less time than bench trials. I know this is contrary to conventional wisdom but have had it confirmed by too many judges and lawyers—as well as by my own experience—to doubt it. Dr. Andrew Watson calls this the "principle of parsimony."

The technique of asking good questions must be learned so well that it becomes habitual. Take an example. The person you want the witness to describe was wearing a tie. How can this fact be brought out and the tie described? Most broadly, you could ask the witness, "What was X wearing?" You would ask the question in this broad form if the information were not very important. You might get the response, "Oh, a blue suit," or "Overalls." If, however, the attire is important, the paragraph of your examination that deals with it must be broken into a number of items. Opening question: "Do you remember what X was wearing?" To this, the answer should be simply, "Yes." Next questions: "Was he wearing a jacket?" "Can you tell us what kind of jacket?" "What color was the jacket?" "Could you see the shirt underneath the jacket?" "What kind of a shirt was it?" "What color was the shirt?" "Was he wearing a tie?" "What kind of a pattern did the tie have?" "What color or colors was the tie?" "Could you see his trousers?" "What color were the trousers?" "Do you remember what kind of fabric?" "Can you recall the style of his trousers?"

And so on. The question is the final and smallest unit of a direct examination. Each paragraph of the examination consists of one or more questions. It is nearly impossible to tell in advance how many questions it will take to fill a paragraph. You can and should have a general idea, but if you decide this matter *a priori,* you will risk either needless repetition or failure to give all the information that the paragraph is intended to encompass. Think of the paragraph as a picture you want to replicate. Ask a question. The witness responds and fills out a part of the picture. With each succeeding question, you fill out more of it until you are done. Then you go on to the next paragraph. In this way, you retain control, you do not fluster yourself or the witness when the answer is not as precise as planned.

Practice this skill. Imagine that you want to convey information about an experience that you have had or a scene that you have witnessed. Break the event down into its important constituent parts. Formulate a series of questions that will convey the event completely yet parsimoniously. You can practice on your way to work or in small blocks of spare time. The only risk is that people will look at you strangely because you will appear to be talking to yourself.

Take another example. Suppose you want the jurors to know the witness's occupation. In many cases, this is simply a biographical detail, so the paragraph that contains occupation information is short. You could fill it with one question: "What do you do for work?"

In another case, however, the witness's occupation may be important to bolstering the testimony. For example, the case may involve something that the witness did as a part of her employment. Then the occupation paragraph requires more questions to fill up, and the picture you want the jury to have is of a competent person who knows what she is doing and who can be trusted to tell it. The questioning might go like this: "What do you do for work?" "How long have you been doing that?" "Did you have any education that prepared you to do this work?" "Did you hold other jobs in the company before this one that prepared you to do this work?" "What part of the company's operations are you responsible for in your work?"

This series of questions prepares the jury to hear what is to follow. By thinking of your direct examination as a movement from one mental image to the next, you will nearly automatically obey the no-leading-questions and no-narrative rules. You will be able to have a normal, conversational relation to the witness without excessive reliance on your notes. After all, it should be easy to keep one mental image in mind at a time, and to fill it up before moving on to the next one, perhaps with just a glance at your notes to pick up the key word that triggers or suggests the next mental image.

# Chapter Three

## *Direct Examination: Neutral Fact Witnesses*

### ARE THERE NEUTRAL FACT WITNESSES?

You have a limited amount of time to devote to any given case. By now the message is clear that for that time you must immerse yourself completely in the story you are going to tell. This lesson is often forgotten when it comes to neutral witnesses, people who just happened to be present when something important happened.

You may, at this point, contradict me with my own teaching. "There are no neutral witnesses, right?" "Everybody is a partisan, right?"

To which I reply, "No." In the old days, you were said to "sponsor" or "vouch for" any witness you put on. This principle led in turn to archaic and convoluted rules about whether, when, or how you could "impeach your own witness." Those rules hardly survive anymore. The Federal Rules of Evidence and their state counterparts have done away with them. So witnesses are no longer "partisans" in the old sense of belonging to one side or the other in the trial context. In most jurisdictions, you can call any witness and interrogate him without suffering the legal consequence of adopting the testimony.

There are exceptions to this principle. Some of your witnesses may be agents of your client or retained by your client to express opinions and conclusions. An expert witness might fall into the latter category. The statements of such a witness may be deemed authorized admissions of your client. This designation might attach to any statement of such a person—in a memorandum done before the litigation began, in deposition, or at trial. I have taken account of these distinctions by giving separate treatment to "interested" witnesses and to experts in other chapters.

True, every witness is a partisan of his *story*, but that does not contradict my description of some witnesses as neutral. Somebody has to conduct direct examination, and usually that must be done with nonleading questions. The other side "cross-examines," and thus is functionally adverse to the witness. That is not what I am talking about.

Of course, you are not going to call witnesses whose testimony doesn't help your case. In that sense, no witness is neutral. I'm not talking about that either.

By neutral, I mean the jury will likely see the witness as not having an ax to grind. I mean someone without provable bias. Such a witness is cross-examinable on all sorts of grounds; see Chapter Eight for an introduction to them. This kind of witness has no connection with your side of the case except for recalling a version of events that fits the story you are telling. A neutral witness is Everyman in the sense that any one of the jurors might have wandered into the same set of events, remembered what happened, and be sitting in the witness chair instead of the jury box.

In summation, you will dwell upon the witness's motivation to tell the truth. In addition, you will stress the particular characteristics discussed below about some important types of neutral witness.

Many of these neutral witnesses are reluctant to "get involved"; they require careful, thoughtful attention. Others have manufactured a view of their own importance that makes them difficult to deal with and, more important, dangerous. The danger arises from their firmness of recollection—leading them to cling to obvious errors or misperceptions and to strike unpredictable poses on the witness stand.

Some neutral witnesses are professionals—police officers, investigators, firefighters, social workers. They have probably been witnesses before now. They may be cynical about trial lawyers, impatient with delay, and unwilling to spend much time discussing nuances of fact and presentation.

One generalization holds for all of these witnesses: Courteous attention to them, their schedules, and their evidence will yield best results. If your law office has an investigator, make sure she follows these principles. As trial approaches, review the file on each witness and identify the points each can make. You, another lawyer in your office, or the investigator should contact each of them. Remember not to do any interview alone, to avoid problems in using prior statements during trial.

How early you are able to meet with witnesses depends on how your firm, your schedule, and the case are organized. Before any witness takes an oath at trial—and preferably before any deposition—the lawyer who will try the case must pay that witness the courtesy of a face-to-face meeting. No matter how good the investigator's notes or how thorough the deposition, the meeting—however brief it may be—is the only way to figure out the best method of presentation.

These witnesses owe you nothing. Neither they, their careers, nor any organization of which they are a part is helped by their appearance in your case. It is always exciting when one of these witnesses takes the stand because all of your careful preparation is likely to go out the window if the witness gets a bright idea. "Independent as a hog on ice," as the saying goes.


## THE PARTISAN

Below, I discuss varieties of neutral witnesses. However, you will find that many themes of witness preparation and presentation are the same, no matter what kind of neutral witness you are presenting.

In one instance, I was called in with a couple of days' notice to try a criminal case. A young lawyer had found and interviewed witnesses, and he had prepared excellent summaries of what they had seen and heard. One witness seemed particularly important to our case. I called him at home the night before trial and made an appointment to meet him the next morning at the courthouse. I promised that we would be sensitive to his schedule and would undertake to have him "on call" rather than waiting around in the courthouse.

As we chatted, I learned that he had been an aircraft mechanic for twenty-five years and was a member of the International Association of Machinists and Aerospace Workers. We talked about the hard times his union had been having and about my dad's experiences as an IAM leader.

The next morning, we talked some more. I warned him that the judge was likely to find his testimony objectionable. I said he should not worry if the lawyers and the judge got to fussing about matters while he was on the stand. He knew what he had seen and heard, and I would be sure to ask him all about it.

"Don't worry," he said. "I've been putting up with Frank Lorenzo all this time; I reckon a federal judge won't bother me." We continued the conversation and went carefully over the events he had seen. I told him that we could not go into his opinions about what he had seen and heard. I was just going to ask what happened, who said what, and where people were standing. We had to try to keep things matter-of-fact.

That's about all we needed. I had the notes of the earlier interview, and I double-checked them. This man had testified in arbitrations. He had held office in his union. He knew about communication. When he testified, he was a superb witness.

The lesson: Honor the witness's abilities to communicate. Warn that opinions are not going to be allowed. Help the witness see the limits on hearsay and how you will have to lay a foundation for any out-of-court statements. Use your questions and manner to keep the witness's effect relatively unbiased and neutral.

This witness recalled events in a helpful way. He was a partisan, not of mine or of my client, but of his truth. In preparing him to testify, I could not appeal to him in the name of anything but his own self-interest. For example, all witnesses must remember that a combative stance on cross-examination, no matter now much suffused with self-righteousness, makes it easier for the examiner to set and spring traps.

In the paragraph above, I spoke of the witness's version as "his truth." So it is. The structure of your direct honors the witness's truth but exercises control (1) to focus only on relevant matter and (2) to guide the places and statements.

"Tell the court and jurors your name, please?" "What do you do for work?" "Do you live here in Austin?" After another personal question or two about family, get right to it with a somewhat leading question. "Were you on the corner on that August day when the collision happened?" Or, "Were you at the meetings in 1961 when the components of crude oil were talked about?" Or, "Were you at the meeting where Mr. Bishop spoke, in Estes Park in April?"

This transition question must remind the jurors of time, place, and event and put the witness there. In the rest of the examination, use the loops described in Chapter Two to keep the story on track. "After the red car collided broadside with the green truck, where did the two cars come to rest?" Use demonstrative evidence to make a record of the answer.

Often, a neutral witness will have described an event in one way, then later have seen the error of her observation. "You say the light was green. Have you ever remembered it differently?" It is difficult to convince anybody, especially a self-willed person, gracefully to admit to being wrong. You must spend enough time with the witness to put your personal credibility behind the assertion that admitting a mistake is the best and inescapable course. "I was wrong about that. As I looked at the diagrams and thought about it, I realized I was wrong." Or, "The man who came to talk to me interrupted me when I was eating. I'm sure I said that, but I just didn't get a chance to think clearly." And, at that, full stop. No amount of coaxing on cross-examination should push the witness into a more complete exercise in self-justification.

I am strong-willed myself. I think trial lawyers tend to be. I know that lead trial counsel must be. Sometimes, though not often, my own sense of where the case should go and my own enthusiasm create barriers between me and a potential witness. Usually, the problem arises with a "partisan." Sometimes I fear that a particularly nervous witness, not a partisan, will choke up if I conduct the direct examination.

If you are not solo at the counsel table, this is the time to consider your co-counsel. Somebody has to be lead counsel, I concede. But I disagree with those who say that a cooperative relationship among lawyers for the same client is inconsistent with the discipline needed for a jury trial.

In a complex case, when co-counsel and I divide up responsibility for witnesses, we try to take advantage of our relative strengths. If a particular witness and I are unlikely to achieve a certain unity in front of the jury, perhaps co-counsel can get the job done. On the other hand, some witnesses feel that their own importance is enhanced based on the lawyer who conducts the direct examination. You will probably have to honor those choices.

## THE RECORD KEEPER

Defending a complex tax evasion case, we wanted to show that the government's principal witness and chief informer was the real culprit. Our theory was that he had stolen the partnership moneys that were being attributed for tax purposes to our client. We wanted to show a pattern of large expenditures for this man's personal benefit.

Witnesses to the true culprit's extravagance were not hard to find, mostly through careful poring over financial records. The problem was to get the witnesses to the courthouse and present them effectively.

All these witnesses shared certain characteristics. They were, of course, neutral in the sense that they did not objectively favor one side or the other of the lawsuit. If pushed, some of them might lean toward the true culprit, who had been their benefactor. None of them wanted the notoriety a court appearance might bring. In one way or another, all of them tried to escape testifying. Our response was the same to all: Come to our offices, bring the documents, and be interviewed. We will not use you if we can avoid it.

Remember that witnesses can stall you if you have no mechanism to make them produce documents and objects before their testimony. If, under the rules, you cannot obtain and enforce early production of exhibits, the witness will play poker with you. "I won't show you the documents until I get on the stand. Maybe they help you, and maybe they don't. Do you want to take a chance?" The discovery and subpoena rules will tell you how much leverage you have. Your rules of practice may permit an application to the trial judge, in the name of trial efficiency, to stop this charade. A good investigator can usually tell you whether the material will do you any good. This problem does not usually arise in complex civil cases, in which waves of discovery have produced mountains of paper. It will surely bedevil you in criminal cases, where discovery is very limited, and in the workaday world of shorter trials.

In our tax case, we talked to the witnesses. "We are not in this case to cause you problems. We have to defend our client the best way we can. We are sure you didn't do anything wrong. Nobody is saying you did." We were reminding the witnesses, and ourselves, that their reaction was the same one that many people, including at least some jurors, might have.

"All we are going to do is go through the records and ask you questions based on those records. If you don't remember a particular situation, you can say so. You have told us that these records are accurate." We are talking about witnesses whose activities left a more or less complete paper trail.

Our potential witnesses included a sales representative of a large New York jewelry retailer, two women who had been flight attendants on the true culprit's Lear jet, a department store fur salesman, and the owner of a well-known restaurant.

The jewelry retailer's records told of jewelry purchases in the real culprit's own name and in the names of others. The latter records turned up because we drafted the subpoena to call for records relating to transactions with or involving X, under any name. The sales representative recounted meetings with X in several locations, including hotel rooms. X had purchased more than $1 million in jewelry in a little more than a year. Other witnesses were able to confirm that most of this jewelry was then given as gifts to women.

We were able to convince the restaurant owner to show us X's charge slips. We put him on a telephone call basis and also agreed to put him on in mid-afternoon, between the lunch and dinner business. We did not otherwise prepare him, although my co-counsel was a regular customer of the restaurant and knew the restaurateur fairly well.

He showed up in white coat and toque. He looked uncomfortable, not only from the experience of testifying, but from revealing the activities of a customer whose assiduous study of the wine list ran checks for a four-person dinner up to $4,000 or thereabouts, plus a generous tip. His discomfiture added to the impact of his testimony.

We did not use all of the witnesses that the records revealed to us. For example, we did not call the flight attendants. Employing a flight attendant on a five-passenger aircraft might seem unusual to a jury, particularly when X bought most of them $10,000 fur coats at a fancy Dallas department store. None of them wanted to testify. Any of them might have volunteered, if given a chance, that X was a generous, caring person and that they liked him. Such assertions would not have been particularly harmful to us, for we were not arguing personalities but the quiet force of financial facts. Nonetheless, we had enough evidence without taking the risk of seeming sensationalistic, or even prurient.

The prospect of a neutral witness's irrelevant detours dictates a structured examination. Arrange the records you have in a sensible order. Perhaps you will begin with a total amount, then backtrack through some significant transactions. Perhaps you will pick out one or two significant events and then double back. Keep the examination short, for two reasons. First, the witness is more likely to detour if you keep him on the stand a long time. Second, the jurors will resent your hammering the point too long and hard. You can usually introduce the records themselves, or even a summary of them, to highlight totals and significant transactions.

You have introduced the witness and her work. Now move right to the main issue: "Did you ever handle cash for Mr. X?" The next question should represent your selection of the best way in to the data. For example, "What's the largest amount of cash he ever gave you at one time?" Or, if the amounts of individual transactions are not so significant, "How much cash did you handle for him in any given thirty-day period?"

If the witness remembers the correct answer, or has been reminded of it in your preparation, you move on to a summary chart, the records themselves, or a fuller development of the issue.

If the witness decides to play cagey, you have the records. Your immediate response to "I don't remember" is, "Would it refresh your recollection if I showed you this exhibit?" Match your action to the question; hand the witness the document, and point to the right place. Then ask the question again, "Please, tell the jury now, what's the largest amount of cash he ever gave you at one time?"

If the witness begins to feign a more complete loss of memory, go through the refreshing recollection routine about twice more. After that, apply to the judge for leave to proceed by leading questions, as against a hostile witness. In the presence of the jury, say, "Your Honor, may I continue by asking leading questions as provided in Federal Rule of Evidence 911(c)? That would save a lot of the court's and jury's time."

## THE BYSTANDER

In a negligence case, the bystander is the one at the intersection. In a store robbery case, the bystander is the one over by the canned goods. In an antitrust case, the bystander may be someone who was at an important meeting or overheard an important conversation.

Bystanders rarely announce themselves. The newspaper ads pleading for automobile accident witnesses to come forward are testament to the desire not to get involved—or perhaps to how busy people are. If you are a witness, people are going to take up your time with interviews. You will probably lose a day from work, in exchange for the puny witness fee, to give a deposition. The secretary or paralegal in the lawyer's office will treat your schedule cavalierly. At least, that is what people fear, and with some justification.

The first task in the presentation of a bystander is to find the witness, get the witness's statement in a form usable at trial, and tell her candidly what to expect by way of further interviews, depositions, and trial testimony. The relationship you build at this stage will carry through the entire case.

Any law firm that litigates should either employ or have access to an investigator who knows how to take a statement. The investigator should be presentable enough to testify if the need arises. You can sometimes use a paralegal, law clerk, or law student for this purpose, although you will turn to a trained and experienced investigator when there is a problem locating a witness or persuading her to give a statement.

Experience has proven to me the importance of moving quickly to find and meet with potential witnesses. In several cases, media publicity has prompted people to call the office to say they know something. I make it a practice to follow up on these calls, and if the caller sounds sufficiently serious, I'll take somebody along and go meet that person myself. Sometimes the caller has nothing admissible. It has been reported that some law enforcement authorities generate phony calls to lure lawyers into doing something that obstructs justice. But if you don't go it alone, and if your ethics are in order, there is little risk there. Quick response pays off often enough.

You must start the factual investigation before the trail gets cold. In one case, a media barrage announced charges against our client. The rumor mill churned out the name of one potential witness. That very evening, my partner and I sent an investigator to the man's house. His wife answered the door, and when the investigator began to ask her about her husband, she said, "Would you like to talk to him? He decided that staying home was as good a place as any." In the interview, the witness confirmed that he had no knowledge of any unlawful behavior by our client. That statement not only carried its own worth, but it left us free to build our defense with other witnesses.

Sometimes witnesses will ask you whether they should have their own lawyer. Examples include coworkers in an employment discrimination suit who are worried about their own jobs, employees of a corporate antitrust defendant who wonder if their exculpatory testimony will trigger hostile scrutiny by a governmental or private plaintiff, and neighbors in a police misconduct case.

In such a case, your answer is governed by the ethical rules. If there is a conflict between the witness and your client, actual or potential, you cannot represent the witness and must make it clear that you are not the witness's lawyer. Beyond the mandatory ethical rules on multiple representation, you must consider the appearance of propriety. Many jurors have a low enough opinion of lawyers to begin with; you harm yourself and your client by appearing to bottle up a witness's story by being that witness's lawyer as well as your own client's lawyer. In deposition or at trial, your relationship with the witness will be shown.

The witness has the right to counsel. It is up to the witness, in the first instance, to exercise or not exercise that right. If you are convinced the witness's interests would be served by having counsel, you should say so. If you represent a corporation, you may be able to invoke corporate bylaw provisions for counsel of the witness's choosing to be paid for by the corporation. A labor or employment agreement may provide for counsel.

When you or someone in your firm first meet with a bystander, you may not yet know the story you will eventually tell the jury. You may not have reference points in other factual research by which to evaluate what the bystander is telling you. You can make only tentative judgments about *what* you are being told. You must, however, begin to make a working decision about *who* is doing the telling. That is, you must begin to decide if this person can be a good witness. One test is to run through a checklist of points that a cross-examiner will seize upon. You would do that anyway in preparing the witness to withstand cross-examination.

For me, the difference between the bystander and the partisan lies in the witness's different degree of suggestibility. The partisan can come untethered by defending even untenable positions on cross-examination. The bystander can be pushed off a position by a strong cross-examiner who appeals to innate doubt. If the bystander backslides, your only solace will be in the positions to which your direct examination has irrevocably committed the witness. You need to conduct a direct examination that almost promises victory but guarantees at least a draw even if the very worst happens.

Your direct examination begins by introducing the witness, her work, and her importance to this case. You ask questions that enhance the witness's believability—her vantage point, how long she looked, or how she came to know what she is going to describe. All of this should take no longer than five minutes.

Q. Ms. Wilson, I am going to ask you to keep your voice up so that everybody within this space can hear you. I'll try to do the same. Will you tell the jurors your name, please?

A. Martha Torrey Wilson.

Q. What do you do for work, Ms. Wilson?

A. I am a clinical psychologist.

Q. What do you do for people as a clinical psychologist?

A. I meet with clients, or patients you might call them, who want to understand their behavior and their lives. I listen to them. I observe them. Then I apply my experience to what I see and hear, and we try to understand how they can make helpful changes in their lives.

Q. Are you a doctor?

A. I have a Ph.D. degree from the University of Texas at San Antonio, but in my practice I don't encourage people to call me doctor.

We have introduced Ms. Wilson. She has told the jury about her work. We have selected that part of her work in which she listens, observes, and interprets what she sees and hears. She is a professional observer. In our case, she is an observer also—a bystander, a witness.

Almost every witness is in some measure a professional observer. In introducing the witness, you must bring out that part of their profession in which observation is important.

Q. Do you know the intersection of Sixth and Lamar, here in Austin?

A. Oh, yes.

Q. How do you know it?

A. I drive North on Lamar from Riverside up to Martin Luther King Boulevard almost every morning, going from my house to my office.

Q. Did you see a car crash at Sixth and Lamar last year?

A. Yes, I did.

Q. I'd like to ask you some questions about what you saw and how well you could see. First, Your Honor, may Ms. Wilson step down to the overhead projector?
[The judge responds:]
She may.

Q. Please step down here. Ms. Wilson, I've put up here a diagram of the intersection. We've got a lot of these diagrams, and each witness has been using one of them to help us see what they saw.

The diagram is schematic, and the witness is going to mark it to show what is on the four corners of the intersection, the crosswalks and signal lights, the path of the cars that collided, and where the crashed cars came to rest. Get the essential facts while the witness is at the projector. Then go into more detail when she gets back on the stand.

Q. What kind of car do you drive?

A. A Ford Ranger supercab pickup.

Q. I guess we want to know how well you can see from the driver's seat?

A. One reason I drive a truck is that I like to sit up a little higher off the road so I can see better.

Your style of interrogation must be easy and conversational. You are interested in a story being told by a neutral nonprofessional observer, not sharing an experience with a partisan. In every way possible, mark off each theme with a tangible exhibit, a prior statement, or a reference to some other witness. A tangible exhibit can include a photograph, a diagram on which the witness makes mark, a chart, or a document. A prior statement can include admissible hearsay or nonadmissible matter used to refresh recollection.

Suppose the witness, in response to the last question, says, "I could see very well." In your office, she had volunteered the statement about why she drives a truck. You could ask, "Is there a reason you prefer to drive a truck?" The approach is rather obvious, but one or two such transparent devices in any given trial day are justifiable.

The reference to another witness will help tie the story of your case together, provide a reference point for this witness, and be a useful anchor to windward if this witness does not do as well as you expect. For example, you might ask, "Can you tell us who else works in that same office?" "How far is his desk from Ms. Rowe's?" Or, "Is there a gasoline service station at that corner?" "Have you been in that station?" "Do they have a 'full serve' line of gas pumps where an attendant fills up your tank?" You have by this means introduced the coworker or the gas station attendant.

In our earlier example, you would make sure Ms. Wilson marked the location of the bus stop at Sixth and Lamar on the chart if you had another witness who saw the accident while waiting for a bus. You are telling a story. Parts of a story are connected. Make sure the connections are proved so you can pick them up and weave them together in summation.

If the bystander is buffeted on cross-examination, redirect can be particularly valuable. Remember, this witness is a neutral who has taken the trouble to come to court. You hope the jurors identify with her. If your opponent has arguably been rude, as well perhaps as effective, you can go back over the markers you left on direct: the exhibits, the statement, and the other witnesses. The scope of admissibility of statements is broadened because prior consistent statements are now more freely usable.

You should not be faced, on redirect examination, with an inconsistency exposed for the first time on cross-examination or with an attribute of the witness (such as a prior conviction of crime) that you did not deal with on direct examination. If there are bad facts about your case, the jurors should hear about them from you first.

Surprises do happen, however. Particularly in criminal cases, where discovery is limited, your opponent may have information that you do not. The danger of ambush on cross-examination can only be lessened by pretrial investigation and preparation.

If you are permitted to talk to the witness between cross-examination and redirect, you may be able to find out enough detail to construct a redirect examination that deadens the sting. You may be prohibited from doing this by court rule or order, and you may thus face the task of rehabilitation without meaningful input from the witness.

If the witness is shaken by the attack, she is in no position to work with you in a logical or sensible way. Asking an open-ended question that calls for an explanation of the damaging matter invites nervous, unpersuasive self-justification that will not pass the straight-face test. The witness will harm herself further in the jurors' eyes. No, you are the advocate. You are in charge. If there is repair to be done, you must do it.

If there is an explanation for a seeming inconsistency or for another impeaching fact, and if you are sure the witness can make that explanation tersely and persuasively, ask for the explanation in so many words. "Ms. Olmstead asked you if you had been convicted of something. Tell us a little more about that." The explanation might be that the offense was situational, the witness was put on probation, and paid the debt. If you are not sure, do the reinforcing redirect outlined below. Then, let the witness go. You cannot try your whole case all at once. You will have the luxury of time to consider the best means of rehabilitation, perhaps through other witnesses.

Your redirect must be short, with gently pointed questions. It is designed to set up an argument blaming the witness's confusion on your opponent: "She saw what she saw."

Preparation should begin by organizing all prior statements of the witness that were not used on direct. The attack will almost surely have opened up your right to use these statements. Do so.

Get back to the basics of the witness's testimony. Most ambush cross-examination is collateral, in the sense that it relates to prior statements, prior conduct, or suggestions about what other witnesses may have seen. If you dwell on the collateral material, no matter how emotionally loaded it may seem at the time, you implicitly vouch for its power to erase the witness's perceptions as related on direct examination.

Q. Ms. Wilson, long before this trial, and one week after the accident, did you give a statement to an investigator?
A. Yes.
Q. Is this it?
A. Yes.
Q. Did you sign it?
A. Yes.
[Offer it.]
Q. I have put it up on the overhead projector. Would you read the part I have highlighted?

The witness complies. Repeat the process with deposition testimony and other prior statements.

After using the prior statements, or at the beginning if you don't have any of them, restate the basics very quickly.

Do not take so long that you bore the jury or excite the judge's ire. Your demonstrative evidence helps you be efficient.

Q. I have put up on the projector the diagram you made for the jurors. Does anything on that need changing based on what's been asked since we made this?
A. No.


## THE PROFESSIONAL

Public and private professionals dog our steps. They investigate disturbing events. Even while dealing with an accident scene or fire, the professional may well be trained to observe and report on possible causes. The investigator from the fire or police department will almost surely be trained, and he may have the kind of legal duty to report that makes that report admissible into evidence under Federal Rule of Evidence 803(8). Most people's medical conditions are documented, in some respect, by doctors. Emotional disturbances may have been chronicled by a psychologist, teacher, counselor, or pastor.

I am not talking here about experts. You are calling the professional as a fact witness, and it just happens that professional expertise may give this witness's observations special force with the jurors.

Also, under Federal Rule of Evidence 701, a witness not called as an expert may nonetheless give an opinion helpful to understanding his testimony; the driver seemed drunk, the woman seemed sad, the child seemed remorseful, the secretary looked agitated.

You will find some of these witnesses' names on accident reports, medical charts, school records, and other such records. Names of others will appear by carefully questioning your client.

Most of these folks are busy. Some of them are subject to rules about being witnesses in litigation; in such cases, their helpful records may also be difficult to get. Public and private entities routinely have their employees sign contracts that confer on the employer a property right in all information gathered by the employee in the course of her duties. The employee is thus forbidden by contract from sharing documents and other information with you unless you have the employer's consent or have used compulsory process.

If your witness is a public servant or corporate employee, go through the right channels to get access to her and to the relevant documents. Public agencies have regulations to look up. Corporations can be approached through their counsel. The witness may be able to tell you the right approach.

If you have an informal way in, use it. Your investigator may have contacts in law enforcement. Your lawyer friends can help you with a public or private entity's rules and procedures. If all else fails, you can use the discovery or subpoena process to get records and obtain the witness's presence. You want, however, to avoid putting a witness on the stand who has not spoken with you.

Privacy or privilege rules may block access to some witnesses and their records—for example, pastors, doctors, journalists, and bankers. Get the necessary waivers, permissions, or legal process before you talk to the witness, or have an explainable plan for doing so.

Unless procedures get in your way, you, the trial counsel, should make the first contact with these professional witnesses. You understand what it means to be busy. You undertake to consume as little of the witness's time as possible. The witness has a special perspective that no one else can give. You will honor the witness's professionalism and schedule, in the interview process, during any discovery, and at trial. Can you make an appointment? What time and place are convenient for the witness?

At trial, when you call the professional to testify, use his title: Detective Jones, Reverend Smith. Your introduction must include a brief recital of the special qualifications that make this witness's story particularly important. "Did you take courses on accident scene investigation?" "How many street accident cases have you had any part in?" Or, "Do you counsel families in trouble?" "Is that part of your responsibility as a pastor?" "What training do you have in that?"

The professional's prior statements are more likely to be admissible on direct examination than other witnesses', because her trade or business may involve keeping records. Those writings may provide you with a way to maintain the chronology of recollection. Even a series of calendar notations can provide this kind of continuity.

If you are going this route, you will move from introducing the witness's qualifications to introducing the writings you will use. If, as in most civil cases, the writings have been premarked and admitted by the pretrial order, you will have them ready to display to the jurors and the witness. If the witness does not remember the episode, then the writings will come in as past recollection recorded. If recollection falters, they may be used to refresh recollection. Different bases for using the materials require different foundations in direct examination.

If the witness has trouble remembering, it is usually better to start him on the story, and then refresh recollection at a convenient point.

Q. How many people were in the car?
A. It was four or five. I'm not sure.
Q. Have you exhausted your recollection?
A. Yes.
Q. Did you make some notes at the time?
A. I sure did.
Q. Would it help you to remember if I showed you the notes?
A. Yes.

Q.  Here they are, and here is a copy for counsel.
    [Handing to the witness or to the bailiff to give to
    the witness.]

I like this method better than asking about notes at the
beginning of the examination, which is often done but
arguably improper. Busy prosecutors do it all the time:

Q.  Officer, can you remember all the details without
    your notes?
A.  Not really.
Q.  Do you have your notes with you?
A.  Yes.
Q.  With the Court's permission, would you take those
    out and refer to them as you go along.
    [At this juncture, the defense counsel interjects:]
    Objection. This is not a proper use of refreshed
    recollection. And there is no foundation for past
    recollection recorded.
    [The judge wearily responds:]
    Move it along, counsel.

Regardless of evidentiary rules, this sort of wholesale
refreshing is unpersuasive. The witness shuffles the notes
and loses eye contact with you and with the jury. He may
not even look as if he is trying to remember what happened. If you have any opportunity to prepare the witness
beforehand, try to avoid such a scene. Sometimes, to be
sure, you will have no choice.

Past recollection recorded requires you to establish that
the witness once remembered, but no longer does. He can
then use the notes to testify, but they may not be shown to
the jury.

If the witness's prior writings qualify as business records
or official records, you have more creative options. Because
such materials are admissible, you can usually obtain them

before trial by subpoena. You can decide if they would make good exhibits for reproduction as overhead projector transparencies or other visual aids to publication. You can then plan the examination to highlight the best aspects of recollection and the exhibits:

Q. Mr. Taormina, what work do you do?
A. I am in charge of helping people borrow money when they come in to our bank to apply for a loan.
Q. Did you work on the loan for the Creekside apartment development?
A. Yes, I did.
Q. In your work as a lending officer at Sunshine Savings, did you make memos and reports?
A. Oh, yes.
Q. Tell the jurors why you would make those memos and reports.
A. Well, when I loan out the bank's money, I have to check that the borrower is qualified and can pay us back, and I have to check that the property that he is putting up is really worth enough to cover us if, for some reason, the borrower can't pay. Those are two of the reasons.
Q. Mr. Taormina, you know that I served a subpoena on the Resolution Trust Company and got the memos you wrote about this Creekside loan?
A. I know that.
Q. I know you've seen these before, so let me ask you to look at Defense Exhibits T-1 through T-12—T for Taormina, I guess—and tell us if you wrote those.
A. That's right.

These are premarked, and you should have had them admitted under the pretrial order. If not, refer to Chapter Six for the litany of admissibility. The examination continues:

Q. Mr. Taormina, would it help you to tell us just how and why Mr. Austin got this Creekside loan if we went through these memos?

A. It sure would.

Q. In your business, why are the memos important?

A. They go in the note case.

Q. I'm sorry. What is a note case?

A. That's the file on the loan.

Q. Who gets to look at that file?

A. My boss does, and the other lending officers. And then the federal regulators come in and inspect the bank. They look at it.

Q. So let's start with this first one, T-1. I am going to put up a copy on the overhead projector here. Tell us about that.

A. This is about my first meeting with Mr. Austin on Creekside. I note that he has been a bank customer, and I have his account balances and credit history.

Q. Based on that information, tell the jurors how you sized up Mr. Austin as somebody who should or should not be trusted with a sizable loan.

One by one, the documents will take you and the witness through the examination. Do not leave the documents up on the screen all the time. Do not have the witness read all of them. Move from a document excerpt to the witness telling the jurors something, and back again. The jurors will then have the documents in the jury room, and their looking at them will help recall what the witness said.

One difficulty with such witnesses is the jargon of their trade. Police officers do not go places and get out of their cars. They respond to scenes and exit their vehicles. In preparing for trial, you may find it difficult to impose a new vocabulary. You should not, however, unwittingly adopt the professional's mode of expression. Sometimes, even, you will want the image of the professional speaking in her own language, as a symbol of authority and therefore of authoritativeness.

If you are not striving to have the professional stand apart by use of language, keep steering back to standard

English. If the witness says, "We arrived at the scene at 1300 hours and exited our vehicle," your next questions can be, "I'm sorry. You got there at 1:00 o'clock P.M.?" and, "When you got out of your police car, could you see anyone lying in the roadway?"

## THE JOURNALIST

A journalist is a sort of professional that deserves separate mention. If the journalist works for a radio or television station, for a newspaper or magazine—as opposed to being free-lance—you may have a long fight on your hands to get the most basic documents and the most limited access to the witness. Some news organizations routinely instruct their news gatherers not to volunteer to be witnesses and routinely resist subpoenas for documents and testimony. Many jurisdictions recognize a qualified privilege for news gatherers' sources, and even for her notes.

Almost all print media journalists carry spiral-bound notebooks, access to which can help your trial preparation and can refresh the journalist's recollection.

Even if you can win a discovery fight, most journalists are reluctant witnesses. Most of them are also agile of mind and articulate of speech. I tried a case some years ago in which my opponent called a local journalist as a witness. On direct, the journalist didn't harm us much, and even helped us on some issues. At the recess, we talked it over and decided the witness had given every sign of wanting to help our side, and we would give him that chance.

I began to cross-examine, and the witness turned on me, being just as sullen and unhelpful to me as he had been to my opponent. He just didn't want to testify at all, and would punish anybody who asked him a question.

Sometimes the journalist will be a key witness who you must call. You will usually do best with a brief, focused examination limited to the necessary material.

# Chapter Four

## *Direct Examination: Difficult Attributes*

### THE DIFFICULT DIRECT EXAMINATION

The sages who say that direct examination is more difficult than cross could point, if challenged, to categories of witnesses that pose special problems. These problems can arise from a characteristic of the witness, such as age or lack of fluency in English. Or they may arise from the peculiar kind of testimony you are offering, such as character evidence.

There are no difficult witnesses. There are difficult direct examinations. You would not be presenting the witness unless she had something important to say. The job of bridging the gap between the witness chair and the jury box is yours. That is the challenge of your art, technique, and skill.

For all the categories of witnesses below, brevity will probably work to your advantage. Jurors, like most of us, may be uncomfortable with difference—the difference between themselves and the foreign language, young, elderly, or physically challenged witness. In addition, the process of questions and answers may be longer for the witnesses of whom we speak. It is therefore particularly important that your direct examination be brief and dignified.

You will not find a category below for every type of difficult direct examination you—or I—have confronted. I have chosen examples that illustrate some useful techniques. For each of these examples, you will find suggestions that can help for other categories of direct examination.

## FOREIGN LANGUAGE TESTIMONY
## AND RELATED PROBLEMS

Court proceedings in most parts of the United States are conducted in English. Witnesses who do not speak English are examined through a translator. Dealing with a translator poses special challenges that I believe are paradigmatic of communication problems in the entire trial process.

The out-of-court event that jurors are to imagine does not recreate itself. Rather, the old reality is mediated by witnesses and objects, as discussed in Chapter One. Translation simply puts another filter between jurors and "the facts." Because the filter is so obvious, we can recognize and address the ways in which it may interfere with the jurors' understanding of the witness, as human being and as testifier. We might use those insights to study other filters through which jurors are to see a story.

In Texas, New Mexico, Arizona, and California border towns, translated testimony is an everyday occurrence. It also appears in multinational criminal cases, complex civil cases, and transnational commercial disputes.

Typically, the translator is a court employee who stands next to the witness. The translator is sworn to translate accurately. *Voir dire* may be available to test his qualifications.

The examiner puts a question. The translator translates to the witness. The witness answers. The translator gives the response in English. The court reporter takes only the English version of events, so the transcript appears as though the witness had answered your question with the translator's answer. There are many cases in which you would seek an audio recording of the entire process, to have a record by which to judge the accuracy of translation.

The principal difficulty of the direct examiner, however, is to maintain a relationship with the witness for the jurors' benefit. Take an extreme, though real, case to illustrate the point. The witness is a criminal defendant, or maybe a key defense witness. The translator is a police officer or other ally of the prosecutor. By manner and intonation, the translator takes a confrontational posture with the witness.

After a few questions and answers, the witness is firmly focused on the translator and not the examiner. After all, the witness is alienated enough to begin with, coming into a courtroom where the formalistic proceedings are conducted in a language she does not speak.

The translator renders the questions in ways the examiner cannot control, and then edits the answers. It would be better to have a deposition translated and read by people of your choice, except of course that the witnesses are "available" and the deposition would not be admissible.

I have seen this scenario dozens of times. Variations include the translation booth for trials in which a defendant does not speak English. One hopes in such a case that the translator, and not the defendant, is in the booth and that the earphones and other translation paraphernalia are relatively unobtrusive.

As your first countermove, try to cut the figurative distance between you and the witness. If you speak the witness's language, move for leave to put your questions in that language, have the questions translated, get the witness's answer, and have that translated. The benefits are great and obvious. Now the witness is focused on you, responding and perceived by the jurors to respond to you. Even if you are not completely fluent in the witness's language, I recommend seeking leave to use this approach; you can prepare your questions more completely than you otherwise would. Your increased rapport with the witness will more than balance the loss in spontaneity caused by using prepared questions.

If you are compelled to use the more traditional method of getting the testimony, you usually have an advantage as a direct examiner because you can prepare the witness. When cross-examining through a translator, you will not have had the chance to meet with the witness, except perhaps in deposition. You may then have to contend with a translator who is trying to protect the witness. At the least, the witness has time to think about answers. Your best bet will be to stick to short, simple, leading questions.

When preparing the witness for direct examination, you should create the courtroom scene. Accustom the witness to the distances and sight lines. Tell the witness to look at you while you are asking questions, then turn to the translator. You must have somebody at your counsel table fluent in both languages. Tell the witness, "If you don't understand my question as it is translated, or even if it seems that the translator is not asking you the same question I did, stop and say, 'I don't understand. Please ask me again.' " When the witness answers your question, she should turn to you or the jurors, not to the translator. Do not be afraid to remind the witness to do this during your direct examination, for example, "Please, when you answer, look at the jurors, so they can hear you clearly."

You and your counsel table assistant should also have an agreed means of communicating so that you are aware of mistranslations and can timely object.

What of the witness who speaks English well enough to testify in that language but whose first language is not English? The trade-off is clear, but you will not value the elements of it the same way in every case. You lose spontaneity and visible rapport if the witness does not testify in English. However, the witness gains valuable thinking time on cross-examination because everything stops while the questions are being translated.

The problems of translation should sharpen your sense of how alienating and difficult all witnesses find the courtroom environment. They should also quicken your appreciation of nonverbal language such as demonstrative evidence, and even gestures. By having the foreign language witness use the same charts, diagrams, and objects as

English language witnesses, you universalize the former's message and tie it to your overall theme.

Dealing with gestures is more problematic. In every culture, communication is both verbal and nonverbal. Yet the gestures that are thought to convey sincerity and openness in one culture may signify the opposite in another. Juror bias toward particular ethnic groups, accents, and mannerisms affects judgments on credibility. The subjectivity of such judgments is one ingredient in the mix of substantial doubts about the value of demeanor evidence.

This problem is not limited to witnesses who testify in a foreign language. It affects all people perceived by the jurors as "not us." Mannerisms of an English-speaking witness that jurors identify as "gay," "black," "Jewish," "Oriental," or whatever, are going to be a part of the cues that jurors use to evaluate the testimony.

You may have to deal with this in summation by stressing the ideal of equal justice under the law:

"Members of the jury, if you get back in the jury room and somebody says, 'Well, look at that witness. You know you can't trust those Japs.' You know you can look right at that person and say to them, 'Hold on there. We took an oath to be jurors here. We swore that we were not going to let any prejudice get in the way. And if we were going to have any trouble, we were supposed to raise our hands and get off the jury. Even the judge told us we had to put all that prejudice out of our minds.' On the marble lintel of the Supreme Court building in Washington, D.C., they have the words 'Equal Justice Under Law.' Equal—for rich or poor, black or white, neighbor or stranger. And we can't let anybody try to get us to go up there some dark night with a high ladder and an ax and chop those words off there."

For such a summation argument to be effective, it is better to have prepared the way in *voir dire* and the opening statement. Tell the jurors who your witnesses will be. Ask whether they would hold it against a witness that she is from another country and doesn't speak English. Will they hold it against the witness because it might be difficult to interpret the words, gestures, and expressions of someone who is different from the rest of us? Venirepersons' nonverbal reactions to these questions may be telling.

When you prepare a witness to testify, you must try to understand how that witness's cultural and personal background affects his mannerisms and gestures. Using a video camera may help the witness see how a particular gesture gets in the way of communication. However, some habits are so deeply ingrained that trying to exorcise them will only add to the witness's difficulty in communicating.

In some instances, you can ask about the gesture. "I notice that you nod your head slightly whenever I ask you a question. Does that mean that you automatically agree with me?" The reply might be, "Oh, no. In our culture, the nod is simply a mark of respect toward another person. So, if I nod at you, or even at the other lawyer when she asks me questions, that doesn't mean 'yes.' "

To help understand a communications problem, you may consult a linguist or sociologist, either in person or through library research.

There are, however, gestures and mannerisms that are universal or nearly so. Pointing at a person, a chart, or part of a demonstrative exhibit; marking on a diagram or map; demonstrating some physical action—all of these recreate a reality and unite this witness to other witnesses and to the story of the case.

Federal Rule of Evidence 611(c) permits you to use leading questions with any witness "as may be necessary to develop the witness's testimony." Usually, one thinks of this provision as permitting leading on introductory matters. The rule has, however, been interpreted to permit leading when dealing with witnesses who are young or who have a disability. The same rationale would permit at least selective use of leading questions if a witness had difficulty in communicating in the English language.

## THE CHILD WITNESS

A child will be ruled competent to testify if he understands the meaning of the oath. We have all seen the kindly old judge leaning over to the kid in the witness box, asking if the kid knows what happens if he lies. The kid usually smiles right at the camera (poised to make it look like the judge is getting it right in the eye) and intones some sacerdotal whizbang about the uncomfortable afterlife of liars. The kid is then permitted to testify and wins the case for the lawyer, who may or may not be played by Jimmy Stewart.

The testimony of anyone, child or adult, who does not understand the legal obligation to tell the truth will not be received. Your direct examination must therefore begin by establishing this precondition.

It is also settled that testimony subjected to undue suggestion is not admissible or, if the suggestion is revealed after the direct examination, will be stricken out or a mistrial granted. Your preparation of any witness, of any age, must avoid these perils.

In some jurisdictions, children who are parties or witnesses may have a guardian *ad litem* appointed for them. The guardian may be a lawyer, someone from a social service agency, or a student in a law school clinical program. If the law permits appointment of a guardian, you may wish to have this done to give the child a sense of security about his testimony, and the testimony itself accrues an added dimension of independence and therefore credibility.

In some cases, one or more expert witnesses will give an opinion for the jury about the weight to be given a child's testimony. The expert evaluates the stresses and pressures on the child and the effect of the courtroom environment.

You will not meet your prospective child witness alone, nor should you. Not only must you not overpower the child, but you must be able to rebut with witnesses any charge of having tried to do so.

You must insist as well that the child not be accompanied and coached by someone with a partisan stake in the testimony. There are several versions of the compelling story of a child witness who on cross-examination repeated the story told on direct—three times, without changing a word of the story as the child had been taught to say it. The story may be apocryphal, or maybe it really happened to all the trial lawyers who say that it happened to them. In any case, the lesson is clear.

You will of course deny a desire to teach the child witness a set speech. It is unethical to do so and destructive of your credibility with the jurors when the tactic is exposed in court. But you must be equally vigilant that no one else has unfairly coached the child before you begin witness preparation.

In sum, the child should be accompanied by someone he trusts but who is not a partisan. "But I want to be there," the mother or father may say. You reply, "I understand, but, if you are, it will actually hurt our case because they'll accuse us of influencing X's testimony." It may be hard to find the relatively neutral person to be with the child—perhaps a child-care person, another relative, or someone appointed as a guardian.

You will be accompanied for the preparation session as well, to have a witness but also to have help. Some of us can talk naturally with a child, and others have more difficulty. Our ability may vary from child to child, issue to issue. Fewer of us are able to tell what kind of impression we are making—on the child or on spectators.

If you can use an inconspicuous video camera to record a part of your interchange with the child, you can better gauge how well you are communicating.

At trial, make sure there is a comfortable chair from which the child can see and be seen. Many courts permit the child to be accompanied to the witness stand by a caring adult—again, someone who is not obviously a partisan but in whom the child reposes trust. The child can sit on that person's lap, or the person can sit alongside the child. Make sure the child can be heard, even if you have to make special arrangements for a sound system.

In your brief and dignified direct examination, make full use of the loops, prologues, and transitions discussed in Chapter Two. Note that Federal Rule of Evidence 611(c) may permit you to use leading questions. When the examination is finished, you will have the satisfaction of having done it well and of knowing that your opponent who is about to cross-examine faces a more difficult challenge than you did.

## THE WITNESS WHO
## WAS WRONG

You may find that your witness has made a statement in a deposition or before the grand jury that is demonstrably wrong. You may have striven mightily to keep the prior statement out of evidence until your witness testifies, thus giving you and the witness the first chance to introduce the prior statement and talk about it.

You must meet such a statement head-on. You and the witness lose credibility by trying to twist and reconstrue words to make them say what they did not. Sometimes context, errors of transcription, and explanation can make the contradiction evaporate. Your efforts along this line must pass the straight-face test; otherwise, abandon them.

In a criminal case, the government alleged that the defendant, a former public official, had lied to the grand jury about the time of day at which he met with another political figure, J, who had allegedly paid the defendant an illegal gratuity. Before going to the grand jury, the defendant had reviewed his typewritten itinerary from the day in question and concluded that he must have met J in the late afternoon.

The itinerary had been prepared as a plan for the day, but the planned order had been rearranged. Most of us have seen witnesses, particularly busy people who keep time sheets or desk calendars, or who generate many memos, being fooled by the written record into forgetting what really happened. In fact, the defendant had met J in the morning, in a hotel room, and a room service waiter remembered serving them coffee.

The direct examiner's job in such a case is to deal with the wrong statement quickly, easily, and naturally—and so bury it that the cross-examiner has nothing to grab. If the inconsistency will be proven before it can be explained, you must anticipate this in the opening statement.

In our case, we asked the defendant, "Did you meet J that day?" "What time of day was that?" "How do you know?" The answer was something like, "It was for coffee in the morning. You know, I even told the grand jury that it was in the afternoon, because that's what my schedule suggested, and I remembered that we met in my room while I was putting my tie on to go out. But my schedule was rearranged after it was typed up, and instead of meeting him when I was getting dressed for dinner, it was in the morning. As soon as I saw that room service waiter—who I've known for years—I knew I had remembered it wrong."

The witness must squarely admit having been wrong. He must have a reason for giving a wrong answer and state that reason. Haste, failing to study the situation, confusion with another event—these are some benign reasons.

Sometimes the earlier statement was wrong because the witness was lying. Everybody is willing to lie for some reason that to them is sufficiently grave: "I was afraid of what my husband would do." "I thought I would lose my job if I didn't go along with it." "I was scared of what would happen if I told the truth, but now that I have told the truth and taken the consequences, I feel better."

Lead up to that moment of admission, move through it, give it a moment to sink in, and then move on to something else.

## THE WITNESS WHO DOESN'T WANT TO BE THERE

There are witnesses whose attitude is somewhere between neutral and adverse. They don't like you much, but you can't get the judge to let you use leading questions. Control, distance, and brevity are the key words. The witness will probably be sullen, an attitude perhaps enhanced by the witness's lawyer having railed at you or having tried to quash the subpoena.

So be it. The testimony is then in the form of truthful reluctant concessions. You exercise control with documents and other tangible objects and with prior statements. You keep distance by setting up the interrogation as an exercise of power: the court's power, not yours. "You are here today because of a subpoena issued under the seal of this court?" "Was the subpoena served on you?" "Did you receive the witness fee that the law requires?" "Did you get your own lawyer to help you understand your rights and your duties?" Now the witness's incipient or overt churlishness seems directed at the neutral institution, the court, rather than at you for any purported discourtesy or *lèse majesté* you might have exhibited to the witness.

Q. I am handing you Defendant's Exhibit 40. Is that your memorandum?
   [With witnesses of this sort, it is far better to have laid a foundation and admitted the exhibits before trial.]
A. Yes.
Q. Did you write that memorandum on July 24, 1990?
A. That's what it says.
Q. Oh, yes. I see that. But as best as you can figure out, is that right?
A. Yes.

In this exchange, the advocate establishes some witness control without acting hostilely. With the memorandum—or patient chart, or notebook—in front of the jury, what do you do with it? If you just leave it alone, the jurors will have little idea of what is there, and you will not have made an impact with this witness. No, you must get the witness to spell it out, even though the witness's manner may lack the persuasive effect you would wish.

Q. I have put the memorandum up on the overhead projector. Will you please read out the brief paragraph that I have highlighted in yellow?
A. [The witness complies.]
Q. Now I am going to show you a patient chart, Defendant's Exhibit 41. That is a chart from your office?

You can ask this because you can lead on foundational matters.

A. It is.
Q. The jurors need to know what you wrote on the chart on July 3, 1990, and how you came to write that. Let me put that entry up. Can you decipher it for us?
A. Right great toe edema, warm, painful to touch, movement. Gouty arthritis. Colchicine, and then a dosage.
Q. You have read us the words on there. Can you tell us what you saw, just as though we were your patient and you were explaining it to us?

You are asking her to talk to the jurors in a way she knows. She will probably take the hint. She may not want to be there, but she has a motive to preserve her professional persona.

A. As you can tell, your right big toe is very swollen and red. You can put your hand over the area and feel warmth. It hurts like the dickens when you touch or move it. I am going to give you some colchicine, which is a traditional drug that has been used to treat this gout.

The pattern is to move from signpost to signpost, gently coaxing the witness along the way. The need for brevity— getting the witness on and off—requires no explanation.

## THE CHARACTER WITNESS

The rules give you choices in the use of character evidence. For example, an accused may call witnesses on a trait of character relevant to the alleged offense or on truthfulness if the accused testifies. The prosecution may then call character witnesses to rebut. A victim's character may be opened up by the accused, again giving the prosecution leave to rebut. A witness's character may be attacked or supported by character evidence on the issue of truthfulness. Under Federal Rule of Evidence 806, you can use the same character evidence against a hearsay declarant as you would have used if the declarant were a live witness.

In a criminal case, sometimes character evidence for the accused, and evidence of a prosecution witness's bad character for truthfulness, will be the only testimony offered by the defense. Most jurisdictions still cling to the rule that, in a criminal case, character evidence standing alone may raise a reasonable doubt and that the jury must be so instructed on proper and timely request.

In the old days, character evidence was surrounded with formalisms, now largely shorn away. The rules required that the witness testify about "reputation in the community," a special kind of hearsay akin to gossip.

Justice William J. Brennan, Jr., tells of being appointed as a young lawyer to defend a vehicular homicide case and calling a police officer as a character witness. He established that the officer and the young defendant were near neighbors, and had been for some time. "And can you tell the jury, what is the defendant's reputation in the community for veracity?" Counselor Brennan intoned. "Well, I'd say he's a pretty good driver," the officer replied. After several more efforts, and when things had quieted down, the judge turned to the officer and asked if he knew the young man.

"Oh, yes."

"And have you ever known him to lie?"

"Oh, no, Your Honor."

"Well, that's what young Mr. Brennan has been after asking you, but he went to the Harvard Law School and forgot how to speak English."

Today, in most jurisdictions, you can take the character evidence by way of opinion, reputation, or both. To elicit reputation—the older form of character evidence—you can ask the witness, as young William Brennan did, whether he lives in the defendant's community, whether he has heard people talk about the defendant, and then to tell the defendant's reputation for some relevant character trait. The witness is not speaking of his personal view. Rather, he is purportedly distilling and repeating hearsay references to the defendant from countless and unidentified speakers. In a simpler time, when one could more meaningfully speak of "community," such evidence made common sense, though its theoretical basis was uncertain.

Character evidence based on opinion is more straightforward. The witness knows the defendant, victim, or witness and tells the jurors how and for how long. The witness has an opinion on a relevant trait of character. What is it?

You cannot use specific instances of conduct on direct examination as evidence of propensity, but you can get the next best thing by asking for the basis of the opinion or reputation evidence. Specific instances are proper subjects for cross-examination.

Relaxation of the rules means that you have fewer barriers between the witness's words and the juror's perception. Know that, and help your witnesses to know it. Character evidence is a kind of relic in our legal system, harking back to the days of compurgation and oath helpers. It has power—if the witness will look the jurors in the eye and perform the vouching ritual.

In Chapter Two, I described the preparation and testimony of Lady Bird Johnson as a character witness. Another character witness in the same case was the Reverend Billy Graham. Frankly, I was worried about the impact he would make on the jury. Character witnesses are often the defendant's very good friends; they often think the prosecution is trumped-up and unfair. They may be anxious to impart this view to the jurors, to "help the case." You have to discourage their ad lib additions to the routine of testimony.

Reverend Graham's unplanned addition worked out fine. One juror carried a New Testament in her purse. She read it during breaks in the trial. Reverend Graham was sworn.

"What is your business or occupation?" Ed Williams asked.

"I preach the gospel of Jesus Christ all over the world."

"Amen!" said the juror.

The court will limit the number of character witnesses you call, and this is perhaps just as well. You will also remember that a witness to someone's positive trait of character may be asked questions about disreputable incidents in that person's life; this inquiry goes well beyond what would be provable if you did not present character evidence. In selecting witnesses, make sure that they are able to handle such cross-examination and that they are prepared for it.

Character witnesses should be as different from the defendant as possible. They should be people with whom the jurors will identify. If you present several character witnesses, they should differ from one another.

You will introduce the witness. How long has she known Mr. X? How did she come to know him? How often do they see each other? At what kinds of events? Has he visited her home? Has she visited his? Notice that this line of inquiry establishes a "foundation" for opinion and reputation evidence, but it also inevitably lets you introduce some specific instances of conduct. For example, "Well, I see him a lot at the school, because for the past ten years he has been in charge of the Booster Club fund drive for the athletic teams."

Continuing, has the witness heard others talk about Mr. X's honesty? Does she know what people in the community think about his honesty? You must, of course, define the community of which you speak. You have some latitude. Most of us in today's complex society live in several communities—at home, at work, in our profession, in performing community service. Familiarity with any of these communities is enough foundation for character evidence, even that based on reputation.

When you have painted a picture of the witness, the person whose character is in issue, and their relationship, there is one more hurdle before asking the key questions. "Before I ask you these last questions, tell us if you are generally familiar with the issues in this lawsuit being tried by these jurors." The correct answer is a simple "Yes, I am."

Now for the key questions: "From all of this, do you know Mr. X's reputation in the community for integrity?" The answer is "Yes." "What is his reputation?" "That he is a person of the highest integrity."

"Do you have a personal opinion about his integrity?" "Yes." "Tell the jurors what that is." "I also think he has the highest integrity."

As the example shows, you should ask separate questions on reputation and opinion, as well as a separate pair of these questions for each relevant trait of character, such as integrity, which may relate to an element of the offense, and truthfulness, which is relevant because Mr. X has testified or will testify. Your questions in this final part of the examination will be crisp, but a small amount of repetition helps to drive the point home.

# Chapter Five

## *Direct Examination: Your Client*

I had read the transcript of a trial. I was retained for the appeal, and won. Now there was a chance to try the case over again. I sat down with the client. "Look," I said, "your testimony at the first trial was a disaster. Your answers on direct examination were unfocused, the direct examination itself did not anticipate the problems you would face on cross, and your cross-examination made you look evasive."

"I know," the client said. "My lawyer was heavily involved in other matters and did not have the time to spend with me. Sometimes, on direct examination, I didn't even know what answer was expected of me. I didn't understand the questions I was being asked."

Can you think of a more damning criticism of that trial lawyer?

Contrast Houston lawyer David Berg's direct examination of his client in a family inheritance feud, of which a journalist wrote rhapsodically: "He turned his chair toward the witness box, sat facing her (not the jury) and asked her about her life. He never let the action slack off, never waited more than a heartbeat to get to the next question, and let shine possibly the best witness he would ever get on a stand in his lifetime. The two became a duet. The rest of the world seemed to disappear." The journalist went on to describe Berg's having spent days with his client, at her home, in his office, at mealtimes, in order to understand her so fully that his direct examination could serve as a window to the soul of her claim for justice.

Not all clients are, in their natural state, woven of such sympathetic material. Their claims for justice may not be obviously worth the jurors' attention. Not all client direct examinations can be structured as a duet for the benefit of spectators or jurors. David Berg was able to find the right set of techniques for this case and client because he listened. He got out of his office to listen to his client on her home ground. He listened to her in many settings, not just in the interpretation of her legal matter.

To restate: The lifeline of a trial is the lawyer earning credibility in the jurors' eyes, keeping that credibility in the heat of combat, and sharing that credibility with the client. So many times the last step does not work; the jurors come back with tears in their eyes and afterward apologize to the lawyer. "You are such a nice person, but I just didn't think your client had a case."

## DOES THE CLIENT TESTIFY?

In civil cases, this is seldom an issue. Of course the client will testify because her deposition has been taken, it can be used by the other side, and there is no principle to explain to the jurors why the client stayed silent.

In criminal cases, the approach differs. Thinking about the issue illuminates the credibility problem for all kinds of cases. My mentor, Edward Bennett Williams, thought it essential that the client testify in almost every case, certainly in white-collar crime cases. I came to disagree with him, and my view took firmer shape after several acquittals in cases where the client did not testify.

In a criminal case, the jury can know on *voir dire*, in argument, and again in the instructions that they may draw no adverse inference from the accused's not taking the witness stand. In summation,

"Suppose you are in the jury room, and somebody looks at you and says, 'Well, you know, that defendant didn't take the stand.' What can you say to that person? You can look them in the eye and say, 'Now wait a minute. We all took an oath that we would follow the law as the judge gave it to us. And the judge said, just as clear as anything, that the prosecutor has the whole burden of proof and the defendant doesn't have to prove anything. You can't hold it against the defendant that his lawyer advised him that this jury was made up of honest people who would follow the law the way the judge laid it out.' "

If you agree with me that jurors care about the law, you will see it is possible that the client not testify. But is it wise in a given case? Here is a lesson that goes beyond criminal cases. The credibility of your client, and of her claim for justice, does not depend only on her. If you try to make victory depend on your client's performance at trial, you will invest it with too much importance and risk overstatement through the client—and perhaps you—losing control and perspective.

Jurors assess the client's credibility from the client's words, deeds, and aspirations, tempered by their own experience and placed into the context created by trial evidence that supports or saps the strength of the client's claim. It is fortunate that this is so, for the reasons given above: Not all clients can carry a load so heavy as the claim for justice they are making. By definition, as well as in jurors' minds, the client has the greatest interest in the outcome, so great indeed that she was disqualified as a witness at common law and is still disqualified in many legal systems. Jurors don't forget that self-interest affects credibility; unfortunately, lawyers sometimes do. Let us examine the question from two perspectives, namely, the practical decision in a criminal case and the client's role in storytelling generally.

## THE CRIMINAL DEFENDANT
## AS WITNESS

Defending a criminal case, you are in trouble unless you are ahead on points at the end of the prosecution's evidence. Cross-examination and consistent exposition of your story are that important. I contend also that most criminal defendants on the stand harm their cause. Most judges allow prosecutors the widest latitude on cross-examination. Thus, it is difficult to protect your client by objecting. In any case, objecting makes you look weak, and in this context makes it appear even more strongly that you and the client have something to hide.

You can endlessly and vigorously prepare some defendants for cross-examination, and they will yet trap themselves by arrogance, anger, or some other misplaced emotion into disastrous behavior on the stand.

The agony of a criminal trial, particularly one that comes after a long and hard-fought investigative phase, puts incredible pressure on the defendant and those close to him. Even when the defendant is articulate and knows information that is part of a credible defense story, he may simply not be a good witness. Looking the defendant in the eye and saying "Don't take the stand" is one of the most difficult jobs you will face as an advocate.

Don't shrink from the decision. If the client insists on testifying anyway, memorialize your advice in writing and redouble your efforts at preparing him for the ordeal. Sometimes you cannot make the decision not to put the client on the stand until you have spent several days preparing him to testify.

And let's face it: By the time the defense case rolls around, you may be tired of your client's constant demands on your skill and emotional support. The most difficult trial decision you face must be made at a time when your personal resources are stretched thin.

A criminal defendant whose case rests on "reasonable doubt" should presumptively not testify. Testifying opens up cross-examination on numberless collateral matters, going to credibility as well as the facts of the case. As the defendant is cross-examined by an able prosecutor, you can watch the ambiguities in the proof, and the jurors' ambivalence, fade away. For example, if the evidence is the testimony of an informer and a collection of ambiguous tape recordings, there is little point in putting the defendant on. This precept can be overruled only if you are supremely confident that the defendant will make a stellar impression.

A criminal defendant who will alienate the jury through arrogance, evasiveness, or provable misconduct should not testify. Arrogance and evasiveness can often be controlled through careful preparation. A prior record or involvement in activities that the jurors will find disquieting cannot be compensated for. Two examples come to mind. In one case, the client had felt persecuted by the government's long-time effort to prosecute and punish him. He resented the prosecutor, who had been involved in the case from the beginning. No amount of preparation could dull that sharp edge of despair. Our theory of the case was that the defendant was a responsible businessperson who had behaved honestly, seeking to conform to conflicting and confusing government guidelines. A few hours on the stand might have wrecked that image. At the time of the alleged offenses, the defendant indeed fit the picture we were painting. By the time of trial, the stresses to which he had been subjected made him someone else—someone we did not think the jury would like.

In another case, the path led in the opposite direction. The defendant had muddled through the business dealings that were the basis of the trial in an alcoholic haze. Some of his conduct supported the government's theory. He had done some things—not provable in the government's case-in-chief—that would have been revealed on cross-examination, perhaps in detail. These things involved booze and women and money. Our defenses were that the defendant's partner—who had become a government witness—was the true wrongdoer and that the defendant's alcoholism made him unable to form a specific intent to violate the law. We were able through cross-examination to present a full picture of the partner's peculations and, in our defense evidence, to paint the defendant and his malady. We did not need the defendant on the stand.

Finally, there will be cases in which the defendant promises to behave on the witness stand, but you know that the promise is hollow. You have to advise against testifying.

## PREPARING THE CLIENT
## TO TESTIFY

To prepare your client for direct examination, start with a set of prior statements and relevant exhibits, arranged and indexed for study. If your client can easily absorb information in this way, she can study these materials on her own. Many people do not profit greatly from written material; for such a person, someone in your office (maybe you) will have to sit down and track through the material.

The key to preparation, however, is understanding. David Berg took the time to know his client in many moods and many settings. By seeing his client on her turf, where she was in control, he not only derived insight but was able to accord her dignity when she testified. Even when the case does not permit so intensive an investment of time, you must adopt some strategy to gain this kind of insight. Take the time to know your client "in the round," not just as a walking legal theory.

I once tried a one-day criminal contempt case. The defendant, a lawyer, was going to testify. One factual issue was whether he had heard something in court that the judge had said; he denied it. In taking the time to talk informally with the client over several hours, we were talking about his habits. One of his consistent habits was also consistent with his denial; while prospective jurors were filing into the courtroom, being seated, and then waiting for the *voir dire* to begin, he sat at counsel table and watched them. If there was a bench conference or some other event that required attention, he would send the other lawyers on his team to cover it. For this lawyer, using every proper and available clue to know the potential jurors was of decisive importance. Not only could we use that on direct examination, but we were able to have other witnesses remark on it as a kind of preview of the client's testimony, as they described having been at the crucial bench conference and noting that the defendant was not there. You will get important clues by breaking yourself and the client out of a rigid mold of witness preparation.

Let us reflect on some typical cases, to identify and critique some usual styles of client preparation.

First case: For prosecutors, the "client" role is often taken by the victim. Why do prosecutors lose perfectly good cases with fairly simple facts? Usually, they lose because their schedules force them to rely on police reports, and they don't take the time to know the victim well enough to conduct her direct examination. Often, the victim has been shuffled through the bureaucratic maze, with little or no emphasis on what she will face at trial. The result is that she looks flat on direct examination and does not do well on cross.

Second case: A busy defense counsel has trouble dealing with the client in any case; appointments are hard to set. Maybe the client is in jail or speaks a different language from the lawyer. The client puts up a facade of bravado. The lawyer makes a few suggestions and leaves it at that. The client takes the stand and looks guilty.

Third case: In a busy negligence practice, the lawyer has the paralegal or secretary schedule the client for a preparation session. The lawyer orders up the file to get ready. The entire session is conducted in a routinized and "usual" way. The lawyer sees the client as an object to be molded into a certain mode of testifying—and according to a certain schedule. The client never truly feels comfortable, and the lawyer misses clues to human strengths and frailties that would have given ideas for direct or sounded alarms about cross-examination.

A fourth case, one in which the lack of preparation is the result of choice and not circumstance: There are lawyers—I have worked with them—who disdain detailed preparation of their clients to testify. They sit with the client, describe the issues, discuss potential problems with the facts and exhibits, talk about the opponent's strategy, and let it go at that. Sometimes they justify this approach by saying that undue preparation distorts the client's testimony.

In all four cases, the lawyers are wrong. In case four, the lawyer is retreating to a position rather like that of the English barrister, who has the solicitor as a buffer between himself and the client. Such a lawyer stands at a physical and emotional distance from the witnesses in court. Arguably, the British trial process is in this respect so unlike the American that witness preparation strategies must differ as well. In my view, however, the best British barristers are those who descend from their lofty perch and learn about their clients.

To begin with the ethical aspect, there is nothing wrong with intensely preparing your client to give truthful testimony in a persuasive way. You serve truth by understanding your client's human predicament and then helping the client to communicate this predicament. This is a process of overcoming the alienating and artificial environment of the courtroom. Your preparation is not building barriers to truth, it is tearing them down. To see this point fully, recur to the discussion in Chapter One.

Cases one, two, and three yield the same result for different reasons. Lawyer one professes to be confined by the system for preparing and trying cases. Lawyer two may indeed be unduly burdened, but he does have the option of not putting the client on. Lawyer three is confined by a self-devised schedule and method.

There is almost always enough time to break through routines that impair your client's ability to communicate with the jury. The prosecutor can find or make a space within which to prepare witnesses. Defense counsel can devise ways of communicating that overcome the barriers imposed by the system. Civil litigators have the most freedom of all—they can meet their clients outside the office or at least outside the structure imposed by undue delegation of functions and unseemly worship of the billable hour.

Clients who are to be witnesses fall into two groups. Some are accustomed to taking control, in their daily lives and in litigation, as a means of fighting back at the system that frustrates them. Others see their existence controlled by others, and the litigation process is merely one more step along that path.

The first type of client risks alienating the jurors through arrogance. That same arrogance may cause the client to disregard your advice at a crucial juncture in direct or cross-examination and "go it alone." The second type may appear uncredible on direct and be malleable during a pounding cross. These types do not describe absolutes. A person may exhibit symptoms of both at different times. Or a person normally controlled may let go a burst of arrogance in frustration.

Your basic response to both types is the same: assert and maintain control. The differences will become important only when you are spotting symptoms of discontrol in the process of preparation or testimony.

For the arrogant client, you can borrow authority from the trial process: "Look, I know how you want to handle this, but the rules don't permit it. The judge wouldn't stand still for it." For the insecure client, the rules are the matrix within which you work to tell his story and to protect against the opponent's unfairness: "The procedures in court permit us to tell your story persuasively and strongly, and that's what we are going to do. That's why I'm here."

The direct examination must not be the sort of wooden performance that turns off the jurors, in part because that is what they expect. Preparation should begin with deconstruction, to sweep away your client's prejudgments, grandiosity, fearfulness, and other assorted imaginings.

You begin with some variation of "Tell me what *you* think your appearance on the stand is going to be like?" Do not be put off; get a full answer to this question. Ask follow-up questions: "Hmm, can you remember how you got that idea of it?" "What do you think the other side is going to do then?" You have to listen to all of this, to drain it off so that you can put back the parts that are real and helpful and throw out the ones that aren't.

In the process, you are going to uncover fears that can be allayed, misconceptions that can be corrected, and underneath it all some important facts about your client. Fears may include revelation of private matters; you may be able to give assurance that the matter has been covered by a motion *in limine*.

Misconceptions include the common one, "Well, I am going to swear to tell the *whole* truth. So when I get up there on the stand, I'll let them have it. They can't cut me off because I swore to tell the whole truth." You can explain that you'd like to do it that way but that choices are limited. If your client is the plaintiff, living by what seem to be silly rules is the price of admission to the courthouse. If the client is the defendant, the rules are just another indignity—one that probably pales alongside being sued in the first place.

The truths underneath are contained in the internal dialogue that almost everyone has about being a witness and that you are asking your client to tell you. They are the parts of the story that the client feels must be told, that she is afraid will not be told. They are the anticipated responses to this or that line of inquiry, by you or your opponent.

Having exhausted all inquiry under the first question, ask your second one, even though you have asked it a hundred times before: "What do you want to get from this jury?" Some clients are going to say "a medal." Some are going to say, "I just want them not to think I am a blithering idiot."

I have had clients who wanted a medal or, as they sometimes put it, vindication. Sometimes that happens, but usually the process isn't built that way. The most dangerous kind of righteousness is self-righteousness. In a criminal case, an acquittal will do nicely. Loud huzzahs from the jury would be nice but are not required. When you lower your client's expectations in such a case, you are bringing the focus down to the realm of facts and credibility that are the focus of direct examination preparation.

The low-goal client needs your assurance that the important process of presentation is part of telling the story that you have agreed is important.

## THE CLIENT ON THE STAND

I don't think much depends on whether your client is the plaintiff or the defendant. You will seldom bet the entire result on the client's testimony. The client is one part of the entire story. Plaintiffs should generally wait to appear until late in the case, to build juror expectation, to let you and the client get used to the jury, and to see exactly how the case story is crystallizing so you have a surer idea of where the emphasis must be. Civil defendants should generally appear first or last in the defense case: first if you need to start really strong to fulfill a promise made in opening, and last as a clean-up hitter. In a criminal case, last is probably best, or almost last: Character witnesses and summary witnesses can follow the defendant to the stand because they are not adding any new pieces to the story.

As you think out the direct, ask, "Who is this person?" Is your client someone who has been robbed by the clever frauds of others? If so, you will not prepare him to take the stand and wade through stacks of financial records to show a discerning ability to spot error; that would be inconsistent with the personality of this client as you have portrayed him. On the other hand, if your client is someone who is habitually careful and was careful in handling the matter in litigation, then she should exhibit that care and attention in handling your questions and the exhibits.

Your questions to yourself always lead to "Am I making sure the client is communicating her true self?" Legendary Chicago lawyer Gene Pincham tells the story of his summation in a criminal case. The defendant was charged with killing his wife, but no body had been found. Pincham urged this as reasonable doubt.

"Members of the jury, who is to say? Who is to say beyond a reasonable doubt that she is not alive out there somewhere? Maybe she is going to walk through the door of this courtroom any minute now. Good God! Look! There she is!" And when the excitement died down, he continued, "You see, you have a reasonable doubt. You all turned and looked at that door, because you were not sure she was dead."

The jury convicted without much deliberation, and a juror explained, "Well, that was a good trick you pulled, but your client was the only one in court who didn't turn his head. *He* knew she wasn't coming back."

The point at which you call the client to testify finally arrives. She has been sitting at counsel table. The jurors met her during *voir dire*. They have been watching her. More important, they have been watching your relationship to her. There are many different theories about what a counsel table should look like, even to how many pieces of paper can be on it. Some lawyers sit alone at a clean table, look at the jury, other lawyers, the judge, or the witness, and just maybe take an occasional note. They do not interact with the client in the jurors' presence.

I think this is a mistake. If the idea of transferring credibility has any meaning, you should visibly be part of a team with your client. Granted, there are times when you will not want to be interrupted, and the client should have a notepad on which to make an *occasional* note. You should put your arm on your client's shoulder, talk to her, visibly pay her deference. You and she are in these moments conducting a direct examination every bit as important as the *viva voce* exercise to come.

When you call the client, make it an event, but without pomposity. Demand respect for the client by the manner of calling her name. This is particularly important for criminal defendants, women, and minorities, whom the other side and even the judge may try to trivialize by demeanor or word.

"Your Honor, members of the jury, we call Ms. Juanita Wilson as a witness." If you have been helping people with their chairs on other occasions, help pull Ms. Wilson's chair. Motion her to the clerk's desk to be sworn. See that she has a glass of water if you have been extending that courtesy to others. If there is a microphone, make sure it is adjusted. Let her get comfortable in the chair.

Custom and rule dictate whether you examine seated or standing and, if standing, whether you must remain at a lectern. Whatever you have done with other witnesses, pick a spot for this direct examination and stay there. Move only when you are helping the witness work with an exhibit or when you are going to stand somewhere to help the witness make a point. For example, if the witness is going to be talking about an opposing party or counsel, you might move over and stand behind that person if the rules permit. People don't like other people standing behind them, especially when they are being talked about; it makes them uncomfortable, and they look it.

Begin. "It is very important for the jurors to hear every word you have to say. Please, could you keep your voice up so that at least everybody within this space [indicating the judge and the jurors] can hear you. Thanks. Tell the jurors your full name. Where do you live? What do you do for work?"

The examination follows the precepts of Chapter Two. However, you must decide where the key points will come. The idea of beginning and ending strong must at times yield to your need to build slowly, accustoming the witness to the rhythm of testifying and the jurors to the witness. Before the witness says anything strong and dispositive, the jurors must be prepared to accept it, and the witness must be prepared to say it in a nontheatrical, natural way.

Therefore, beginning strong usually means telling the jury why this person is here and who she is. After "What is your work?" the next question might be, "Why are you in court?" The answer will be partial, preliminary—for example, "I sued the insurance company because they wouldn't pay me what they owe." That answer packs a lot of information, but can be given in a fairly matter-of-fact way. If the client begins too intensely and combatively, there is little room for more intensity—the entire examination will be on one high note.

Now, move through background, experience, and on to the events that led to the lawsuit. In organizing this material, make sure you punctuate it. Identifying people and exhibits will give natural breaks to the examination. Your loops and prologues will do this as well.

When you first set, then vary, the tone of interrogative discourse, you are also trying to set a pattern that will hold for cross-examination as well. Your client listens to each question, pauses for a moment, then answers it directly and simply. You cue the level of intensity by your question, although you will also have discussed this in preparation. Your loops and prologues can signal that the mood changes up or down. The client responds to you in the same collected way she will respond to the cross-examiner.

You must ask your questions and listen to the answers as though you want information, and as though you are getting what you want. You cannot expect the jurors to be interested if you are obviously not. You signal noninterest by fussing with elaborate notes, checking off questions as you ask them—in short, by any technique or mannerism other than complete focus on the witness. If the interrogation looks rehearsed, it will be judged to be. If you have more than a few words of notes, easily readable without bending over, you have too much.

Your understanding of the client's personality will not so much affect the kinds of demonstrative and tangible evidence you use as the way in which you use it. The witness who radiates competence walks with you through the documents and helps explain them to the jurors. The witness who was bamboozled by the documents shares your wonder at them and keeps them at arm's length.

Let me illustrate. In a medical malpractice case, the doctor defendant wants the jury to believe that she operates efficiently and carefully. She therefore displays a confident familiarity with patient records, medical journal articles, lab reports, and the like. Not arrogance, mind you, but the ability to grasp and then to interpret the material. "Yes, I saw that report. When one of my patients is in the hospital, I look at the chart twice a day to see what tests the hospital has done, to get the results of tests I have ordered, and to make sure that my instructions are being carried out. This particular report told me that Mr. Johnson had responded to the medication in a normal way and that we had given him the right amount for his condition."

By contrast, a defrauded investor looks at and readily acknowledges having seen documents—letters, proxy statements, a prospectus, advertisements—but wrinkles his brow at them and talks about his understanding of them rather hesitantly. "Yes, I got that proxy statement. I don't remember reading all of it carefully, because it is about forty pages of little type. But I did read what the president said about these recent setbacks the company was having."

Both witnesses are testifying truthfully because they are communicating to the jury how they really did view the documents and exhibits they are now looking at. It is important for you, however, to ensure that the client in each case is for the jury the same person you know him to be.

Let us take a leisurely example. The client is charged with bank fraud. Your examination begins by setting the stage, introducing the client, and making him comfortable on the witness stand. Your story of the case turns on understanding the relationship between smaller banks such as the one your client owned and ran and larger urban banks.

Q. Tell us your name, please.

A. Ronald Marshall.

Q. [Softly, not stridently.] Did you commit the crimes that you are accused of in this case?

A. [Softly, directly.] No, I did not.

Q. In the brief time we have together, I want to ask you about your background in banking, so the jurors and the other lawyers here can understand how you made some important decisions. Then I want to ask you about some specifics that other witnesses have tried to describe. Along the way, I'll ask about people like Mr. Dandridge [the bank examiner]. Where did you do your growing up?

A. I was born in Port Arthur, Texas, in 1931.

Q. Where did you get your schooling?

A. I went to the schools in Port Arthur until I graduated high school in 1948. Then I went to the University of Texas at Austin for two years.

Q. Was that all the schooling you had?

A. No. I enlisted in the Army and served a little more than two years, then I went back to school.

Q. Where did you see Army service?

A. They sent me to Fort Ord in California for training, then to Korea.

Q. Did you get an honorable discharge?

A. Oh, yes.

Q. Any commendations?

A. I got the Silver Star for gallantry and a Purple Heart for a sniper bullet that I took.

Q. After you returned to the University of Texas, did you finally get to graduate?

A. Oh, yes, I took an accelerated course and got a degree in finance in 1954.

Q. Now, this case is about banking. So can you tell us what work you did in banking?

A. I got a job in Victoria, Texas, at the State Bank of Victoria. It was a small bank, so I did every job in the place to learn how to do it.

Q. Now these days we are used to big statewide banks, and even to these multistate banks. How was it different then?
[The prosecutor interjects:]
Objection. What is the relevance of the banking structure?
[The defense responds:]
The nature of Texas banking, and how this witness understood it, is central to the loan at issue.
[The court decides:]
Overruled. He may answer.

Q. I'll ask it again. How was the banking system different then?

A. There were no branch banks in Texas in those days. Other states, like California, permitted statewide branching, but Texas did not. Every bank had to stand on its own.

Q. Why is that important?

A. A bank that stands on its own is all in one building. The senior officers, the loan officers, the tellers, the secretaries—they all work right there alongside each other. If you have business in the bank, they are more likely to know you.

Q. What kind of management style did you learn in those days?

A. In a single-branch bank, you count on the people who work with you. You have to work together, and a lot is based on trust, not on formulas and memos and all that bureaucracy.

Q. But how could a little bank in Victoria survive against the competition of larger banks?

A. Well, a little of it was artificial. We survived because the law said no branch banking. But I learned very quickly the most important element of small bank survival—both for our financial health and to be able to serve our customers. And that was that you had to go and work out a cooperative arrangement with a bank in the nearest big city. That's what they had done in Victoria, and that's what I did in every single bank I ever worked with.

Q. Does that include this case?

A. Sure. I was President of the National Bank of Seguin, and our relationship was with SouthBank in Houston. They cleared large checks for us, so we could get the money quicker. Sometimes a customer would come in and want to borrow more money than we could lend since we were a small bank. SouthBank could participate in the loan. Or maybe somebody needed an introduction to a potential business partner in Houston.

Q. Can you give the jurors an example or two?

A. Sure. We had a Western wear designer in Seguin who was doing pretty well and starting to sell to the major department stores. But she needed capital to finance expansion of her workshops. We want her to succeed because all of Seguin benefits. But we are a small bank. We don't have the funds to make a loan that size. At the same time, we don't want her to go off somewhere else and borrow. We lose the interest that she would pay, and we just might lose her as a customer, lose that banking relationship. So I call up Abner McDonald at SouthBank and work out a deal where they will participate with some of their funds, although we will be the lead bank.

Q. How can you count on Abner McDonald taking your phone call when you call up there?

A. Like anything else in business—we try to work out an arrangement where both sides make a fair profit on the relationship.

Q. Is there any particular thing that smaller banks in Texas did around that time to make sure they had a good relationship like that with a big city bank?

A. Oh, sure. It went by different names. The economists might have one word for it, the business people another. Basically, a smaller bank builds a relationship by putting funds in the big city bank—you can call it a correspondent account, a demand deposit account, or sometimes even a compensating balance, but it all means the same thing.

The subject matter of inquiry is not the main concern. Our banker is talking about something that he has done for years—and knows inside and out. He is becoming comfortable with the idea of testifying. Under your guidance—to prevent shows of ego and self-importance—he is displaying himself as the kind of person you hope the jurors will see him to be. From this point, you can carry the examination to the transactions at issue in the case.

It should not be necessary to say, "End strong." Do so. Take your client in summary fashion over the high points—to emphasize those points and build a kind of semantic wall for your opponent to try and deconstruct.

Q. The indictment says, sir, that on January 10, 1971, you got money from Will Winston. Is that true?

Q. Did you, on January 20, 1971, get any money from Will Winston?

Q. During the whole time that you were secretary, did you ever accept money from Will Winston?

The answer in each case should be, "No, I did not," or something more than a monosyllable.

# Chapter Six

## *Demonstrative Evidence and Illustrative Materials: Say It with Pictures*

Demonstrative evidence, for our purposes, is any evidence other than the live testimony of a witness. In my opinion, everything that happens in a trial except the witnesses' testimony, lawyer arguments, and judicial remarks is governed by a single, coherent set of principles of presentation. This "other time" can go by various names—demonstrative evidence, visual aids, writing on the chalkboard, "publishing" the exhibit—but the same basic ideas govern, whatever the name. Works on demonstrative evidence are usually limited to charts, summaries, and graphic aids. They consider tangible objects a different subject and use of depositions still another area. I think the similarities of tactics and basic principles are greater than the differences. You might also call these things "tangible evidence."

Wigmore reminded us

> We are to remember, then, that a document purporting to be a map, picture, or diagram is, for evidential purposes simply nothing, except so far as it has human being's credit to support it. It is mere waste paper—testimonial nonentity. It speaks to us no more than a stick or a stone. It can of itself tell us no more as to the existence of the thing portrayed upon than can a tree or an ox. We must somehow put a testimonial human being behind it (as it were) before it can be treated as having any testimonial standing in court. It is somebody's testimony—or it is nothing.

Because neither the law nor lawyers know a bright line between demonstrative evidence and "other" illustrative materials, I am going to discuss them together. There is, I think, a continuum from the single document shown to the witness and then read to the jury, all the way to an interactive video reconstruction that may not be "in evidence" but may be exhibited to the jury as "illustrative" or even "argumentative."

The question here is the impression that pictures and physical objects make on jurors, and for this purpose we can put aside the rules of evidence after a brief introduction.

## BASIC PRINCIPLES

Five sets of rules govern the use of demonstrative evidence. I hold in my hand a chart. I want the jury to see it.

1. Is it authentic? That is, under Federal Rules of Evidence 901 through 903, is it what it claims to be? A letter is what it claims to be if the sender or recipient says so. A rock is what it claims to be if a witness says it was found in such and such a place. A gun is what it claims to be if "chain of custody" is established.

2. Is it the "best evidence?" This question arises only for "writings" and "recordings," but Federal Rule of Evidence 1001(1) makes those terms cover a lot of territory: they include any "form of data compilation." Federal Rule of Evidence 1002 says: "To prove the content of a writing, recording, or photograph, the original writing, recording, or photograph is required, except as otherwise required in these rules or by Act of Congress." Rule 1003 adds that "a duplicate is admissible to the same extent as an original unless (1) a genuine issue is raised as to the authenticity of the original or (2) in the circumstances it would be unfair to admit the duplicate in lieu of the original." Rule 1003 thus creates a rebuttable presumption of admissibility, but one must still prove that the item offered is a duplicate.

3. Is the item admissible hearsay or admissible nonhearsay? If the exhibit contains statements of a witness other than while testifying, offered for the truth of the matter asserted, you must find a hearsay exception.

4. If the chart is a summary of other data, does it meet the standards of Federal Rule of Evidence 1006? This rule is one of the trial lawyer's most valuable allies, especially when you want to present complex data persuasively.

5. Finally, does the chart tend to make a matter in issue more probable than it would be without the evidence, and can you overcome objections phrased as "cumulative, time-wasting, misleading or unduly prejudicial?"

If the chart does not meet these tests, you may still be able to use it as "illustrative," in the opening statement, the closing argument, or even while the witness is on the stand. It will not be "in evidence," however, and it will not go to the jury room. This is not necessarily a disadvantage, as we shall see, provided it brings to life evidence that the jury will have—and which they will be more likely to remember in deliberation.

The term "authentication" takes in a lot of territory. The Federal Rules of Evidence and their state counterparts have simplified the matter by suggesting easy ways to authenticate and by providing for self-authentication as to some documents.

If the exhibit is a stack of complicated charts that purport to summarize boxes and boxes of data, authentication by the proponent may require putting a live witness on the stand. By the same token, the opponent can challenge admissibility by showing that the summary is incorrect or misleading in some important way. Again, this is a tactical question. You may decide that the inaccuracies, in the venerable cliché, "go to weight and not to admissibility." That means, as the opponent, you will lay behind the log and cross-examine about the errors when your turn comes. There is no better way to rattle an expert than to conduct a disciplined cross-examination that tears apart the factual basis of the expert's conclusion.

The most sophisticated authentication problems arise in connection with computer animations, video recreations, and other complex representations of a past event. Consider, for example, a computer reconstruction of the last ten minutes of an airplane flight that ended in disaster when the airplane missed the approach, skidded off the runway, wound up in the bay, and caused death and injury. Using data about weather, airfield lights, the airplane's flight recorder readings on speed, altitude, flap settings, and so forth, with an overview provided by the recorded conversation between the cockpit and the tower, a computer animation expert can recreate on a video screen the conditions as the pilot "must have seen" them on approach. Drama may be added by using the flight recorder as a voice-over. Computer animation is also used to recreate vehicle accidents. For example, to show what happens to a passenger belted inside the cab of a car, truck, or other vehicle on impact.

The computer animation technique, which results in a sort of cartoon, is subject to a high risk of error. First, there are simple calculation errors; the designer may have misinterpreted the data. Second, the designer must fill in some information gaps by making more or less educated assumptions. Third, the resulting animation can be very dramatic, heightening the effect of any errors and of all the choices made by the originator.

To figure out what demonstrative evidence you will use, first decide your goals, then choose the best technique for reaching them. Only then should you try to decide the details of admissibility. Admissibility theories and limits vary from jurisdiction to jurisdiction. Because the trial judge has so much discretion on what to permit, individual judges in the same courthouse may have widely differing attitudes.

I can recall having invested money and time in video- and computer-based demonstrative evidence in a complex case, only to have the trial judge say that he "didn't believe in all that stuff." Fortunately, the investment was not great, and we had already decided that high-technology evidence was not going to present the persuasive picture that we wanted our client to sponsor.

It is a good idea to have a file memo on admissibility and nonevidentiary use of illustrative materials, with cases on both sides. Then, when an issue arises, you can quickly generate a short memorandum of law to support use of your materials or oppose your opponent's plans.

## AGREEMENT OR RULING?

In addition to reading up on evidence law and finding out the judge's attitude toward your proposed techniques, you will have to figure out the mechanics of admissibility rulings. Some of the methods we will discuss are expensive and involve a lot of lead time. Your opponent knows this—and will delight in having the court limit or reject your presentation on the eve of trial.

I don't run into this problem as much as some lawyers do because I happen to think that fairly simple, noncontroversial, and easily amended methods happen to be best. The pretrial order in your case should provide for exchange of demonstrative evidence and other illustrative material, whether or not the party will seek to offer it in evidence. The timing of this exchange can vary depending on what is involved. Obviously, a party cannot be expected to produce opening statement graphics until motions *in limine* are resolved.

With exchange, and with understanding of the judge's attitude and the law, agreement usually follows on most items. Remember, if your opponent's materials are misleading, you may want to withhold an objection in favor of conducting a scathing cross-examination of the sponsoring witness. If agreement fails, the trial judge or, in federal civil cases in some districts, the magistrate can make rulings before trial.

In every case, subject to the limits imposed by the pre-trial order, there will be an exhibit that you want to introduce at trial or a graphic representation that you decide to use at the last minute. Then, as Professor Pat Hazel says, *MIAO*. *M*ark it; ask the witness to *I*dentify it; *A*ccredit it by going through as many as necessary of the five steps set out above; and *O*ffer it.

You usually mark exhibits with press-on stickers furnished by the court clerk or purchased from a legal supply store. The court is likely to have a preference about the exact kind of sticker to use. Check with the clerk's office, and get a plentiful supply. Have a bunch of blank stickers in your litigation bag to use on exhibits that must be offered at trial.

If your materials are computer generated or otherwise not able to be marked in the traditional way, work out an arrangement with co-counsel and get approval of the judge or the courtroom deputy clerk. If you have not resolved admissibility issues before trial, the litany of admissibility is fairly standard.

Q.  Ms. Bolger, I am showing you [or asking the bailiff to show you] what I have marked as Plaintiff's Exhibit 3.

The exhibit has now been "marked."

Q.  [Continuing.] Is that a memorandum from your company?

You can lead on preliminary matters. If you are not permitted to lead, ask this:

Q.  Without telling us what's in there, what is Exhibit 3?
A.  It is a memorandum from the vice-president of our company, EnviroScene, to the comptroller of EnviroScene.
Q.  Is it the original memorandum?

A. No, it is a photocopy of the original.

Q. How do you know?

A. By looking at the distribution list at the bottom and noting that one of the names has been checked on this copy.

Q. Is that memorandum made in the regular course of business of EnviroScene?

A. Yes.

Q. Is it the regular course of business of EnviroScene to make and keep records like this?

A. Sure. That's the way we keep track of things, with memos like this.

Q. Were the entries made on this memorandum done at or about the time of the events that are described, and by people with personal knowledge?

A. Sure.

Now we have almost finished "accrediting" a business record. An admission of a party opponent would require fewer questions. A chart summarizing many documents would require additional questions, first, to lay an authentication and hearsay exception to the underlying records and then to inquire if the witness knows that the chart or summary is accurate.

One step remains to "accredit." You must show that the memo is relevant.

Q. What is this memo about?

A. It is the memorandum with the August sales figures on the Micromanager pocket PC.

Q. I offer Exhibit 3.
   [The court:]
   Without objection, it will be received.

Q. Your Honor, I have a copy of Exhibit 3 on a transparency, and I'd like to put it up now so that the jurors and Ms. Bolger can see it.
   [The court:]
   Move along, counsel.

Once a chart or other visual aid is in evidence or used in argument, you have a powerful motivation to keep it where the jurors will see it. Your opponents have the same motivation about their materials.

## BASIC PUBLICATION
## STRATEGY

I confess a love of archaisms, the words our legal forebears passed along to us. So I catch myself saying, when I have successfully completed a *MIAO*, "Your Honor, may I publish this to the jury?" And she either says, "Why, certainly, counsel," or, archly, "Well, you can sure *show* it to them."

Jargon aside, you must decide when the jury will see your exhibits, to enhance, not interrupt, the flow of testimony. The first limitation on your power is Federal Rule of Evidence 106, the "rule of completeness." When you offer something in evidence, your opponent can ask that the rest of that something, or a related something, come in at the same time. When you show the jury the part you are interested in, your opponent may ask that some other part be shown at the same time, to make your presentation not misleading.

The trial judge has latitude in applying these principles. The paired arguments are "Your Honor, let each side try its case in its own way " and "Your Honor, let's not mislead the jury by unduly one-sided presentations."

Suppose your witness has just identified an important letter. What are you going to do with it? Don't pass it to the jurors. Even if the judge would let you stop everything while they all read it, all the jurors but one would be unoccupied at any given moment. You could make twelve copies and pass them out, so that everybody could read at once. Don't laugh; this technique may sometimes make sense.

The best way to "publish" is to have the witness read aloud the portion you want to emphasize while you simultaneously display that portion on a screen. What kind of screen? The choices are discussed below.

For now, the point is that you have choices about handling exhibits, and your choices influence the kind of graphic material you decide to use. There is an industry of graphics/demonstrative evidence/illustrative material specialists. The approaches, techniques, and fee structures of these outfits vary widely. Some of the best of them are members of the Demonstrative Evidence Specialists Association (DESA). Some DESA members are first-rate, but I would not retain anybody to help you with graphics until you know the story of your case. Much money and time spent on visual evidence is a substitute for thinking about how to try your case. I am an experienced procrastinator, and have a lot of on-the-job training in it, so I know whereof I speak.

A final word about publication: No experiments in the courtroom, please. The device you or your expert builds to go whiz, pop, or bang will fail in the jury's presence. Do the experiment under controlled conditions, and videotape it.

## SKEPTICISM ABOUT HARDWARE

I am skeptical of expensive gadgets. You can spend hundreds of thousands of dollars on hardware and software for your exhibits. Be careful before doing so. One good reason will pop into your mind if you think about the week you tried to install a new computer system in your office. If you didn't have any trouble, then talk to another lawyer because you are in a distinct minority. I am not knocking the folks who sell this stuff. Usually, the problem is with the humans trying to run the system.

It's sort of like the sign just east of El Paso: "Last Gas for 100 Miles." It's tough to halt the trial while you dial the toll-free number to ask the technical wizards to help you show the jury the next document. I do not say, "Rule out

the high-tech stuff." Rather, I urge you to climb the technological mountain a step at a time, pausing often to see if
you are high enough to enjoy the view.

Here are some stops on the trail.

## READ IT

Asking the witness to read something can be effective.
Almost always, that alone will not put the contents before
the jury in a memorable way. There is one exception. When
the real evidence is not so much the words, but the fact of
the witness saying them, reading may be enough.

Example: A former Secretary of the Treasury was accused
of having accepted a $10,000 illegal gratuity from a lobbyist
who had been his good friend. The former friend was now
a government witness. Cross-examination covered informer
perfidy, motivation to lie, and prior inconsistent statements.
The informer had written to our client, after the alleged
payment but before he became a government witness,
expressing friendship and gratitude and professing undying
respect. The precise words are not so important. Indeed, if
you think about it, the letter could even be double-edged.
But the informer had been painted a liar, and we wanted
to make him an ingrate as well. We laid the predicate for it,
got it admitted, and had the witness read it out to the jury.

Another example: Your client sues an insurance company for bad faith refusal to settle a claim. The insurance
company has sent one of those officious letters denying a
claim. The letter is just one step in a series of relevant
events. To keep the examination moving, you may decide
to have your client read aloud the relevant part of the letter.
You can wave it around, and even show parts of it, in
argument or with a later witness.

## OVERHEAD PROJECTORS

You remember these. You put 8-½" x 11" transparent
sheets on them, and they project the sheets onto a screen.
Depending on the lamp power and lens magnification, the

screen can be quite large. The item being projected sits faceup on the machine so you can write on it with a felt-tip pen and have the marks show on the screen.

These machines have more persuasive potential than any other courtroom aid. Consider the ways in which a simple overhead projector can do the jobs usually reserved for much more elaborate and expensive gear. Mind you, we are talking about a good machine, one that is easy to set up and focus and that throws a powerful, clear image. You may have to bring your own.

Almost any copier can reproduce a document onto a transparency. If yours cannot, the neighborhood copying service can do it, even in color. A felt-tip pen highlights key images or phrases. You can do the same with a deposition transcript.

In a major antitrust trial, Chief Judge Singleton insisted that all documents be reproduced on transparencies and shown to the jury on a screen. The original paper versions were available to go to the jury room. In the suit by William Tavoulareas against the *Washington Post*, which Tavoulareas won, though the verdict was reversed on appeal, plaintiff's counsel used the overhead projector effectively. You or the witness can read the key words while the jurors both listen and read along.

Any image that your computer can devise and that your laser printer can print can be printed on a transparency and used immediately. In cases involving financial information, the spreadsheet programs—Lotus, Excel, Quattro—permit you to present information in graphs and charts of many different forms, and with a variety of typefaces. A color printer—or an assistant with marker pens—can dress up these exhibits for copying on transparencies.

Or suppose you have several documents that are marginally legible or very long. You want to publish key excerpts. You want the witness to read them out. You can type these excerpts out, with a citation to the exhibit number and page, and print them on a transparency. These are not exhibits; they are a method of publishing the exhibit to the jury.

You place the exhibit number on the image because you want the jurors to begin remembering numbers of key exhibits. They will remember. I can recall a jury coming out after an acquittal in an eight-week trial, and the prosecutor asked, "What did I do wrong?" They began right away to analyze a key exhibit in the case, referring to it by number.

A related concept requires expert help, although if you or somebody in your office is handy with computer graphics, you can home-grow these things. Some documents are so dense or illegible that they do not show up well on a transparency. Take the document itself, shrink it, and move it to the left side of the page. Box the relevant language, and point to another box on the right side of the page. In this box goes the language you want to emphasize, in large, easily readable type.

You can provide further emphasis by putting a heading on the page and by using color. Some computer printers generate color transparencies. You can also make a multi-color exhibit on 8-½″ x 11″ white paper and use a color copier to reproduce the image on a transparency. Advertisements abound for computer graphics programs that work with one or more word processing systems, and the technology is changing so fast that one can only recommend checking to see what's available this week.

In a recent case, we had a big budget for graphics—and therefore plenty of choice. We had bar graphs, physical exhibits, summary charts, charts with words that highlighted key arguments—in short, a full array. We tested all of these with several focus groups of mock jurors.

Those with a refreshing "keep it simple" attitude have already figured out the result. So have those who go to rodeos and know that the cowboy whose eight-second ride wins the event is the one with a horse trailer on an old Caddy and faded jeans, who just gets on the bull and remembers "hold on with the left fist, hang on when the stock twists." The cowboy who looks like he just toured Nieman-Marcus is probably only a spectator. Fancy and expensive is not necessarily better.

The jurors preferred the documents. They liked the physical exhibits, too. On the whole, they disregarded the charts and summaries unless a given chart followed in sequence after the documents that it summarized.

Why did jurors have so much more faith in the more down-to-earth materials? In our case, we were arguing a position that was against many jurors' intuitive feelings and preconceptions. If they were going to adopt our story, they would do so only on their own, by testing it themselves against hard evidence.

I think our insight from this study holds for any case. A position that a juror has taken and held on her own will more likely survive the rigors of jury deliberation than an undifferentiated sense of how things should come out. Your highest and best service as a lawyer is to take the evidence itself and put it in a form that jurors can use.

You can create graphic images of a stack of papers, representing a long exhibit, with several boxes containing key excerpts. You can create boxes that summarize. As you get farther from the raw data, keep an "icon" in the picture that represents the exhibits themselves. Never let go of the power represented by "the evidence."

Transparencies are useful for illustrations that go beyond the documents. The artwork for transparencies can be computer generated, computer edited, and constantly up-dated to accommodate changes in your trial plan or hostile rulings from the court. The final product can even be enlarged to become a chart. Charts produced in the more traditional way may be more expensive and harder to change.

You can use transparencies with your witnesses. Suppose you have a map or a diagram. The witness can mark on it with a felt-tip pen to describe the action. If several witnesses are going to be describing the same scene, you can have several copies of it on transparencies, each as a subexhibit—for example, Plaintiffs Exhibit 55A, 55B, and so on. Each witness can then mark his own descriptive material—location of the cars before and after the wreck, where the witness was standing, etc. In argument, you may find it useful to superimpose these images by stacking the transparencies. Using exhibits in this way gets the witness off the chair and down in front of the jury, talking and illustrating in a more natural way.

If you are going to use transparencies in argument anyway, consider starting with an overview of main points. Make an outline. Simplify it so each concept is expressed in a word or two. Do the outline on a word processor in large type. Print it on a transparency. In a long opening statement, you might put up this summary graphic several times to remind everybody (including yourself) where everything fits.

In one closing argument, I thought the timeline of events was persuasive in making our case. I also thought that a key phrase in the correspondence was a good recurring theme because it showed that my client had a deal with the other side based on a common understanding.

I headlined a chart with the key phrase, followed by the words "A Deal Is a Deal." If a bargain is fair to both sides, and fairly negotiated, most jurors will enforce it. Anybody who thinks "a deal's a deal" is not powerful rhetoric should reread a book on the Pennzoil-Texaco case.

Under this heading—this is argument, remember—I had a list of dates, and next to each one an exhibit title, a phrase of description, and that all-important exhibit number.

I know a lawyer who uses two overhead projectors and two screens in situations like this, one for the outline that stays up on the screen, and one for the changing array of exhibits. That is too much hardware and motion for me and, I suspect, for most courts and jurors as well.

As you see yourself using the overhead projector, there is one more image to capture. If permitted by the court, handle the transparencies yourself. Get used to the required order, and learn how to operate the machine. If somebody else on your team is assigned the task of running the projector, the inevitable foul-ups will create awkward moments in which you will be tempted to say or do something that makes you look overbearing, uptight, or pompous. If you are out there making your own mistakes, you can only look vulnerable, and that is preferable.

## MULTIPLE COPIES

In a complex tax evasion case, the government served the charts and summaries on us the night before their summary witness was to testify. We had not been using an overhead projector in the trial up to that point. There were several charts for each of the four tax years at stake, and they were complicated—in part, the result of being prepared at the last minute.

I had already planned my cross of the expert and would now need to refine it in light of these charts. The government was not using large posterboard charts or an overhead projector.

I wanted to deconstruct this witness, his conclusions, and his charts. I wanted to go after his credibility as a witness in addition to refuting his numbers. The cross was structured, but I was not locked in. I had a stack of documents on which to examine, a list of the problems with the witnesses on which he had relied, and some errors of arithmetic.

I was stuck for graphics because I didn't have the time to do anything elaborate. Nor did I want to be hemmed in by some visual image I had chosen to use. So I made twenty-four copies of the government's exhibits and brought a supply of pencils to court. When I reached the point in the cross where I attacked the numbers of the first calendar year, I gave the witness his chart and passed a copy to each juror, each alternate juror, counsel, judge, law clerk, and court reporter.

I could then direct everybody's attention to a particular entry and quiz the witness about it. If I wanted to make sure everybody was watching the witness and not reading the chart, I would say, "Now, Agent, please look right at the jurors and tell them. . . ." A side benefit was that the technique almost guarantees that the judge will follow along—and the jurors see the judge doing so.

Here is an edited sample:

Q. Agent Smith, I want to ask you now about the $50,000 item for the year 1976. Do you see that, sir? Will you tell the jurors please how they can find it on their copy?

A. It is on page 3, about half way down the page.

Q. Do you remember, sir, the accountant who testified here telling the jury that this check for $50,000 was marked "Expenses"?

A. I remember that.

Q. In fact, sir, let me show you the check, Government Exhibit 472. That's the check?

A. Yes, it is.

Q. It shows, at the bottom, "Expenses"?

A. Yes.

Q. Would you tell the jury why you on your chart here, you included $50,000 as part of Mr. X's taxable income, when everybody knows that expense reimbursement isn't taxable income?

A. I didn't think the evidence sustained the idea that it was a deduction rather than income.

Q. You are a Special Agent of the IRS, aren't you?

A. Yes.

Q. That means you get to carry a gun?

A. Yes.

Q. You weren't always a Special Agent, were you?

A. No.

Q. You used to be a Revenue Agent?

A. Yes.

Q. When you were a Revenue Agent, you used to do audits on people just like members of the jury, and make them justify their deductions. Isn't that right?

A. Yes.

Q. In those audits, who had the burden of proof?

A. The taxpayer.

Q. But this is a criminal case, isn't it, Agent?

A. Yes.

Q. Look at the jury, Agent, and tell them who has the burden in a criminal case of proving things.

A. The government.

Q. That's right. And what is the burden of proof that the government has to meet?

A. Beyond a reasonable doubt.

Q. But you decided to count this check as income rather than expenses, which is what it says on the check, because *you* didn't think that the proof sustained the proposition that it was expenses? Is that what you've told us?

A. Yes.

Q. Who has the final word here about whether or not you have sustained your burden of proof?

A. The jury.

Q. And if the jury decides that you have not sustained your burden of proof on this $50,000 item, how would they have to adjust your figures on this sheet where you claim that you show Mr. X's income for 1977?

A. Well, it would be deducted from the total.

Q. So, the jurors would look down here on the lower right-hand corner of the sheet where you have the figure $375,000, and they would just subtract the $50,000 right off of there? Isn't that right?

A. Yes, that is what they would do.

Much later, the judge—by then retired—told me that the cross of the summary witness had done a lot to change his own perception of the case and his prediction of how the jury would vote. The judge gave the jurors permission to use a pencil to follow the testimony, although we had to collect the copies when the witness stepped down.

On reflection, transparencies might have been better, or at least as good. But the multiple copies strategy put the jury more into the process of my cross-examination and I think contributed to the jurors' assessment that the agent was the government's "worst witness."

You may ask how we learned of this assessment. The jurors took seriously the admonition not to deliberate on their verdict until the case was submitted to them. Among their ways of not deliberating was to take a daily informal vote on "best witness" and "worst witness." The defendant's former wife (who testified for the defense) won "best," and the testifying case agent won "worst."

## LARGE POSTERBOARD CHARTS

Most of the work of large charts is better done by overhead projector transparencies. When you consider the costs of a first-class version of each one, the relative benefits of large charts diminish even more. However, modern photographic and xerographic reproduction techniques make some sophisticated chart work easier than before, so it may be possible to generate smaller images on a computer and have them blown up.

There are some jobs for which charts are the illustrative material of choice. If you have an image that you want the jury to see as much as possible, put it on a chart. Suppose your case involves a collision at a dangerous crossroads. The danger, you say, is immanent in the way the streets come together, or perhaps the terrain. Witness after witness will describe the scene. You want them all to use the same sketch map but to be able to compare their versions. You need a chart, sized to fit your courtroom, but large enough to be seen by the judge and jurors without squinting or straining. You may get away with leaving the chart on an easel near your counsel table, even when it is not being used. You couldn't do that with a transparency. To use the chart for multiple witness examinations, put a couple of alignment marks on it, and use large acetate overlays clipped to the top.

The professional chart makers, of whom there are many, can create charts with as many layers and image changes as you like. For example, you can use Velcro strips, so that additional materials can be added to the display. In a recent case, I wanted an expert witness to talk about the development of sophisticated crude oil refining techniques. Most people think that crude oil is used pretty much as it comes out of the ground and that refining it into products is neither expensive nor complicated. We needed to address these issues.

We had a choice of themes to present the information. One can visualize refining techniques developing in at least four ways—technological innovation over time, relative cost, the range of products that can be made from a particular crude oil, and the use of given processes as a stream of crude oil moves through the refinery. Interestingly, in this example, the order of topics will be the same no matter which of these you choose as an organizing theme because developments in refining have mainly consisted of adding additional, expensive units that produce a greater amount of high-end product like gasoline from a given quantity of a given type of crude oil.

Our expert begins with some crude oil and product samples. He could also use some models of hydrocarbon molecules. Now we turn to the chart. The large posterboard depicts a schematized version of a simple refinery, which basically takes crude oil and obtains the products of distillation. On the right side of the poster is a dollar figure, representing the cost in today's dollars of this unit. There might also be an indication of the product mix obtained. With time, progress, and money, we can use less desirable crude oils more efficiently to make more "light" products such as gasoline and jet fuel. Our expert uses schematic models of additional parts of the refinery, which are revealed as he takes away blank pieces of posterboard that have been covering them up. As he reveals each new component, he takes away a blank rectangle from the right side, exposing the cost figure for the new unit. When the expert has finished the description, the chart shows a modern refinery as well as complete cost and production figures.

If the chart summarizes evidence, it may itself be admissible. In that case, take a large-format Polaroid shot of it in its final form, because your photo stands a much better chance of going to the jury room. Alternatively, if the chart began as a computer-generated graphic, you can make a smaller copy of it. The copy should, however, be larger than a standard sheet of paper, and on stiff stock, so that the jurors can find it easily among the exhibits.

This example shows the power of the chart. You can use the same technique for any linear event, regardless of the "line" you choose, which may be time, money, the expert's trip through the data, or something else.

Two technical notes: Notice that I have the expert taking away blank pieces of posterboard to reveal the finished work. In this way, the finished chart is on a single surface that you want the jury to continue to see. Second, the "posterboard" is in fact a foam panel covered with art paper, which you can get at an art supply store.

You can glimpse the power in this process in preparing an accounting or economic expert's testimony, illustrated in understandable segments, as described in later chapters.

In a wrongful death case, it can become difficult to separate the items of damage and to quantify each of them. If the case is to be submitted on special issues, the plaintiffs' damage presentation must be precise, detailed, and memorable. You risk overpowering the onlookers, including the jurors. I have chosen a plaintiff's expert, but the same technique can be used to deconstruct damages in the defense case, as discussed in Chapter Thirteen.

The numbers expert builds conclusions an item at a time. He uses a chart that groups the items by topic; as the blank rectangles peel away, the column of numbers becomes larger until it is time to add them all up. This chart, or a good copy of it, should be admissible in evidence. Again, the expert is up at the easel while testifying, helping to put the points across.

## THE OBJECT ITSELF

If you doubt the power of symbols in litigation, your lawyer cynicism has so far overcome your humanity that you need a rest cure. The courthouse in which you try cases is probably filled with symbols, from the image of justice in the lobby to the seal behind the judge's bench. Maybe, where you live, the symbols have fallen on hard times. I wrote this more than twenty years ago about a courtroom in New York:

> Someone, in a forlorn battle to preserve the trappings of justice, had put a large plastic bag over the American flag in the corner to keep it clean. The bag itself had yellowed and was covered with grime. And in back of the judge's bench—not a bench really, just the most comfortable chair in the house—an incomplete set of aluminum letters proclaimed

> IN GOD WE   RUST

In all societies, symbols of life, belief, or state are given a special place. Our totemic ancestors understood not only the value of the symbol itself, but the special consideration given to those who were permitted to handle it. If the totem of the tribe was an animal, the priests and elders were thought to gain or possess special powers by eating it.

The exhibits in evidence in your trial are symbols that have significance not only as rational instruments of persuasion, but in the handling and keeping of them in the presence of the trier of fact. The ways you stand, walk, and speak are part of the symbolism of the trial process.

Mocking a symbol that has acquired significance in trial can bring unexpected instant rebuke. I was sitting in court waiting for a jury to return, and, as the deliberations promised to be long, another trial was being held. The case involved allegations that the defendants had falsified the records on firearms shipped in interstate commerce in order to obtain a cache of weapons for some political group—Croatian, if memory serves.

The prosecutors had patiently amassed the records of falsified purchase slips. Knowing the power of symbols, they put these exhibits on the corner of their table closest to the jury, so that the jurors would always be aware of them.

Whenever a prosecutor examined a witness about these documents, he would meaningfully pick them up from their assigned place, conduct the examination, and carefully replace them when he was through.

In the closing argument, defense counsel sought to challenge the symbols, failing to understand the power they had acquired. Striding to the prosecution's table, he picked up a fistful of the documents. He waved them in the juror's faces and declaimed, "Look at this! Look at this, now what does this mean? What does this mean?"

Juror number 5 responded equably, "Illegal dealing in guns."

Defense counsel compounded the error by quickly putting the papers back on the prosecution's table and moving for a mistrial. The motion was denied; after all, while the rhetorical question is recognized as far back as Aristotle, in the real and modern world one ought not to ask unless one is prepared to listen to the answer.

In one case, our story was that the other side was using the lawsuit to get out of a contract that was fair to both sides. The contract was the center of our case. I had a copy of the contract to use in the opening statement, with an official certificate on it attesting that it was a true copy. The contract had a special place at counsel table, in an easily identifiable folder. Whenever it was time to examine a witness about the contract, I would use that copy. I might put the exhibit itself in front of the witness, but that copy became one of our symbols.

If you represent a person or entity with a symbol, consider using the symbol throughout the trial. Defending a multidefendant antitrust case, I directed that our exhibits all carry our company logo to set us apart from the plaintiffs and the other defendants.

What are the lessons? First, that a major exhibit, identified early, can become a powerful symbol. Second, and more important, the thing itself is often more powerful than a reproduction. In most cases, the documents were originally handled by the witnesses in their paper form. I think something is lost when you don't have the witness handling the piece of paper as she handled it to begin with. Moreover, I want the witness and the jurors to have the chance to see the documents and to arrange them as they wish when they deliberate.

In a product liability case, your symbol might be a report showing that a safer alternative existed. In a civil rights case, maybe a pamphlet copy of the constitution will do. Perhaps a few key depositions will always be on the counsel table.

Of course, objects can both empower and disempower. A gun or knife may be scary enough that its message is lost—no matter who is brandishing it. If you try cases in a community where gun racks and pickup trucks are familiar sights, the symbol means something different than in another place.

In the courthouse where I first practiced, old-timers told of a suit over allegedly inflammable children's clothes. The lawyer for the company thought it significant that the clothes would not catch fire unless exposed to an open flame—or equivalent heat source—for many seconds. So he had some of the clothes in court—and had a witness set fire to them. Sure enough, it took some doing to set them alight.

The jury brought in a plaintiff's verdict. The courthouse observers—whose view I tend to share—said that the image of kids' clothes burning canceled every other message, including the one about how hard it was to set them afire.

There is another good story in here. In all big cities, and not a few smaller ones, there is a group of court buffs who sit in on interesting trials. Mostly these are older folks who regard trial watching as better than the soaps. Often, they will share powerful insights with you about your trial technique. I was in the middle of a political corruption case when my partner reported that the court buffs had foregathered in the men's room and were imitating one of my favorite cross-examination gestures. It made me stop and think whether I was appearing too contrived.

## PAD OR BLACKBOARD?

Almost every courtroom has one of those blackboards on a stand that can be carted or wheeled around. You can use the blackboard while examining a witness. A witness can, with permission, step down and illustrate something. You can write things to use in closing argument. Sometimes the board swivels around so you can write something on it to be revealed when the time is right.

I do not like blackboards. Buy and use "whiteboards" instead. They are better than chalkboards because one can use washable felt-tip markers in many colors. They can be taken to court. When you write on them, the jurors are not gritting their teeth in fear of that fingernails-on-the-blackboard screech.

Sometimes you cannot easily get whiteboards to court. You can buy large tablets of white paper that serve a similar purpose. Take along some large binder clips to attach them to a blackboard, or invest in a folding easel.

Hardware aside, the blackboard, whiteboard, or tablet gives you a lot of freedom. You can use it as an excuse to move from the lectern or counsel table to make your examination more animated. You can ask the witness to move down in front of the jury box. You can underscore key concepts that have appeared in the opening statement and are going to reappear when other witnesses testify and in the closing argument.

In many criminal fraud cases, there is a serious issue of valuation. The prosecutors, supported by an informer-witness, argue that the defendant has inflated the valuation of property as part of a scheme to cheat the bank regulators, the revenue collectors, or the investing public. Typically, the government calls an investigator as a summary witness. Laden with charts, the witness summarizes the testimony and exhibits. On cross-examination, use your paper tablet or the whiteboards. You might begin by writing "Collateral," "Insider," and "Documents." As the examination begins, the juror is more likely to be looking at the cross-examiner, not at the government's charts. This examination is a composite of several:

Q. Agent, let me begin by asking about collateral. The price of land in this corner of Texas has been up and down a lot, hasn't it?

A. It has varied some, yes.

Q. In fact, you have seen situations where the valuation of a parcel of real estate will double overnight, correct?

A. I have seen that, but not very often.

Q. You are not a real estate appraiser, are you?

A. No.

Q. You do not live in Texas, do you?

A. No.

Q. So you cannot tell us the history of land prices in Texas, can you?

A. No, I cannot.

Q. I am showing you Government Exhibit 5407. That is an appraisal on this Circle J land that supports the amount of the loan that was made, correct?

A. On its face, it does.

Q. On its face. I will come to that. Your answer is that the document supports the loan?

A. Yes.

Q. And the jury can look at this Government Exhibit 5407 and see that, right?

A. Right.

Q. They do not need a CPA or a Special Agent from Washington in order to see that, do they?

A. No, I guess not.

Q. Well, do you have any doubt about it?

A. No.

Q. Coming to the phrase you used, "on its face," you want to say that this appraisal sort of fudged, right?

A. That's right.

Q. You were not there in that bank when this appraisal was discussed, were you?

A. No.

Q. The people there were my client Tim Ransome, the appraiser Mr. Wolfert, and a bank vice-president named Lou Anthony, correct?

A. That's right.

Q. Mr. Wolfert and Mr. Ransome say that the appraisal was honest, right?

A. Right.

Q. Mr. Anthony says it was phonied up?

A. He did. The jury heard him.

Q. Exactly, sir. And who is going to decide whether Anthony is telling the truth or whether Mr. Ransome and Mr. Wolfert are telling the truth?

A. The jury.

Q. And that's the American way, isn't it? Trial by jury?

A. Well, yes.

Q. Tell the jury about Mr. Anthony. Did you ever talk to him before August 5, 1983, when he did not lie his head off to you?

A. I would not say he lied his head off. He was not candid with us until he made a plea bargain.

Q. I am sorry. I didn't understand your answer. It is a fact that Mr. Anthony habitually lied to you, right?

A. That is right.

Q. And Mr. Anthony's story is one basis for your saying that this loan did not have enough collateral?

A. That is right.

You might draw a line through "Collateral."

Q. And when we come to "'Insider,'" sir, you told this jury that there was a silent partner in Circle J who was a director of the bank, correct?

A. I said that there was a silent partner, and that your client knew that, right?

Q. I am sorry, Agent, I don't mean to fuss with you. But please look the jury straight in the eye and tell them the name of the only human being in the world who ever told you that Mr. Ransome knew a bank director was in this deal.

A. Well, it was Lou Anthony.

Q. I am sorry. Could you repeat that?

A. Lou Anthony.

Q. This is the Lou Anthony you just told us a moment ago was a liar.

A. I didn't say he was a liar. I said he had lied.

Now is the time to draw a line through "Insider," and pause briefly. In one case, I turned back to the witness absently and said, "Would you buy a used car from Lou Anthony?" The prosecutor stood up. I started to say, "Withdrawn." The witness blurted out, "If the price was right." Some jurors actually looked at one another and shook their heads, and, in a postverdict discussion, they said that was the "worst answer" by the "worst witness."

Most of the time, your use of the blackboard, whiteboard, or paper will be illustrative and evanescent. Sometimes, however, you can offer this material in evidence, and you had best be prepared to do so. If, for example, a police officer is describing an accident scene with a handmade sketch, you can mark the sketch and offer it, provided you have asked him to write on a large pad of paper.

If your witness starts out on a whiteboard or blackboard, admissibility presents a practical problem. Your options are to use one of those electronic boards that delivers a color copy of what is written on it when you push a button or be prepared with a Polaroid camera.

## MODELS

A model can make spatial relationships understandable. If you are trying a tractor accident case, the important portion of the tractor—from real life or in a model—can help the jury see how the plaintiff got his hand in the machinery. If your case involves a refinery, an apartment block, or some other complex collection of objects, a model can help.

A large model will sit in the courtroom as a silent teller of your story even when a witness is not talking about it. Jurors do not listen attentively to the witnesses all the time.

Besides being admissible, the model must satisfy another canon. It must never lend itself to uses that cast doubt on your case. You have passed off the model as a substitute for the real thing, or even as a piece of the real thing. If it fails to work satisfactorily when required to do so, your credibility suffers. This is a special instance of the general rule to avoid experiments in the courtroom.

The model maker, or someone who supervised the work, should be called to describe how the model was built. What scale is used? Are any parts simplified or left out entirely?

Why? The final question will always be, "Based on what you have told us, does this model fairly and accurately represent [whatever you have said it does]?"

## PROJECTING COMPUTER IMAGES

Several companies make devices that plug into the serial port of a computer and replicate the monitor image on a screen that can be placed on an overhead projector. The computer display then appears on a large screen. Other devices put the small-screen computer image on a large monitor or television projection system.

This form of demonstrative evidence can be useful, but it poses dangers. An example shows its utility. The plaintiff has put on evidence that damages were $X million. The damage study rests on three or four key assumptions, in addition to the obvious one that there is any liability in the first place. Your expert says that the key assumptions are wrong.

You are in a classic muddle at this point. You do not want to put on any damages evidence that seems to concede liability, but you want to attack those figures. One way to present the evidence is with color transparencies. A more telling way would be for your expert to replicate the plaintiff's theory on a pie chart, bar graph, or $x$-$y$ graph. The expert can then go through the fallacious assumptions and show in each instance the impact on plaintiff's numbers. The jury can watch as the expert enters calculations on a laptop computer at the witness stand and the screens show the dramatic results as the graphs and charts change shape before them.

You can save these exhibits in any of several forms, depending on the basic hardware. These include color printer printouts (paper or transparency), diskette, and videotape.

The danger is that witness examination is a game that two can play. Your opponent can cross-examine and ask that the expert plug in alternative calculations fairly arguable from their side's evidence. The graphs or charts change shape again, this time as dictated by your opponent. This opportunity is denied to the other side if your expert uses color transparencies, a videotape, or a computer program made in the office.

## VIDEO IMAGES

The books on demonstrative evidence, and the commercial providers of this high-tech persuasive material, tell you what, how, and—often most important—how costly. I focus briefly on issues relating to examination of witnesses.

Videos can be live or animated. If a live video was taken at the event, it is admissible as a photograph. Video reconstructions can be live, animated, or a combination of the two. They may be offered in evidence or used only for argument and illustration.

All torts lawyers have seen or heard of the "day in the life" video designed to show the plaintiff's disability. These videos work best when narrated by a family member or treating physician. They can backfire when the plaintiff looks to be very much the center of a loving, caring family; the jurors are likely to reduce the damage award in such a case.

A professionally produced video can explain complex events and processes to a jury better than any competing evidence. For example, in a case involving recovery of crude oil, the oil company produced a video that showed personnel and equipment moving to a drill site. It then used animation to depict the underground processes by which crude oil was recovered. The overall impact was positive. In an antitrust case, the court permitted the parties to show a fifteen-minute video, combining actual footage with animation, on how a refinery works. Note that the video was shown by agreement, which avoids knotty problems of admissibility.

More controversial is the animated, often computer-generated re-creation of a disputed event from information gathered by the expert.

The expert sits in the witness chair next to a video screen, holding a light pen. At any point, the image can be frozen, and the expert can use the light pen to show significant details with circles and arrows.

In another use, the animator takes available data and makes a video of what must have happened to a driver, inside the cab of an industrial vehicle, when it was struck by a passing truck. The video can be stored in any number of formats, of which videotape is the least expensive, but the most difficult to handle in court because it takes time to cue the tape. CD-ROM technology has the quickest retrieval capability and the most exhibition options, and it can be integrated with a computer central processing unit with an interface card.

Production of these exhibits is so expensive, and revising them often so difficult, that admissibility issues should be resolved long before trial. The root question is whether the video fairly represents an event without unduly trespassing on the jury's function. The jurors' job is to make inferences from evidence of an event; it is often arguable whether they need an expert computer graphics person to re-create an alleged reality.

Moreover, the information on which the graphic material is based may be questionable and, if presented through witnesses, can be cross-examined. Counsel cannot cross-examine the video, though the sponsoring witness is fair game.

To make the video effective and admissible, take the witness through the process of making it. I have interviewed jurors who spoke scathingly of a computer graphics video expert who arrogantly overstated his own abilities and the reliability of his product. Suppose your witness has prepared a cartoon or animated version of an air crash, using the FAA tapes, the cockpit flight recorder, known information about the weather near the airport—including radar data, charts of the airport area, and investigators' reports. All of this background information is itself admissible in evidence, and you should pile it up on the counsel table. Establish the witness's qualifications to reconstruct the events. Move efficiently through the evidence used as the basis for the exhibit. Then offer it.

Technology in this field is moving faster than one can write about it. The basics are that a computer screen is a bunch of dots (pixels). Each dot can be a different color. The dots make up an image. We are all accustomed to making the screen image change by using the computer keyboard, a mouse, or by running a program. You can, however, import images into the computer's memory by other means, a process sometimes called digitizing. You can do this with a photograph or even a video "movie." Then you can add text, rework the image, and combine images. This technology is becoming less expensive and more accessible, but the strategic and tactical principles remain the same.

Be not afraid of your opponent's pixels, and be skeptical about making your own case too fancy. A high-tech exhibit is no more reliable than the evidence on which it is based and therefore is no better than the reliability of the sponsoring witness. In a homicide case, a witness made a video graphic reconstruction based in part on a tape recording of a 911 emergency call. The witness claimed, in addition to technological expertise, the ability to tell the differences among different kinds of gunshots on the tape recording. Cross-examination of such a claim uses the same techniques as with any "expert" who was not present when the events happened but who is willing to imagine how things must have been.

Sometimes the technology comes prepackaged. If so, use it. Many doctors, engineers, architects, physicists, and others use computer imagery in their day-to-day work. For example, a doctor who has done a CAT scan probably has a videotape of the scan that appeared on the screen as the test was being done. This is different from a re-creation; it is the real thing. Using the principles discussed in Chapters Eleven and Thirteen, you can guide the doctor through the video and make the expert opinion truly accessible to the jurors. They are empowered to see what the doctor saw. The same technique can be used with any expert whose ordinary duties include use of computer modeling.

I have vetoed the use of high-tech exhibits when they would look obviously expensive and would reinforce my client's image as a "win at all costs" party. I always look carefully at the vulnerability of the exhibit, whether I am thinking of using it or considering how to oppose its introduction. As a proponent, you must anticipate your opponent's moves.

As an opponent, I usually ask for the right to take the sponsoring witness on the *voir dire* out of the jury's presence. I use the same cross-examination techniques as with an expert witness. The basic principle is the computerese acronym *GIGO*, which stands for "Garbage In, Garbage Out." A computer, whether it is making spread sheets or animated graphics, does no more than rework the data it gets. If the data is unreliable, the result is, too. Since the visual impact of the animated material is great, it is often not sufficient to reply that the opponent can cross-examine after the jury has seen the exhibit. The risk of misleading and unfair prejudice may be too high.

There is nothing inherently wrong with video. Indeed, jurors are accustomed to getting information from television. However, your first instinct must be to keep it simple; you do that by first choosing a witness who can persuasively teach the principles you want to get across, then working with that expert to develop the visual aids with which she feels most comfortable. If a high-tech wizard dictates the form of your case, your props may get in the way of your story.

## LASER DISK DOCUMENT STORAGE AND RETRIEVAL

A laser disk is like a compact disk from the record store or a videodisc from the movie store. I have been before a good judge who strongly urged us to invest in laser disk technology to show documents to the jury. He was convinced that the investment of several hundred thousand dollars would greatly help the lawyers, judge, and jury during a multimonth trial with thousands of exhibits. My client settled out before trial, so I cannot know with certainty if he was right.

The nonsettling parties went to trial with a truncated version of the setup. The courtroom was a mess, with video equipment blocking movement and vision. In my opinion, the system did not do its job. What is the "job?" The system retrieves documents and shows them. Witnesses and counsel can use light pens to underline and point. Deposition transcript can be called up. The same system can be used, if it is expensive enough, to play videotape deposition excerpts or deposition summaries. Some judges and lawyers like the idea of summarizing and extracting depositions rather than playing parts of them. They will tell you that the impact of a multimedia event based on video rendering of documents and testimony is overwhelming.

For almost every case and almost every lawyer, simpler is better. Every trial lawyer needs to assert courtroom control and case control. You lose the former when the equipment is in the way and the latter when the mass of documents and depositions obscures the story you are trying to tell. My response to the laser disk is that both sides should be compelled to reduce the number of exhibits on their lists to a manageable number. The jury cannot keep track of thousands of exhibits, except perhaps through summaries that are independently admissible. There is, therefore, no rational reason to have a machine capable of storing and displaying thousands of exhibits.

When my opponent says, "We need a laser disk system because we have 20,000 exhibits," my response is, "Nonsense, Your Honor. You cannot try a jury case with 20,000 exhibits. The other side has not done the hard work of choosing the documents that really count and preparing a good faith exhibit list." Exceptions to this principle—true megacases or some nonjury proceedings—will be very few. Even then, the megatrial should probably be severed into manageable morsels.

While high-tech methods permit quick retrieval and easy highlighting with light pens and other techniques, these methods are inferior to the deliberate and well-organized action of a well-prepared lawyer who shows mastery of the case through efficient handling of its visual symbols.

If you are compelled or convinced to use an electronic retrieval system, make sure that you know it so well that your interaction with witnesses and jurors does not suffer. And learn the art of courteous interaction with the support personnel, just as with the lawyers and paralegals on your side.

# Chapter Seven

## *Adverse Examination: Inviting the Enemy in to Dine*

It would be better to abandon the Federal Rules of Evidence term "hostile witness," blessed though it be by decades of use. Real or feigned confusion marks the use of the term. In a famous Chicago conspiracy trial during 1969 and 1970, the defendants called Mayor Richard Daley in their case and tried to ask him leading questions. Objections were sustained. "But, Your Honor," defense counsel said, "Mayor Daley is a hostile witness." "Oh, no," said the judge, "his manner has been that of a gentlemen." The judge was wrong about the law of adverse witnesses and wrong about Mayor Daley, who had been seen on national television mouthing the f-word about people with opinions similar to those of the defendants.

### RULES AND CASES

Before deciding when, whether, and how to call an adverse witness, you must thread your way through a maze of evidence rules and case law. Federal Rule of Evidence 607 says, "The credibility of a witness may be attacked by any party, including the party calling the witness." Rule 611(c) says, "When a party calls a hostile witness, an adverse party, or a witness identified with an adverse party, interrogation may be by leading questions." Finally, Rule 801(d)(1)(A) permits substantive use of a witness's prior sworn statement.

The trial judge has discretion to permit leading questions on cross-examination of an adverse witness, although the practice is frowned upon because the witness is most likely friendly to the cross-examiner. In a deposition taken by your opponent, using leading questions to "cross-examine" a witness identified with your side may lead to exclusion of the answers.

The Rule 801(d)(1)(A) provision has proven to be a powerful incentive to call a hostile witness. The interrogator is able to use prior statements that might otherwise not be admissible and that the witness now disavows. This tactic is sometimes so transparent that judges forbid it. Appellate courts have reversed judgments when the trial judge permitted a party to call an adverse witness only to offer an otherwise inadmissible prior statement.

You can impeach any witness, but using your right to do so does not guarantee that you can use leading questions. Unless you are calling the adverse party, there is room for argument. The Eleventh Circuit has said that Rule 611(c) "significantly enlarged the class of witnesses presumed hostile." The Advisory Committee Notes to Rule 611(c) as proposed say that the language "witness identified with" is designed to relax the old Federal Rule of Civil Procedure standard, which required that the witness be an agent or employee of the adverse party in order to be deemed hostile without further inquiry.

The combination of case law and rules says that if a witness is identified with the opponent in the sense described in the admissions rule, Rule 801(d)(2), hostile witness status is virtually automatic. Beyond that, you must make your argument to the trial judge.

Going back to our Mayor Daley case, Seventh Circuit law today would make it an easy question. In a suit against the City of Chicago and a police officer for killing the plaintiff's dog, the court held that police officers should have been regarded as hostile witnesses. One might argue that the police are there to serve everybody, just as the mayor is, and that they cannot be termed "hostile" to either party. The case law is more realistic than that.

## WHEN AND WHETHER TO CALL
## AN ADVERSE WITNESS

No matter what the rules say, there is a great difference between the witness, called by the other side, who counterpunches on cross-examination and the witness, called by you, who savages you. The jury expects parties to move the ball and score during their case. This is the usual understanding of the adversary system, and modifications such as Federal Rule 607 cannot change the popular perception.

Jerry Solovy and Robert Byman cite a telling example of the misfiring adverse witness. In a recent trial between two brothers who are fifty percent shareholders of a closely held company, the dissenting brother (call him Cain) claimed, among other things, that his brother (Abel) had purchased $200,000 worth of gold with company funds and attempted to conceal the purchase from Cain. In his deposition, Abel was asked, "Did you have the gold stored at the Jefferson State Bank to keep Cain from finding out that you had bought the gold?" Abel answered, "Yes, I did not want him to find out."

At trial, Cain's counsel called Abel as an adverse witness and asked, "You stored that gold at the Jefferson State Bank in order to keep your brother from finding out that you had bought it, isn't that right?" Abel admitted, yes, he had done that because they needed gold to run the business, and every time Cain had heard that Abel ordered gold, Cain called the supplier and canceled the order. So Abel decided to keep the purchase secret, but only for a few days, to keep Cain from "destroy[ing] the company's business out of spite."

The surefire impact of reading the deposition transcript and letting Abel and his lawyer explain it was lost. Of course, one could fault the plaintiff's lawyer for giving the witness a chance to explain instead of simply getting him to acknowledge the prior statement and making him read it to the jury. But many judges will let witnesses on cross-examination explain answers, and in any case the explanation will arrive just as soon as cross-examination begins.

The deposition was admissible as an admission of the party-opponent, whether or not the defendant testified. If the plaintiff had simply offered the choice morsel, subject of course to the rule of completeness, the defense would have had to wait until its case-in-chief to give the explanation.

This example captures the dilemma. If your principal purpose in calling an adverse witness is to gain admission of a prior statement, the cost may not be worth the benefit. The prior statement may be admissible in any case, as in our example. If the statement is not admissible, the trial judge may well forbid you to call the witness for so transparent a purpose.

The other horn of the dilemma is that to avoid being hurt by the adverse witness, you would ordinarily not call her unless you had enough prior statements in hand to guarantee control of the examination.

In sum, I agree with Solovy and Byman that almost every bit of evidence you can get from an adverse witness can be presented more easily and safely, provided that you have taken proper discovery.

We can test this assertion by thinking of cases in which adverse testimony is usual, for example, where a plaintiff calls the physician in a medical malpractice case, or a plaintiff calls the other driver in a negligence case. If there will be other witnesses to the same events these witnesses describe, and if you are going to argue that these witnesses are mistaken (or even untruthful), it is better to wait until you have firmly established your own version of events before you give them a platform.

Should you ever call an adverse witness? Of course. Plaintiffs will often want to call witnesses identified with the other side, perhaps even the opposing party. In a product liability, antitrust, or securities fraud case, the defendants' agents and employees may be crucial witnesses. Of course, they are not going to admit liability, but they have documents, they went to meetings, they signed papers, they conferred with others—they performed actions that are consistent with the plaintiff's version of the case. The more the other side's witnesses can be compelled to admit facts essential to your case, the fewer matters over which to argue to the jury.

In the kinds of cases we are discussing, you will have depositions. You may not be able to use them because the witnesses are available. If the depositions give you sufficient control so that you can elicit the helpful information and then quit, calling these witnesses in your case can be persuasive. If you plan such a tactic, you will need to take precautions. First, tell the jury in the opening statement: "We are going to start by calling as witnesses a lot of people who work for the Squamus Corporation. The rules here let us do that. Now, you wouldn't expect they will agree with our whole case, and they won't. But they will admit to you the following things. . . ."

The other precaution is to move *in limine* under Federal Rule of Evidence 611(b) to limit cross-examination to the scope of the direct, and then reconsider your position if the motion is denied. In one case, plaintiff's counsel announced that they would call several dozen employees and former employees of the defendants. The defendants quickly moved for leave to cross-examine beyond the scope of direct, so that they could turn each adverse witness's appearance into an endorsement of the defense position.

If the judge is going to permit this kind of interruption of your case-in-chief, calling the adverse witnesses becomes a much more risky business. It is unlikely that the court of appeals will reverse a trial court judgment for rulings under Rule 611(b), regardless of which way the judge leans. In jurisdictions that permit wide-open cross-examination, the chances of an adverse witness inflicting damage are greatly increased.

Your best tactical and evidentiary position is this: "Your Honor, I am going to call Dr. Jones for a brief examination, limited to the following items. It serves no purpose to permit a cross-examination broader than those limited issues. Indeed, a shotgun cross-examination simply makes the entire case much more difficult for the jury to comprehend."

You will sometimes call an adverse witness who is so marginal for the other side that they will not call him. A technician may have conducted a test whose results are inconsistent with the other side's theory but which do not really support your case. An agent or employee of the opposing party may have authored a series of memoranda that make it unlikely the other side will call him but that are helpful enough that you will take the risk that the employee may explain them away.

Sometimes you cannot get the evidence in as an admission because the employee's duties do not include making statements on this subject matter. Some judges will let the other side mousetrap you in this way: The judge is convinced it is unfair to let the written evidence in without calling the employee and giving the other side a chance to "explain" the documents. The risk/benefit calculation will depend on the extent to which the jurors will think that someone in that witness's position is so accustomed to saying exactly what he means in memoranda that the subsequent explanation must be discounted.

In one case, an employee of my opponent had handwritten some very powerful comments on drafts of reports. There could be doubt whether the handwritten comments qualified as the opponent's admission. The employee had at one time worked for one of my codefendants. With candid explanation in the opening statement about the evidence, how it came to be, and what it was and was not worth, I opted to call the witness if the plaintiff did not.

Sometimes you have little choice. You learn of the witness after discovery is closed. Or it is a criminal case, and you get only derisory discovery to begin with. You simply have to take the risk.

This brings me to the final tactical consideration. If you are the defendant, you have the luxury of parading statements of witnesses before the jury and then saying, "And if they don't call Mr. Jones to testify, we are going to call him in our case." The plaintiff can try to wait until rebuttal to call the adverse witness, but can hardly announce that strategy in the opening statement because there are limits on rebuttal, and the defense might not open the door.

## HOW TO DO IT

In adverse examination, you should hesitate to do anything that will give the witness a platform. The ideal examination consists of a series of short statements with which the witness must agree or be impeached.

"You are Miriam Wilson?" "You were a registered representative at Squamus Corporation?" "That was in 1985 and 1986?" "Can you give us more exact dates?" "Mrs. Albertson was your client?" "You called her on January 5, 1986?" "You don't recall the date?" "Here is your call slip, Plaintiff's 105. Does that remind you that it was January 5, 1986?"

Take the witness through the documents.

"Mrs. Albertson said that she would follow your advice and buy the stock?" If the answer is "Well, she said she would buy it, yes," your response is the same as if you had encountered an evasion on cross-examination. One repetition for emphasis, and then the impeachment:

"Mrs. Albertson said that she would follow your advice and buy the stock?" If the answer is other than "Yes," go through the routine of making the witness read out the deposition answer in which she admitted that Mrs. Albertson bought the stock on the witness's advice. After all, you wouldn't ask that question in that form unless you had an impeachment answer in that form. The surest method of control is to have the witness's prior statements—in whatever form—and to make the witness acknowledge them one by one.

Get through the items that compelled you to call the witness—and then quit. Give thanks for your good fortune that no disaster befell you.

If the witness begins to unravel the adverse evidence that you are trying to introduce, or is otherwise making a fool of you, what do you do? You cannot just give up. You will hear in summation about how quickly you backed away when confronted with powerful opposing evidence. You are permitted some repetition, as on cross-examination, so consider yoking the unfavorable answer with a favorable one, and then quickly moving on. For example: "It is your testimony, then, that you did not tell Mrs. Albertson that company's financial reports looked funny, but you thought she knew that? Correct?"

In addition, you must save one or two surefire strong questions so that, no matter what happens, you end strong.

The need for control should not lead you to write out your questions or to stick so closely to an outline that you miss gifts from the witness. Often you can call an adverse witness with little or no notice. Even when you have subpoenaed the witness and kept her waiting awhile in the witness room, the witness is nowhere near as ready to testify as someone your opponent called, examined on direct, and then tendered to you for cross-examination.

Perhaps your opponent did not foresee that this person would be a witness and did nothing to prepare them. The short time available between the summons and the testimony may not cure that problem. Or perhaps the opponent has simply not yet had time to prepare the direct examination and ready the witness for cross-examination. All I know is that some adverse witnesses take the stand and look like a deer in your headlights.

In one case, plaintiff's counsel had seen that the defendant had done a fairly lackluster job of preparing its witnesses for depositions. At trial, a fairly senior executive of the defendant was sitting in the courtroom, presumably to "represent" the entity. Plaintiff's counsel took a calculated risk, betting that the executive had not been prepared to testify, or at least not yet. He turned right after the opening statement and called him as a witness.

The scene was dramatic, and the tactic successful. The problem, of course, is that we litigators love dramatic gestures and sometimes do not think beyond the gesture to the risks of playing out the gambit thus begun.

This lack of preparation is your signal to get right to work, ask your questions, display your exhibits, and make your point before the witness settles into the routine of testifying. By all means finish your examination before the trial day is over, and plan enough time so that the cross-examination should be over as well. I have scored points against adverse witnesses and left them overnight only to find that in the morning they are full of explanations and theories that undercut the previous day's work.

Also be alert to the witness's expressions and gestures. Often an adverse witness will start looking at your opposing counsel, to try and check how things are going or even to get a cue. Sometimes the witness will grimace or even smirk. If the gesture or expression has been obvious to at least some jurors, call the witness to account.

"Mr. Johnson, why are you looking at the plaintiff's lawyer before you answer every question?" I know a lawyer who followed up by saying, "You won't get wisdom, or knowledge, or courage, or anything else you lack, by looking over there." That was, however, in a deposition, and it is not recommended courtroom commentary. If you catch a smirk, you may be able to ask, "I'm sorry. Do you find this funny?" It depends on the mood and tenor of your questions and the witness's answers.

The adverse witness will be a rarity in your practice. There is no type of witness whose use depends on thoughtful answers to so many preliminary questions: Does this witness qualify as adverse? Will I be permitted to use the evidence that is responsible for my calling this witness? Do the rules of evidence permit me a risk-free way to admit the same evidence? Will my opponent use the opportunity to break the rhythm and flow of my case, through extensive friendly cross-examination? Will my risks be less, or the impact of this witness better for me, if I defer my questions until I cross-examine?

# Chapter Eight

## *Cross-Examination: Venial Violations of the Ten Commandments*

Paeans to cross-examination abound. Wigmore's "greatest legal engine ever invented for the discovery of truth" is most often quoted. The Supreme Court has repeatedly emphasized the fundamental role of cross-examination in criminal cases and has insisted that the lawyer be given the tools to do it and the arena to perform it. Even in civil cases, undue limits on cross-examination will trigger reversal.

Cross-examination and confrontation are central to the adversary system, but they are not merely talismanic rituals. Nor are they solely a means of putting questions and getting answers. They are devices for letting the jury see how the witness reacts, to assess whether they want to believe him. They are a part of empowering the jury, of giving it the tools to decide, and of jurors participating in building the story of a case.

Of course, you can get hurt on cross. There is a Zulu warning about cross-examination: *Bhasobha ingozi! Izoshaya wena? Noma ufakazi?* It means: It is a boomerang. Will it strike you? Or will it strike the witness?

Cross-examination is about immanence, about what is inherent and indwelling. It is the process of finding and revealing the contradictions in a story told by a witness. You cannot expect to get what is not immanent. Most of cross-examination simply traces the inherent deficiencies in any human perception of events.

The rules limit your ability to ask the witness on the stand to explain or comment on the testimony of another witness. This is a marked contrast to other legal systems, such as the British and South African, in which putting others' versions to the witness is often done. Almost all your cross will consist of uncovering different aspects of the same story told on direct. This will especially be true if your opponent is wise enough to anticipate on direct examination any troublesome areas of cross.

Because cross-examination is a process of extracting good from someone who has been placed there to harm your case, and because you are limited by the principle of immanence, cross-examination is said to require control of the witness. Control is important for two reasons. First, the witness has already hurt you. She has gone through all the harmful details of a story. You should exercise control in order not to invite or permit her to repeat.

Second, the witness wants to hurt you. The witness is at least situationally against you. Even a neutral observer is cast by the adversary system on one side or the other. The abolition of sponsorship and vouching rules does not change the human desire to be seen as right. (Have you ever noticed how the tenor of a friendly pickup game of basketball or tennis changes when a couple of people stop to watch the action?) The cross-examiner necessarily challenges rightness. The witness looks for chances to reaffirm the right—"Yes, but. . . ." You exercise control to stay in charge.

The goal is to have a working plurality of jurors say "Aha," meaning "We see now the flaws in what this witness has said." Many lawyers do not understand that the "aha" can come at many possible times during trial, and need not even be the result of cross-examination. The jurors can choose to discredit a witness because of what some other witness has said or based on some other evidence; effective lawyer argument shows the contradiction and points to the right result. In short, you don't have to cross-examine every adverse witness.

Even when you do cross-examine, the "aha" needn't occur while the witness is on the stand. Trying to make it appear may lead you to take excessive risks with the witness.

When Edward Bennett Williams had Jake Jacobsen, ex-Treasury Secretary Connally's accuser, on the stand, much of the cross-examination was derided by journalistic on-lookers as boring. Ed was taking Jacobsen through a long series of prior inconsistent statements, most of them under oath. In some measure, Ed was showing Jacobsen power—that he had mastered all these facts about Jacobsen, making Jacobsen reluctant to hazard disagreement with the examiner.

The main purpose of the cross was to lay the basis for the closing argument, where the inconsistencies could be spread out again and made part of the story of the case. Then the jurors would say, "Aha!"

It is important, however, to make the witness agree with one or more important elements of the cross-examiner's story. Later in this chapter, we discuss the how and why of that exercise.

The leading writers and speakers on cross-examination ask whether it is a science or an art. If it is a science, its precepts can be taught. If it is an art, they cannot. Or so the argument goes. I reject any such distinction. There are basic principles of cross-examination that every lawyer can and should learn. These principles distill experience and honor the essential characteristics of an adversary process. Following these rules can make any lawyer a reasonably good cross-examiner.

In this chapter, however, I want to go beyond rules. It is possible to acquire an art of cross-examination based upon one's sense of case theory and storytelling. For this process, one can suggest approaches and ideas but not rules. If there are indeed "ten commandments" of cross-examination, I am going to advocate constructive sin.

## THE TEN COMMANDMENTS

The best-known rules of cross-examination are derived from the need to control the witness. Irving Younger's list is:

1. Be brief.
2. Short questions, plain words.
3. Ask only leading questions.
4. Never ask a question to which you do not already know the answer.
5. Listen to the answer.
6. Do not quarrel with the witness.
7. Do not permit the witness to explain.
8. Do not ask the witness to repeat the testimony he gave on direct examination.
9. Avoid one question too many.
10. Save the explanation for summation.

Other lists abound. Some savants add "No why questions," "Begin and end strong," and "Have a point" to the list. The attentive student adds "Consider not doing any cross at all."

These rules summarize the basics. But in a career trying cases, good sense and good tactics will tell you at some time to violate every one of them. When you do, however, understand *that* you are doing so and *why*.

But even on their own terms, the ten commandments do not tell you how to cross-examine. Like the original ten, they are largely negative warnings about pits into which you should not fall.

## THE TRUE RULES OF
## CROSS CONTROL

You want to know *how* to cross-examine, not how *not* to. The witness has finished the direct examination. "Pass the witness," says your opponent, or the equivalent in your jurisdiction. The jury expects you to do something.

If your case plan includes not cross-examining, tell the jury in the opening statement: "In this case, we are not going to waste your time on the obvious. When the other side puts up a witness to testify about something that isn't even being disputed here, we will just say, 'No questions.' Or, if the other side puts up a witness that the other evidence shows is just plain wrong about something, I might not cross-examine. Instead, I'll leave it to the closing argument to show how that witness can't be trusted. And, of course, we'll be trusting you to keep an open mind until the case is all over."

But the witness currently before you is not that "no cross" witness. You have to do something. As with every other form of examination, you have internalized the Rules of Evidence. For example, you may ask leading questions, you have great latitude in asking questions about bias, you are limited on using extrinsic evidence to impeach on "collateral matters."

You know also what a leading question is. It is, according to Bergen and Cornelia Evans's *Dictionary of Contemporary American Usage*, "simply a question so worded as to suggest the proper or desired answer." By contrast, the classic "Have you stopped beating your spouse?" inquiry "is not a *leading question* but a *misleading question*," at least unless the witness has admitted the predicate facts.

Of all the principles of cross-examination, two stand out:

1. Begin and end strong.
2. This is not a deposition.

The second one should be unnecessary. If you think it is, go to court and watch lawyers in your town. What passes for cross-examination is often as inconsequential as a pillow fight in a pizza parlor.

The first principle reminds you that however much sinning you do against the ten commandments, you should always come home to virtue with a tight, strong close in which the witness agrees with a fundamental point.

To begin strong, you must choose an area in which the witness will agree with you. Preferably, the witness will also want to agree with you. What do I mean "want to"? If you are going to cross-examine a police officer on a defect in his report, you will begin by establishing how careful a report writer the witness is. The witness wants to tell you this.

Face the witness. Smile at the witness. The smile need not be friendly, but it must be polite. Remember, you want this witness to agree with you. You will see British barristers take a superior attitude toward the witness, lofty and disdainful. You will see American lawyers—real or on television—sneering and snarling. Don't do any of that. With whom will the jury identify in a contest between a witness who is just sitting there and a snarling, sneering, supercilious lawyer? Oh, maybe later, when the jury is brought along to your point of view, you can change mien. But for now, a polite smile.

The next idea is borrowed from Terry MacCarthy. Actually, all good trial lawyers have done what he suggests, but Terry has refined the technique into a "method." The idea is this: Don't ask questions. Make *statements* with which the witness must agree or suffer impeachment. Most good cross-examiners use leading questions:

Q. You were in charge of the city's oil properties, right?
Q. It was your job to review the prices the city was
   paid, isn't that right?

You can even eliminate the words "right" or "isn't that right."

Stand up. If the rules where you practice require you to examine from a seated position, start your cross with a document or exhibit that requires you to approach the witness so you have a reason to stand. After the obligatory smile, look the witness in the eyes, and make a positive statement, all the while smiling and nodding.

Q. You were in charge of the city's oil properties?

Q. You reviewed the prices the city was paid for its crude oil?

If the witness agrees with you, but does not answer audibly, give a reminder.

Q. That's "yes"?

This method is particularly effective when you are leading the witness through a series of assertions, each one part of a picture.

Q. You were in the bar?

Q. You were with John?

Q. Somebody came in?

Q. He had a gun?

Q. This person had on a jacket?

Q. Red?

The last in the series illustrates MacCarthy's shining example of brevity: a one-word question. Brevity is, however, not a result but a means. This style of questions encourages the witness to agree with you by a series of "yes" answers. It leads from point to point, giving the jurors a picture of the action.

Best of all, the method lets you jettison most of the ten commandments as unnecessary. You will almost automatically be brief, short, plain, and nonrepetitive. Because your statements are questions only because you verbally punctuate them as such, you are not likely to ask "one question too many," "permit the witness to explain," or "ask the witness to repeat" the direct examination.

If the witness does not agree with you, have your impeachment material ready, to be used in the same fashion:

Q. You gave a deposition in this case? [Pulling out the deposition, or cueing the video recorder, or doing

whatever gesture symbolizes deposition
impeachment in your case.]

Q. You were under oath to tell the truth, just as you are
   now?

Q. Your lawyer was there?

Q. You were asked this question and gave this answer?
   [Reading.]


In this style of cross-examination, you must have the
impeachment material so ready at hand that the flow is not
interrupted by your pulling it out and using it. You "listen
to the answer" in part because you want to administer the
discipline of impeachment if it is not what it should be.

Preparing for this kind of cross-examination consists of
making a list of points that you want to make and taking
the witness through them. Almost the entire list should be
made before the witness begins direct examination. If you
have not anticipated the direct well enough to make such
a list, something is wrong with your preparation.

In preparation, you have kept in mind (using the Federal
Rules of Evidence as an example) that you may ask leading
questions under Rule 611(c). You are generally limited to
the scope of the direct examination and matters bearing
upon credibility, as controlled by Rule 611(b). However, in
many cases efficiency and jury comprehension will be
served by a more expansive cross, and case law supports
your right to move for relaxation of the rules. On collateral
matters, you will not be able to impeach the witness's
answer with extrinsic evidence.

When you internalize these rules, you can anticipate
problems with your cross-examination. You should consider making a written motion *in limine* on doubtful matters to protect your rights and to limit your opponent's
chance to derail you. At a minimum, you should be prepared with a case or rule citation to justify your actions.

If you are shut off, promptly make an offer of proof out
of the jury's presence as to what you would have done if

permitted. If the court denies leave to make such an offer, ask to do it at the end of the day. Failing that, write it up, and file it. In any case, you may wish to file a motion to reconsider, listing authorities.

In the heat of cross-examination, as at no other time in the trial, preparation wins the little battles over objections. Making a thorough record can also provide grounds for appeal.

## THE THEORY OF MINIMAL CONTRADICTION

Up to now, we have been concerned with the techniques of cross-examination. Most of the essays and checklists deal with technique, as do all of the ten commandments. Lawyers who know the rules often do bad cross-examinations because they do not have a point—and expect from cross-examination more than it can give. They violate the principle of immanence.

What do you want to accomplish with this witness? How will you argue that her testimony fits the story of the case? How will the jury think about the story? You will seldom be able to argue that all the other side's witnesses are liars. Jurors are looking at witnesses and trying to figure out how to make sense out of what they say. They are trying to sort out contradictions and to explain them. By the time you rise to sum up, the jurors will have pretty well figured out what they think of each witness who has testified. The summation is a means of gathering facts for the jurors who lean your way, to use as ammunition in the jury room. It is a time to emphasize pieces of evidence that might be overlooked, such as documents that may have been alluded to but not published in full. It is a time to evoke the memory of testimony and to weave it into a coherent pattern.

Looking through the record you have made, you want to maximize the number of things that fit and minimize the number that do not. Claiming that all the opposing witnesses are liars violates this principle and calls on the jurors to perform the distasteful job of labeling an entire group of testifiers as perjurers. You will, in trying cases, come to label many witnesses as liars and should not shrink from this duty when the occasion demands. The occasion demands, however, far less frequently than some people think.

I call my view the "theory of minimal contradiction." It directs attention to all four of the defects in evidence that cross-examination is designed to show up. These four are meaning, perception, memory, and veracity. A potential cross-examination must focus on all four. Let us see how this works.

## MEANING

The witness may have used words that convey one impression to us but which the witness was using in a different sense. This is the problem of expression, or meaning. It is the stuff of which a classic story was told by Dan O'Connell, the great Irish advocate:

> There was this lawsuit over the validity of a will, and one of the attesting witnesses swore on his oath that, at the time the will was witnessed, "the deceased still had life in him."
> So I crossed him: "On your oath as a Kerryman, are you telling this jury he was alive?"
> "He had life in him, Mr. O'Connell."
> "Well, isn't it the fact that you put a live fly in the dead man's mouth before you attested the will?"
> "That's what I've been after saying. He had life in him."

In your case, the witness may describe someone as "tall" or "hairy." You may want to make the evaluative word precise. Without some prior statement of the witness, this course risks creating additional unfavorable evidence. With such evidence in hand, there is no reason not to let the witness explain what the imprecise word means.

Q. You told the jury this person you saw was "tall." Can you put a number on that? How tall?
A. Well, I don't really know . . .
Q. You told the police he was six feet two. Was that about right?

The tone is conversational. The questions are not leading. You have violated the commandments. To what purpose? You have given the jurors a tool to use in evaluating this witness. It is not that the witness lied. The witness told us the literal truth, but used a word that might lead us to get the wrong impression.

Sometimes you can go on to blame the problem on your opponent, who claims after all to be presenting a true story. You end up saying, in effect, "There is no contradiction here. When we take what Mr. X said in the way that Mr. X was trying to tell us, it all comes together."

The problem of meaning is particularly acute when a witness interprets a document. Perhaps it is a document prepared by our witness, and we have the luxury of taking the witness through it on direct, to clarify meaning.

The trouble starts when one of our client's documents is offered by the other side. Sometimes the authentication and admission in evidence come without any chance for cross-examination. The offending document is then like a sword plunged in, for us to pluck out later, after we have bled a little or a lot.

If we are lucky, there is a witness to cross-examine. That witness can help the jury understand that the words on paper may bear more than one meaning—and even how best to see what meaning is right. Your cross can include major themes such as "the person who wrote it knows best what is meant" and "often when you write something, you go back later and find out that somebody has misinterpreted it." Smaller themes might be based on meanings used in a particular company or office for particular words.

I once had a translator on cross-examination. His relentlessly literal translation of my client's letters was damaging. One major theme was the danger of literal translation. The male witness had worked in a military setting and knew a lot of barracks idiom in three languages.

"Making a literal translation can be very misleading, can't it?"

"Well, it might be sometimes?"

"Let's take an example. Suppose I said to you in French, '*Il y a du monde sur le balcon.*' Literally, that is a very polite statement: 'There are a lot of people on the balcony,' correct?" The witness looked at me warily and wide-eyed.

"Yes," nodding.

"But you know from all the soldiers you worked with that it doesn't mean that at all, don't you?"

"Yes."

"Tell the judge and jurors what it really means."

The witness paused, made a suggestive gesture, and gulped. "Stacked," he said. The judge and jurors laughed out loud.

"It is something that men say about women they are looking at, right?" The witness's insistence on literalism was seriously undercut.

The problem of meaning also arises in cases involving videotapes and audiotapes. Sometimes cross-examination alone will not present the issue clearly. An expert witness may be able to explain how meaning depends on context.

## PERCEPTION

Chapter One explains that we are all victims and beneficiaries of the Gestalt. We want to remember an event as a whole, and we tend to embroider our recollection so that we can tell a coherent tale. A witness may swear to having seen something that objectively she could not have seen.

She may not be a liar, and you need not argue that she is. She may simply not have seen what she thought she saw.

The controversial comedian Lenny Bruce was on trial in New York for making an obscene gesture during a night-club performance. A police officer swore he had seen the gesture. Defense counsel set the scene carefully. Where was the officer sitting? How was the club arranged? Did this sketch seem to be accurate? Was the stage right here?

The cross built up the objective picture that the lines of sight made it unlikely that the officer had a good view. Counsel unfortunately tried to end with a dramatic gesture, and his verbal shaft went astray. He strode masterfully to the end of the jury box, wheeled, pointed at the witness, and declaimed, "So isn't it a fact that you couldn't actually *see* Mr. Crotch put his hand on his Bruce?"

You can do the perception cross with short, sharp shocks. You can make a series of statements about where the witness was standing, the lighting, the time available to observe, and the witness's emotional state. Prefer this method when the witness has been trained to hurt you by repeating the direct or injecting prejudicial matter.

If your point is that the witness is honest but mistaken, you may wish to tread a gentler path—and to violate a commandment or two. Set a scene with the witness. Ask where she was standing. Ask how many people were around. Ask what kind of lights were shining. You do not need to structure this examination as a series of tight, leading questions. You will know the scene. You will have impeachment material at hand. Let the witness talk. Let the jury see the witness tell the facts that objectively contradict her version.

Of course, you would not make the mistake of asking the witness to admit that her direct examination does not make sense. The "one question too many" commandment is valid, but it may now be derived from a different premise. You are letting the witness answer questions so that the jury can see her and make up its mind. You are not doing lawyer tricks to keep the witness from talking. By the same token, there is no reason to let the witness argue conclusions by reaffirming some ultimate reality that has now become improbable.

In exploring perception, you may wish to invite the witness to mark on a diagram or map. If you want to work toward a comparison of vantage points, you will have an agreed diagram with multiple clear overlays so that the various witness descriptions can be compared at trial's end.

It may be objected, here as with other sins against the commandments, that the witness who is not on a short leash will very likely jump out at you with a repeat of the direct. For example, an eyewitness may bridle if during your cross-examination you keep referring to the one the witness has identified as "this person," or may react to a suggestion that he cannot accurately identify the accused. That's when you may hear "I picked out that man right over there." Or, "I just know it is this defendant."

These are said to be the untoward risks of letting the witness run free. What should you do? One commandment says "Never quarrel with the witness." There is a judge who will enforce the rule against argumentative questions. The problem with this commandment is that it derives from a faulty premise. Here is the sinner's response. First, I reject such statements as Irving Younger's that the "clever advocate controls a witness, . . . making him say only what the advocate wants him to say."

Too clever by half, I say. The jury knows when you are straining to prevent the witness from completing a thought. Sometimes you want to shut the witness off; the liar, the crafty, and the ruffian deserve no quarter. But the honest witness whose errors you are trying to probe deserves better treatment at your hands.

So you will need to be able to respond to sallies such as "Well, it was your client." Understand that the jury knows which side everybody is on. You could just let it go by, figuring that the jury understands the adversary system. But

I like to use these episodes to quarrel openly with the witness in a permissible way—and thereby carry the argument back to the jury.

Q. I understand you have already told the jury that. But you do understand, Ms. Johnson, that the jury has to decide this case?

A. Yes.

Q. You don't mind my asking you these questions, do you?

A. I suppose not.

Q. Because the jury needs to know all the facts that both sides bring out, don't you agree?

A. Yes.

Q. I mean, neither you nor I am going to decide this case, are we? That's the jury's job, don't you agree?

A. Sure.

Q. That's the American way, isn't it—to give both sides a fair chance?

A. Yes.

Q. Well, then, let me go back to this group of photos that the policeman picked out for you to look at.

And back to the job at hand. This is the "Do you believe in America?" line of cross-examination, and I am proud of it. This cross helps discipline the witness who is taking unfair advantage of being permitted to answer civil questions. It reminds the jury of their power and helps them to anticipate your argument about how they should use it.

## MEMORY

Most of what passes as "memory" cross-examination is nothing of the sort. The witness says the light was red. In a deposition, he said it was green. The lawyer impeaches with the deposition, then adds, "Was your memory better when you gave your deposition than it is today?" or the only marginally better, "Your deposition was only six months after the accident, and now three more years have gone by, right?"

We know from experience and science that memory of an event drops off quickly and sharply, then continues to fade at a slower rate. Whether memory, once lost, can be refreshed or even revived by such techniques as hypnosis is controversial. It is certainly likely that much allegedly refreshed recollection is a tribute to the powers of lawyer suggestion.

Yet the system of jury trials is based on the idea that public oral recitation of recollected events is the best way to decide disputes. A witness who claims to remember clearly an event three years ago may not be lying. He may simply be laboring under our human need to tell a whole story and our consequent willingness to latch onto devices—such as lawyer suggestion—that fill in the gaps in our memory. This is called "confabulation." The witness may even be unaware that such a process has occurred since, at each retelling of the story, the new version has become superimposed upon the old in the mind's eye.

So here is the problem. Faulty memory is not mendacity; however, witnesses can tell remembered stories quite convincingly because they truly believe they are telling the truth. Only occasionally will you be able to develop the entire theme of inherently defective memory and inevitable confabulation. You get nowhere by violating the theory of minimal contradiction. Your style must aim to develop the objective facts that support your version of events and call into respectful question the contradictory statements of the witness. The contradictory witness, the prior statement, pretrial preparation, and the objective facts are four prime ingredients of a lapse-of-memory cross-examination.

The contradictory witness is not wholly available, because you usually cannot ask witnesses to comment on one another's testimony. You can establish that others were present or know "the facts." You can ask about their qualifications and whether the witness knows any reason

why they should not be credited. If this witness did not
make a report or statement soon after the event, but
another witness did, you can bring this out. You need not,
in this process, "ask only leading questions." Your mien
need not be hostile. You are simply making a list of
reasons, to be added to your closing argument, why one
point of view is better than another.

The inconsistent prior statement need not be used to
suggest fabrication. You can take the witness through the
contradictions and use them to observe later what a jumble
memory can be. The drill is almost the same no matter what
your ultimate objective. Accredit the statement by a short
litany of positive statements, then go through the contradictions.

Q. You made a statement to Mr. Johnson, the
   investigator?
Q. He came to your house?
Q. This was about a week after the accident?
Q. He took notes on what you said?
Q. He wrote up a statement?
Q. He gave it to you to read?
Q. This is the statement?
Q. It says here that you read it?
Q. It has some changes in your handwriting, on pages
   four and five?
Q. You signed it right here?
Q. In the statement, you said . . . ?

Sometimes you can tell why the witness has changed
some detail, and help the jury to see why the change is so
important. I wrote this in a tribute to Edward Bennett
Williams:

> In the *Connally* case, for example, he confronted
> the witness Jacobsen, who had testified on direct that
> Connally counted money with a "glove or gloves" in
> order to leave no fingerprints:

Williams: You told us that Mr. Connally and you had a meeting in his office alone, that he excused himself, left his office for ten minutes and came back with a cigar box and a rubber glove or rubber gloves on top of a pile of money in the cigar box, is that right?

Jacobsen: Well, it was something like that.

Williams: No, tell me what it was, Mr. Jacobsen, not whether it was something like that or not. You tell us exactly how it was, Mr. Jacobsen.

Jacobsen: I believe the rubber glove was on the side of the money in the cigar box. The rubber glove or gloves was on the side of the money.

Williams: I'm sorry?

Jacobsen: I say the rubber glove or gloves was on the side of the money, not on top of the money.

Williams: Now, when you told Mr. Tuerkheimer in your interview with him back last year about this episode, you told him it was *a* rubber glove, did you not?

Jacobsen: Yes.

Williams: And when you testified before the grand jury on March 23rd, you told the grand jury it was *a* rubber glove, did you not?

Jacobsen: Yes, sir.

Williams: But when you testified on Thursday here in this courtroom before His Honor and this jury, you said it was a rubber glove or gloves; is that correct?

Jacobsen: Yes, sir.

Williams: When did you decide it might have been a glove or gloves?

Jacobsen: Between the time I testified before the grand jury and the time I testified here.

Williams: What was it that changed your recollection from it being a glove to it being a glove or gloves?

Jacobsen: Just the logic of it being gloves instead of glove.

Williams: It was the logic of it, is that right?

Jacobsen: Yes.

Williams: Was that because, Mr. Jacobsen, the prosecutors pointed out to you that nobody could count money with one glove on one hand and a big pile?

Jacobsen: No, sir.

Williams: Well, what was the logic of it that changed your mind . . . and caused you to testify on Thursday that it was a glove or gloves?

Jacobsen: Well, the fact that you couldn't hardly handle money with one glove.

Williams: Well, that was what I just asked you, Mr. Jacobsen.

This cross has it all. Control: "You tell us exactly how it was." Pace: we get each prior inconsistent statement and the witness agreeing to it. Preparation: The prior grand jury testimony *and* the prosecutor's notes—produced after a hard fight—are deployed. Daring: There are at least four non-leading questions in the series, including the ones laden with the most significance. Closure: Ed does not stop until he has the devastating admission that this witness kept working on his story until it was "logical," and then Ed moves on to another topic. This cross, like all of them, was sharp and clear.

Many lessons can be drawn from this excerpt. The present lesson is that some changes in the witness's story are driven by the need to make things "consistent." Uncovering this fact is effective summation fodder.

Williams's cross-examination suggests the pretrial preparation theme mentioned above. In criminal cases, where discovery is limited, I almost always start cross with a hunt for prior statements. I get the witness to catalog all the meetings with the police and prosecutors and then demand all the notes and statements that resulted from those meetings. In a civil case, I use the hunt only to fill in gaps in what I have.

Where preparation has apparently been lengthy and the witness tells a much more polished, directed, or damaging story in court than in prior statements, I want to help the jury see just how this story was built up over time. I assemble the prior statements and a time chart of meetings with lawyers and their minions and put the puzzle together. I am not leading toward accusing the witness of intentionally lying. I am showing how the fickle memory that all of us have can be cudgeled or persuaded.

The objective fact cross-examination uses the same techniques as one employs when getting at problems of perception. Confront the witness with time, place, vantage point, and other undeniable details.

## VERACITY

Most commandment-based theories of cross-examination are designed for the witness you will claim is a liar. There is some merit in virtue, and there are greater penalties for sin when you confront such a witness.

We seldom find a witness who is a liar through and through, like the Kerryman who was charged with stealing chickens and confessed to the crime under fierce cross-examination by Crown counsel. His lawyer, wise in the ways of a Kerry jury, argued that the defendant should be acquitted because he was such an obvious liar that you couldn't believe a thing he said.

Some lying witnesses are professionals, with long experience on many witness stands. Some are informers recruited for the particular case, and they are promised not money but that reward that only a grateful sovereign can bestow: immunity from just punishment.

Such witnesses usually want to hurt you. They will take advantage of lapses in control. For your part, you will use them as objects not only to enhance control but to diffract moral and tactical superiority.

Let me explain this. When you ask a series of short, tight, leading questions on cross-examination and obtain the witness acknowledgment of each, you say two things to the jury. First, you demonstrate that the only facts from this witness that anybody should care to hear are those that support your version of events. You know all the important facts. This is tactical superiority.

Second, you are saying to this witness and the jury that the only truth of which the witness is capable is that wrung from him in the form of circumstantial evidence that his main message is untrue.

But have you considered the possible delights of a petty sin or two, even in the face of such a witness as this? Remember that jurors still want the chance to make up their own minds about whether and what to believe.

Let us take the paradigmatic liar: the informer. I have, to my sorrow, assumed sometimes that exploring the informer's deal would inevitably undercut what the informer has to say about my client. Maybe that worked in days now gone. Maybe it works in places where I do not try cases. But I doubt it.

Sure, the jury wants to know what rewards the witness will receive and what threats of harm may have influenced her testimony. But jurors understand what it means to cop a plea or do a deal. They understand that somebody who is guilty might do that and still be telling the truth about her cohorts.

Jurors will not reject an informer's testimony unless their consciences are shocked by what she is getting away with—or unless they can find some circumstantial evidence of mendacity beyond the objective facts of an "immunity for truthful testimony" deal.

One must also keep in mind that the theory of minimal contradiction limits the extent to which you can attribute a malign motive to the informer. The informer is often a person that committed a crime and got caught at it. She is offered a way out of trouble, or a way to minimize consequences. She takes it. Whose fault is that? More important, whose fault will the jury think it is?

Let me suggest a sinful scenario. You know the witness once told a story that exculpates her and your client. You know she was jailed, interrogated, and eventually counseled to make a deal. You know that the deal recites that she must testify truthfully and that she will be subject to prosecution for perjury for lying. Here is an example based on an old National Institute for Trial Advocacy file, *United States v. Peters*. The witness is the informer, Laura Hobson.

Q. Let me take you back to that night when you were arrested. Where were you when they arrested you?
A. In the car.
Q. Do you remember who arrested you?
A. A bunch of agents. I think there was somebody named Johnson.
Q. Did they have guns?
A. Yes.
Q. Were you scared?
A. Sort of.
Q. Then what did they do?
A. Well, they warned me of my rights, and handcuffed me, and put me in the police car.
Q. Where did they take you?

This line of inquiry paints a far more compelling picture than one pursued with leading questions to which the witness must answer "yes" or "no." You have the chance, by reflecting the rising tension in your voice, to have the witness relive the terror she must have felt. Arrested, with a prior drug record, facing near-certain jail, she took the deal that was offered.

Q. What did you tell the agents when they first talked to you?

A. I told them I didn't know anything about it.

Q. Was that true?

A. No.

Q. Why did you lie to them?

There it is. A sinful nonleading question that also begins with "why." There are dangers here. Maybe the witness will say that she was afraid of your client. If there is any real prospect of that, leave the question alone unless you have some surefire impeachment for that answer.

But, in the usual case, the answer will be "I was afraid" or "I was confused" or "I don't know." You want to stretch out the fact of the witness lying, and the pressure she felt. You want her to face the jury and try to argue around the plain facts. Her exhibition of fear, uncertainty, and plain old unbelievability is more powerful than anything your leading questions can do. If your questions build a box of the right size and shape, you can drop the witness in and let her run around.

Q. In fact, you were involved in that drug deal, weren't you?

A. Yes.

Q. So you lied, right?

A. Yes.

Q. If you admitted you were in the drug deal, what did you think would happen?

A. I guess I would go to jail.

If you don't get this answer, prompt for it with a leading question. Leading questions can be used to keep the witness on track, but the point here is that sinful open questions are all right—and even preferable.

Q. So you are a person who would lie to keep from going to jail, isn't that right?

As you build the theme, you will be letting the witness tell of her fall from grace, induced by prosecutors who made her an offer she could not refuse.

There will, almost as surely as sunrise, be two themes the witness will try to develop: (1) her bargain to tell the truth and (2) her desire to protect your client when she lied in the first place. The "control" commandments teach you to prevent the witness from blurting out these themes.

But I tell you to violate those commandments, and sin with glee and confidence. You are going to hear about these themes on direct examination or on redirect. The jury will not think well of you for dancing around them. Let them out, and then deal with them. You will have to do it at some time, in the summation, if not earlier.

A.  I lied to protect Fred [the defendant].
Q.  Are you saying that you would lie to protect a friend?
A.  No.
Q.  You have just told us that you lied to protect Fred Peters, haven't you?
A.  Yes.
Q.  And you told us earlier that you considered him a friend, didn't you?
A.  Yes, I suppose so.
Q.  Tell us, Ms. Hobson, who is your best friend in the world, an even better friend than Fred Peters?
A.  I don't know.
Q.  Aren't you your own best friend?

You might get a variation such as "My family," to which the answer is: "They would be really upset to see you go off to Club Fed—that's the federal prison—wouldn't they?" You can then follow by pointing out that she is her own best friend.

The second theme is: "Well, I'll only get off if I tell the truth. If I lie, they will prosecute me." Your inquiry must focus on the witness's understanding of who makes the decision whether her testimony is true or false. It's not defense counsel. The decision of what to believe is for the agents and the prosecutor.

Certainly, summations without number have told the jurors that they must decide who is telling the truth and who is not. Jurors will not brand someone a liar without a reason and an objective basis. The reason is given by bringing out, usually with short leading inquiry, the facts showing implied bias—relationship, plea bargain, employment, friendship, preparation, or prior statements not admissible for their truth.

The objective basis can be supplied by a prior statement admitted for its truth but more completely and powerfully by demeanor and evasive answers that the jurors will see only if you let the witness run a little. To do that requires strategies based other than on the commandments.

## MINIMAL CONTRADICTION REDUX

Nothing said here authorizes a departure from the principles "Have a point" and "End strong." Pointless doggedness not only elicits more harm than benefit, it tumbles into time wasting and witness harassment, both of which trigger juror resentment. Never abandon tight, controlled, "look good" cross without a careful plan.

Ending strong can help cure some problems that may have arisen when the witness runs on a little too much. You can bring it all home and show you always had control—even when you didn't.

## WITNESS AS OBJECT, WITNESS AS OBSERVER

To help you decide when to depart from the commandments, you may wish to distinguish between the two roles a witness can play.

In some cross-examinations, the witness is an object, like a talking rock or a ventriloquist's dummy. This is the witness generally imagined in the commandments. So the saying goes, the lawyer on direct examination is telling information—or letting the witness tell it. On cross-examination, the lawyer is "showing" information by making a series of statements with which the witness is asked to agree. The witness is an object of the trial lawyer's action.

The theory of minimal contradiction tells us that sometimes we must not *use* the witness as an object of action but must *see* him as a subject of it. When you ask a well-planned open-ended question, or explore areas in which the witness agrees with your story, you are letting the witness be a subject. You are letting the jurors see you treat the witness with dignity. You are giving the jurors information to use in evaluating the testimony.

You will seldom have the unalloyed pleasure of a witness breaking down on the stand and admitting perjury. Cross-examination is an exercise in circumstantial evidence. Because the witness received a certain benefit, or was threatened in a certain way, her testimony should not be believed. Because the witness was standing in a certain place, or only saw the assailant for a few seconds, one may doubt the accuracy of his description.

You must take this circumstantial evidence and weave it into a coherent argument about credibility. You must empower the jury to evaluate what the witness has said. The commandment approach of staccato questions can make an excellent and lasting impression on jurors. Do not abandon this approach.

You should, however, consider adding more leisurely, open-ended lines of inquiry, turning from witness-as-object to witness-as-subject. Giving the witness a chance to perform in front of the jurors gives you a store of shared experience to interpret in summation.

The jurors are smarter than the commandments theory gives them credit for. They know when a lawyer is cutting off the witness from saying something damaging. They know when lawyers are using technique to mask substance. Make the jurors part of your quest to tell the true story.

# Chapter Nine

## Cross-Examination: Difficult Witnesses, Witnesses with Difficulties

Once you grasp a theory of cross-examination and tailor it to fit your style, almost all that remains is practice and study of examples. I agree with the preachers of commandments that there is a science of cross-examination; I contend, however, that it is more complex than they say it is.

Beyond the science is an art. The art cannot be gathered from study, however intense, of general principles. The Cartesian deduction cannot be adapted to say, "I think, therefore I cross-examine." You will build up the art through personal and vicarious experience, gaining the latter through observation and reading.

There are, however, some categories of witness for which generalizations can be made.

### THE EYEWITNESS

Among the most powerful cross-examinations based upon perception are of eyewitnesses who identify the defendant. Studies abound on the unreliability of these identifications and of the ways in which improper suggestion can taint the testimony. The Supreme Court has set out rules about line-ups and photo spreads designed to place a due process floor under eyewitness testimony. Some courts will permit expert witnesses to comment on the questionable value of eyewitness testimony in particular circumstances.

For me, however, cross-examination is the most powerful tool for attacking eyewitness testimony and helping the jury to see that what seems to be most valuable is in fact counterfeit coin.

Most eyewitnesses are not liars. They may have the natural desire to see their prior impressions vindicated, and so they are, to that extent, hostile to the examiner's purpose. They are often victims of a crime or citizens drawn into the judicial process by the happenstance of being near a crime. They did not control the lineup they viewed or make up the photo array they were shown.

Neither they nor the jury will appreciate your trying to "control" every response. The witness is not, in short, an object. She is someone who in many cases has had a frightening experience, with which the jurors will empathize.

Q. For how long a time did you see this person?
A. Oh, for a minute or so.
Q. Let's think about that. Would you just close your eyes and imagine the robbery. When you can see this person in your mind's eye, say, "Go." When you stop seeing him, say, "Stop." I'll time it.
A. [The witness complies.]

This little experiment works often enough to be worth trying in most cases. People tend to overstate the time it takes for things to happen.

Q. Were you scared while all of this was going on?
A. Sure I was.
Q. Was this person pointing a gun at you?
A. Yes, he was.
Q. Did you happen to notice whether the streetlight was on?
A. I think it was.
Q. That streetlight is up at the corner, isn't it?
A. Yes.
Q. How was this person dressed?
A. He had on a black jacket and white shirt. I didn't notice what kind of pants he was wearing.

Q. If you didn't notice what kind of pants he was wearing, did you notice his shoes?

A. Not really.

Q. When did you first tell the police about this person?

A. Well, they got there pretty fast. Half an hour or so.

Q. When you talked to the policeman, was he making notes of what you said?

A. I suppose so. I think so.

Q. Do you remember telling him that this person had a white shirt or a blue shirt?

A. No.

Q. Do you remember saying that you couldn't really tell because the light wasn't too good?

A. I may have done.

Obviously, if the witness signed the police report you are using for these questions, you will want to make that point now. A little later, the examination might continue.

Q. The policeman showed you some photographs, didn't he?

A. Yes, he did.

Q. How were the photographs arranged?

Notice what is happening here. The advocate has a point, uses simple questions, puts things in bite-size pieces, and controls the flow of examination. But the witness is telling us something, so the jury can make up its mind about her testimony. In summation, the advocate can recall this testimony with pride because the witness was not pushed around.

Cross-examination that permits the witness leeway to answer is not uncontrolled because the indicia of eyewitness unreliability are well established. The examiner uses these as an outline but gives the jurors a chance to size up the witness.

This sort of latitude should not be extended to a professional identifier such as a police officer. If the witness becomes too talkative, you can use the "Do you believe in America?" series noted in Chapter Eight and resume inquiry with more controlled questions.


## THE REPRESENTATIVE

It is often a good idea to present a witness to represent an institutional—government or corporate—party. However, few lawyers wisely select the representative. Thus, they sow seeds of effective cross-examination for the opponent to harvest. There are many kinds of representatives, ranging from the custodian of documents to the chief executive officer. All of them share two characteristics, one in the law of evidence and the other in the dynamics of trial.

In evidence law, admissions of a party opponent or its cohort or representative are broadly admissible. Any representative can be confronted with a broad array of such admissions and be asked if she knows about them and has an explanation.

This leads us to the trial advocacy dynamic. A representative *is* the entity. There is no exception to this principle. The chief executive or other senior official is *presented* as a representative. But you can make any employee of your opponent into a representative by your questions.

In summation, you may remind the jury that a corporation cannot do, say, think, or believe anything. Only humans who do the corporation's business can do those things. So we have the rule that a corporation is bound by and responsible for what these humans do or fail to do. I have even used a Mr. Potato Head kit in summation to illustrate how a faceless potato—the corporation—has eyes, ears, nose, and hands. I took a potato and stuck the body parts on, one or two at a time, each time recalling what one corporate employee had done, failed to do, or testified.

Often your opponent will choose a low-level corporate employee to testify to try to limit cross-examination. This strategy can be undone. Suppose an engineer is called to testify about how a part is made and what it is designed to do. Your case rests on a corporate decision to ignore available technology in choosing to make the part one way rather than another.

Confront that witness with evidence of the choice you are assailing. If the witness knows nothing of the matter, you have strengthened the image of the uncaring entity whose right hand feigns ignorance of its left-hand doings. If your opponent objects that the cross is too far-ranging, remember that the federal rule limits you to the subject matter, not the scope, of the direct examination.

Some chief executives are excellent witnesses on direct and cross because they take the time to prepare and the care to understand the issues and concerns that the jury must face. More often, the chief executive representative is often a good cross-examination target because of the structure of corporate life. The time of today's executive is protected in many ways. He lives a relatively cloistered existence. The executive may not have genuine and sympathetic insight into the views and aspirations of those who oppose corporate goals. At a more practical level, the chief executive is accustomed to ordering lawyers around. The corporation's trial counsel may well find that the executive has not set aside enough time to really prepare for testimony. If you are going to depose or cross-examine corporate executives, go to the video store and rent a copy of the motion picture *Roger and Me*, about a documentary film producer's quest to interview General Motors president Roger Smith.

The result: a wooden witness, by turns evasive and arrogant, when confronted with hard questions about details and basic issues. This evasiveness and arrogance cannot be made to appear if your examination is a staccato burst of focused inquiries. You have to let the witness talk, which he is usually willing to do. The jurors will get the idea.

True, not all executives fit this mold. Some of your opponents will have read this book also. You must be prepared for a controlled and controlling cross-examination as well as for a more leisurely one.

## THE INFORMER

Perhaps "informer" conjures an image of that 1930s movie about the Irish Republican Army, or possibly some celebrated criminal case. Think again. An informer, for purposes of worthwhile generalization, can be any "turncoat" witness. The informer, once identified with one side, to gain reward or avoid punishment, changed her story and allegiance.

A former employee or disaffected friend, testifying in a civil case, is cross-examined on the same principles as a Mafia hit man in the federal witness protection program.

We have already shown that a change of allegiance may not itself give the jury a reason to disbelieve the witness. After all, a change of allegiance can as well be the sinner being redeemed as the veracious being suborned.

Why did the witness turn her coat? Why is she now telling a new untrue story in place of the old true one? Witnesses switch allegiances for different reasons: some in a cynical trade of testimony for freedom, some from a misplaced sense of duty, some because their lawyers led them to it, still others because an unscrupulous prosecutor led them into doing it.

Consider, for example, a witness who held a responsible position in the defendant's corporation, who once told the grand jury a story that the defense can live with and now says that the defendant is a scoundrel and a defrauder. If you attack her directly as a conniving liar, the jury may begin to feel sympathy for her. If it is already your theory that the prosecution's case is ill-motivated, your best line of attack is to show that the witness turned only after being subjected to unreasonable pressures.

If the witness has made prior statements that you believe are true, begin by accrediting and using them. Then move to the events that led the witness to recant the prior statements.

Q. Ms. Bonthrone, you were vice-president of the bank?
A. Yes.
Q. You were responsible for making loans?
A. Yes.
Q. In fact, my client, Mr. Wilson, consulted you on loans?
A. He did.
Q. He consulted you on the Bar-C loan, didn't he?
A. He may have done.

You are accrediting the witness, putting her into the picture. Your questions are tight and controlled because in the early stages of examination you cannot give the witness maneuvering room. Indeed, the questions are almost entirely statements, made in an interrogating mode, to which the witness must agree.

Next, move to the prior statements.

Q. I show you what I have marked as Defendant Wilson's Exhibit G. Isn't that a memorandum that you sent to Mr. Wilson, responding to his asking you for advice on the Bar-C loan?
A. Yes.
Q. He asked for your advice, and you gave it to him?
A. Well, yes.
Q. You don't have any doubt about that, do you?
A. No.
Q. Let me show you Wilson Exhibit H. Isn't that a memorandum you gave the bank examiners on April 15, 1985?
A. It is.

If the rules of court permit it, go and stand next to the witness, and ask her to read out the parts of the document that show her vouching for the loans. Alternatively, you can have an overhead projector transparency on a screen.

Remember not to block the jurors' view of the witness, at this of all times.

You may have other, similar documents or prior statements in other forms. Then comes the turning point.

Q. Sometime after April 15, 1985, you met Mr. Snyder?
A. Yes.
Q. That's the Mr. Snyder sitting over there at the prosecution's table?
A. Yes.

If you are permitted by the rules, walk over and stand behind Mr. Snyder. You are about to have the witness refer to him unflatteringly. If you are standing behind him, you emphasize your point, and there isn't much that he can do about it.

More generally, standing by the witness and then standing by the prosecutor is thoughtful use of courtroom space. Symbolic claims to courtroom territory are a part of trial strategy.

## CHARACTER WITNESSES

Many character witnesses should not be cross-examined. You will wait until the closing argument and point out that almost nobody is entirely friendless. "We can all remember people in our neighborhoods that we thought were the very soul of honesty. Then it turned out one day that they had stolen or cheated or done something else that is very wrong. And many friends and family members, if they were honest, would have to say, 'Gee, I never thought he was like that.' "

However, offering a witness to vouch for good character opens up a wide field of cross-examination. You may inquire into prior bad acts of any relevant sort, even if the conduct did not result in conviction or even arrest. The cross-examination is said to bear upon the weight that ought to be given the witness's opinion or upon his knowledge of reputation. If the character evidence is in the form of opinion, the questions on cross-examination are in the form: "Did you know that Mr. Johnson was arrested for bookmaking?" If the evidence was in the form of reputation, the form is: "Have you heard that Mr. Johnson was arrested for bookmaking?"

## SPECIAL CARE WITNESSES

In a mock trial demonstration in London, England, a few years ago, I defended and former Attorney General Benjamin Civiletti prosecuted John Burns, an alleged robber-murderer whose defense was alibi. The defendant had a criminal record. His wife was the alibi witness, but she concededly had been in the basement of their home during a part of the afternoon and might not have heard the defendant go out.

There was no quarreling with those objective facts. Each side had the advantage of being able to select the people who would portray the witnesses. I was lucky. The exquisitely talented film and stage actress Estelle Parsons agreed to be "Mrs. Burns." Estelle created a working-class Massachusetts housewife, concerned about her errant husband and believing profoundly that he could make good if the cops would just stop hassling him.

When Ben Civiletti began to home in on her being in the basement doing the laundry, "Mrs. Burns" burst into tears. "Don't you think a wife knows? Don't you think I listen for Johnny?"

"Like trying to cross-examine the waterworks," Ben muttered.

The experience brought up a vivid recollection of a witness I tried to cross-examine in a weapons trial many years ago. She had changed her story and made a most advantageous bargain with the government to avoid criminal prosecution. Every time I got close to these uncomfortable facts, her voice dropped and the tears welled in her eyes. The judge protected her with clucking noises, signaling to the jurors that I was badgering her.

We will all confront witnesses—of both genders and of any age—who present us these problems. Here the ten commandments come in handy. Get up, do your stuff with dignity and control, and sit down. Make a series of assertions with which the witness will agree, and quit.

Be sure, however, to cover meaning, perception, memory, and the implied bias part of veracity. Save the summing up for the summation.


## FOREIGN LANGUAGE WITNESSES

I have probed this subject in Chapter Four, with greater attention to direct examination. There is little to add. Sometimes a witness who is presented in a foreign language understands and speaks English quite well. He elects to testify in another language to have extra time to consider responses to questions on cross-examination. By keeping your questions short and plain, you cut the time between question and response.

You should also attempt to get as much demeanor evidence from the witness as you can. If you succeed, you may get the witness looking at you and reacting to your questions in English, thus giving away the pretense of nonfluency.

I was at a political trial in South Africa. The witness was testifying in Xhosa, although he had been educated at an English-speaking school. The defendants were charged with committing a politically motivated murder—a daytime shooting of people at a taxi stand. Siraj Desai, a brilliant black South African advocate, took the witness through his prior statement. He impaled the witness on contradictions between the statement and his direct testimony. The witness said on direct that the shooters were wearing police-type blue uniforms, with police caps and jackets. In his statement, he had said they were dressed in coffee-color overcoats with balaclavas on their heads, which they pulled down over their eyes just before they started shooting. Desai wisely did not show the witness his statement until he had finished with all the contradictory material.

The witness attributed the contradictions to errors in translating his statement. He said he had spoken to the police in Xhosa, and they had prepared a statement in English, which he admitted having signed. He claimed to be unable to read and write English, though he admitted having attended school.

Desai handed the witness the statement to authenticate it. The bailiff put it between the translator and the witness. Desai let it stay there. The court could see that the witness was in fact running his eyes over the statement, belying his assertion that he could not read.

Desai concluded his examination. During a recess, I suggested we ask the defendants the Xhosa word for balaclava. As I expected, there is none—it is a borrowed foreign word, as it is in English, so the Xhosa word is "balaclava."

The next advocate asked a few questions on other subjects, then in a matter-of-fact voice demanded, "What is the Xhosa word for balaclava?" The translator translated, using the word "balaclava." The witness, without thinking, replied, "Balaclava." His Lordship could not repress a smile, and he looked at me with a knowing grin.

The witness quickly recovered, and said the Xhosa word was a compound word meaning folded cap. By that time, the damage was done. If the Xhosa and English words were the same, the witness would have understood the word when it was read to him before he signed the statement. At the very least, he had sworn he knew the word in both languages.

In a demonstration that it is possible to do effective cross-examination through a translator, Desai won a judgment of acquittal for his client at the close of the state's evidence. His Lordship found the witness utterly unworthy of belief.

# Chapter Ten

## Cross-Examination:
## Preparing Your Witnesses
## for Its Rigors

This chapter suggests ways to accustom your witnesses to cross-examination. These hints are also useful in preparing witnesses for hostile depositions. Indeed, because there is no referee at a deposition, the hostile examiner will sometimes take liberties that he would not take in court. By the same token, you can protect your witness more in a deposition than you can in court.

If you doubt that a deposition gives more leeway for protecting your witness, think again. Sure, some judges in trial will warn your opponent not to insist unfairly or belligerently on a "yes" or "no" answer. Some judges will remind counsel that the witness may explain a seemingly categorical answer. Another judge, or the same judge with a different witness, will equally firmly say that a "yes" or "no" answer is required—and will upbraid objecting counsel in the jury's presence to leave the impression that counsel is trying unfairly to protect the witness from legitimate inquiry. You will probably know enough about the judge in your case to predict her behavior, but you may not know the judge's identity until the morning of trial, when it is too late to prepare your witnesses for that particular jurist's idiosyncrasies.

The moral: Your witness needs to be prepared to fend for himself, but to do so while remaining composed, controlled, and credible. Preparation falls into two parts: the locker room speech and the scrimmage.

## THE LOCKER ROOM SPEECH

"When I finish my questions, I say, 'Pass the witness,' or, 'Your witness,' or 'That's all I have,' or whatever. Then I sit down or shuffle my papers, or look up if I am already seated. One of the lawyers on the other side gets up. We don't know which one it is, but I can tell you about them. Old Phil Jones is, well, just like he was at your deposition—gruff, always looking like he doesn't believe you, always pausing at the end of your answer to see if you'll get uncomfortable and add something else or qualify your answer. He's even been known to look at a witness like he doesn't believe them and pick up a paper as though it has something on it that contradicts what that witness has just said. It is a game he plays. If he has something, he will ask a question about it. It will probably be something we have looked at and talked about.

"Then there's Paula Wilson. She is polite but insistent. You relax. You stop thinking there is danger. Then she asks a complicated question, and you're not ready for it.

"So what do you do? Remember that I asked you to trust me, for the direct examination? Well, trust me some more, but it's a different kind of trust. As long as you tell the truth, you're going to be all right. But you need to follow some rules, because it isn't like direct. I don't ask the next question. I can get up and ask more questions of you after the cross-examination is done, though.

"Here are the rules, just as we discussed in talking about direct examination. First, listen to the question. I mean, really listen to it."

The next part depends on your witness. Maybe you have to warn him, "I know you are a quick study. You see the issue even before the question is finished. You want to jump right in and answer it and get on to the next topic. I tell you: Don't do that. Listen to the question. All of it. Every word. Do not be thinking about your answer until you have heard the question."

Maybe the warning is this: "From what I can tell, you like to make sure your answer is right before you give it. Good for you. Obey that rule. Listen to the question, and consider it before you answer."

Back to the more general version:

"Second, pause for just a bit after every question. This helps you to enforce the first rule. It also gives me time to make an objection if I need to. Now you can't expect me to jump up and object every time you are asked a hard question. The judge will make remarks about it, and we'll both look like we are trying to hide something. Believe me, though, if you are asked a question that is improper, I'll stand up.

"Third rule, if the question isn't clear, say so. And, fourth, if the question is clear, answer it. Remember how I asked you to just answer the questions on direct examination? I was getting you ready for cross. We want you to look like you are treating the cross-examiner the same way you treated me. So listen, pause, and answer what was asked. Do not feel the urge to explain your answer. If explanation is needed, we can do that when I get to ask questions again, on redirect examination.

"You see, if you just answer the question asked, the cross-examiner has to think up another question. If you try to tell him what you think he was asking, you make his task easier. There is no reason to do that. Also, by just answering the question, you avoid suggesting a line of inquiry he may not have thought of. You avoid, in short, being taken advantage of."

Add a fifth rule, which is particularly important for partisan witnesses. So far as the jurors are concerned, your opponent has a right to cross-examine. They are unlikely to have the deeply felt feelings about the case and its personalities that the witness has. At least, they will not have such feelings until late in the case, and even then it is unwise to presume that you know what their feelings are. You are navigating by dead reckoning, after all. Here is the fifth rule:

"Fifth rule, and this one is a little hard for me to say correctly. Don't start off the examination with a chip on your shoulder. I know you think their case is bunk—and that old Jones or young Wilson is trying to trap you. Don't project a combative attitude. The jurors expect you to answer the questions. They are looking to you for cues about how to judge you, and we want them to think you are composed and truthful."

There are a lot of variations on the fifth rule. In one criminal case, a public figure was on trial for allegedly taking a bribe. He thought the charges were trumped-up. The prosecutor had been personally obnoxious—arrogant and self-righteous. The defendant was used to being listened to. We needed to state and restate the fifth rule, and to work on it in the scrimmage portion of preparation. We promised our client that he could have one moment of pique, and just one. We trusted him to limit himself in that way. If, after he had courteously answered questions for a long time, the prosecutor came at him with a sort of supercilious air of disbelief, he could look at his wife and children and say that he swore in their presence that what the prosecutor was claiming was untrue.

I am not saying that every witness, or even most witnesses, should be told they can have that luxury. Far from it. That sort of thing can look maudlin. But this client believed it and was believable in saying it.

For another witness, the fifth rule might be restated: "Look, your accent, your manner, your clothes, the way you treat people—all come across as arrogant as hell. We are going to work on that." The point is that the rule must be tailored to fit every witness, and then you must let the witness see during the scrimmage how to apply it.

"Sixth rule: Maintain the right eye contact and *never* the wrong eye contact. Look directly at whoever is asking you a question. Usually, it will be the cross-examiner. The judge may pipe up and ask something. If she does, turn around and look at her. Refer to her deferentially as 'Your Honor.'

"It is all right to keep looking at whoever is questioning you. If you feel it is right, look at the jurors. We will work on that when we prepare you in detail. No matter how much trouble you feel you are in, do not look hopefully, balefully, or in any other way at me or anybody else on our side unless you are referring to one of us, or unless one of us is speaking—for example, to make an objection.

"The jury wants to hear your story. They haven't heard it before. They need to be convinced. Go ahead and convince them, but take it easy."

Of course, the witness will have questions and will need more detailed reassurance. You can give some of that during the scrimmage.

## SCRIMMAGE—
## THE GROUND RULES

Even practice games have rules. If you take down the statement of a witness, or even make detailed notes, during a cross-examination scrimmage, those may be producible to your opponent. If the witness is your client, the risk is slight. For witnesses you do not represent, the work product privilege shields much of your note taking. It would be wrong to assume that the privileges will always be enough. Be careful with your notes, and leave off vivid interpretive comments.

At trial, the witness may be asked about preparation on cross-examination. You are going to find a lot of disagreement among lawyers about how to handle a scrimmage to head off that kind of inquiry, and how the witness should respond when asked. I always think *KISS: Keep It Simple, Stupid.* Keep the preparation simple and direct, and tell the witness candidly what to expect.

First, preparation. In some cases and for some witnesses, you may hire a trial consultant to advise on presentation. The consultant will meet with you and the witness to talk about demeanor, dress, and issues in the case. Do not let the consultant burden the witness with theories. This is just a conversation about making sure the witness understands the process and is prepared to answer questions.

To do a mock cross-examination, try to use another lawyer or a law clerk. A fresh insight will help you anticipate problems by covering them in direct examination. An observer will see problems with the witness that you may not see. Also, if the mock cross gets adversarial, someone other than you is being the "heavy."

I think it a mistake to have the mock cross-examiners portray specific people on the other side. This fact has a way of slipping out at trial, and I think it looks too cute. Certainly, the preparers ought to be probing, and there is nothing wrong with them using different styles of attack. But no names, please.

Use videotape if you think it will help. You will have to do careful research on the rules in your jurisdiction about videotapes. Can you use the same tape and just keep recording over it? Are you ethically bound to keep it, in order to produce it at trial for the judge to determine whether it should be turned over to the other side? Are the rules clear enough that video of this kind is work product? I hope that witness preparation videos are work product. They certainly should be. If there is the slightest risk you will have to turn the videos over to the other side, I would use video only for a few fairly neutral questions and answers.

Now, what should you tell the witness? The witness should be able to make these truthful responses:

Q. Now, did you get together with some people to prepare for cross-examination?
A. Yes, I met with Mr. Tigar and some of the people helping him prepare for trial.
Q. Who did you meet with?
A. With Mr. Tigar, of course, and then at different times with Ms. Doyle, Mr. Alford, and a Ms. Arbogast.
Q. Ms. Doyle is the one at counsel table?

A. Yes.
Q. Who are the others?
A. They are people who work with Mr. Tigar and Ms. Doyle on the case.
Q. Ms. Arbogast is a trial consultant, isn't she?
A. She was introduced to me as a consultant, yes, working on this trial with Mr. Tigar and Ms. Doyle.
Q. Who is Mr. Alford?
A. He is a young lawyer who works with Mr. Tigar. Or perhaps he is a law student. I'm not sure.
Q. How long did you meet with them, altogether?
A. I met with different ones at different times, but, all in all, for several hours.
Q. On more than one day?
A. Yes.
Q. How many meetings, and how much total time?
A. Well, at least five meetings, and a total time of at least ten hours.
Q. Did they ask you questions as if they were cross-examining you?
A. Oh, yes.
Q. Did they videotape you?
A. Yes, they did. Twice. So I could see what I looked like.

This examination may be prolonged. The witness may be asked more detail and should candidly describe reviewing all the exhibits and papers in the case and discussing it with the lawyers and those working with them. Personally, I think it is a waste of time, unless the cross-examiner can show that the preparation session significantly influenced the testimony. For example, a witness may have changed her story from deposition to trial, or from arrest to grand jury to immunity to trial. The examiner may want to blame the new version on opposing counsel. Unless you have got that kind of an issue, dwelling on preparation looks bush league.

## IS THERE A GENTLER WAY?

I know some very good lawyers who do not believe in intensive mock cross-examination. They take the witness aside and explain the issues, talk through some of the questions that may be asked, make sure the witness knows the document trail, and leave it at that.

I disagree. I would never give up a chance at scrimmage-type preparation. I will not retain an expert who will not subject herself to such a process because an expert who behaves on direct examination can, on cross, turn either arrogant or equivocal. The very witnesses who think they are too smart or too busy to need preparation are the ones who need it most. For examples of how such witnesses become easy targets, see the chapters on cross-examination and imagine how the characters portrayed would benefit from scrimmage.

## PERCEPTION, MEMORY, MEANING, VERACITY

Cross-examination, as I have said, is about perception, memory, meaning, and veracity. Preparation for cross must therefore cover these areas.

You must anticipate and work on problems of perception. The witness must candidly concede every objective fact that casts doubt on the ability to perceive—lighting, time to observe, relative position to the event, responsibility for seeing and reporting, and so on.

Memory poses problems, but you will have anticipated most of them on direct examination. If the witness has refreshed her memory with a document or by talking to someone, you will have made that clear. She remembers what she remembers. For the rest, she may not have remembered it until reminded by seeing or hearing something. Some events she does not remember at all, but she certainly recognizes her signature on a memorandum that may then be admissible. Some cross-examiners delight in taking witnesses over gaps in their memory that have been filled in this way.

Meaning arises in distinct contexts. If the witness has sponsored her own prior statement, or is explaining it, she is open to cross-examination on that interpretation. The cross-examiner may also seize upon a statement made on direct. The witness has the options of denying having made that statement or of accepting or refusing to accept the interrogator's interpretation of it. If the witness admits having made the statement, the examiner may stop right there, leaving his preferred meaning dangling in the air. This confuses some witnesses, who wonder how to correct matters. The witness must be warned just to answer the questions and wait for redirect. If the tactic is obviously misleading the jury, you may object, but only if you have a good chance of succeeding.

Veracity in the sense of truth-telling should not be much of a problem by this point. In your direct examination preparation, you have dealt with the witness's obligation to tell the truth. Veracity issues remain, however. The witness may have made a prior inconsistent statement that is now being used substantively or for impeachment. Or she may have an implied bias from circumstances—relationship to a party, employment, a plea bargain. The cross-examiner is entitled to probe those circumstances.

## HOW TO SCRIMMAGE

The first scrimmage session should be based on your direct examination and be handled by someone other than you if at all possible. If you are really solo, videotape the direct and watch it, taking notes for cross-examination.

The examiner should focus on the issues raised in notes taken during the direct examination. You know the drill. A vertical line slightly to the right of center on the legal pad. Use 8½″ x 11″ paper; I use the kind with three holes punched, so it goes into a notebook binder. On the left, you note the questions and answers. On the right you make notes and symbols on the cross-examination you plan to do.

The first scrimmage should focus on how well the witness has assimilated the rules laid down in the locker room speech. It needn't take long. You will be evaluating answering the question, pausing before answering, the appearance of credibility versus combativeness or discomfiture, eye contact—the appearance issues.

For this purpose, focus on meaning, memory, and the implied bias part of veracity. Meaning issues will be drawn from the direct. Memory issues will bring in any prior statements. Implied bias issues are a good indicator of witness behavior because the natural tendency is to react when someone seems to be questioning your integrity.

As the bad guy snarled at Mae West, "Have you ever heard my integrity questioned?" "Honey," she purred, "I've never even heard it mentioned."

Remember that all answers must pass the straight-face test. There are explanations of human conduct, even true ones, that defy belief. If your witness comes up with one of these, particularly when challenged on cross in a way that invites an explanation, the witness, you, and your cause lose credibility. I cannot explain this. I just know that in many cases the witness's earnest and truthful first recollection is not enough. You have to probe deeper.

"Watson," said Holmes, "I don't believe in coincidence."

Let me illustrate. A corporation makes a decision on product design. It had several choices. Nobody can remember why they chose design A over design B—it just seemed to the deciders that was the right thing to do on that day. I tell you that if it turns out in a lawsuit that there was a material difference between A and B, the answer "It got down to those two choices, and we just chose the one we liked that day" will not pass the straight-face test. The answer is, as far as the witness is concerned, truthful, but it is not good enough because it is incomplete. You must independently research the setting in which the decision was made and the background to it. Then probe until you get more persuasive detail. You must help the witness recall the perhaps unspoken reasons why he would have made that choice on that day. He may even then be unable to tell you that these were the reasons; he will only be able to say that these factors were present and it seems reasonable to say they were dispositive.

After the first, relatively short scrimmage, later sessions should focus on documents, objects in evidence, and prior deposition testimony. In a complex case, you can divide this work among others, and let them conduct some of the scrimmages.

All the examiners should carefully note the witness's difficulties so you can talk about them. Keep circling back over issues, questions, and tactics that make the witness forget the rules. Reinforcement must be as a good trial advocacy class—repetition, very short critique, learning by doing, plenty of positive reinforcement.

You want the witness to appreciate that she is not working without a net. You are there for some purposes. The truth is there as a constant reference point: "What though the tempest 'round me roar, I hear the truth, it liveth." There can be redirect examination. In most cases, no one witness takes the entire case on her shoulders.

When should you do the scrimmage? Do most of it before trial. In a long case, you can use weekends and off days. Evenings should presumptively be free for the lawyers to do other work, including the urgent work of preparing a last-minute witness. Do not scrimmage with the witness once direct examination begins, and surely not after cross begins. You may in any case be forbidden to talk with the witness about her testimony once your opponent has started cross, unless the witness is your client. But it certainly looks bad when the jurors find out you are intensely prepping the witness to shore up the performance on cross-examination.

# Chapter Eleven

## Expert Witness: Soft Subjects— Choosing and Presenting Your Expert

In my first trial, I was so junior that I sat at a table behind the counsel table—more distant from the action even than our case expert. The defendant was charged with tax evasion. Edward Bennett Williams was lead counsel. The redoubtable Boris Kostelanetz was co-counsel.

One defense was that the items of income and expense had been reported as the defendant was advised by Kostelanetz's partner. The partner took the stand and testified, on direct and cross, at great length. This virtuoso performance included a detailed treatment of the distinction between ordinary income and capital gains.

The jury was sequestered. The next morning, one of the marshals reported that one juror turned to another during the walk back to their hotel at the end of the day and said, "Who's this Captain Gaines they were talking about today?"

The other juror replied, "He's going to testify tomorrow."

I reflect often on this experience. I have added to its lessons with the passing years. This chapter and the three that follow are based on two basic principles. First, most jurors discount expert testimony as the set speech of a hired gun. They think that you can find somebody to take an oath in support of almost any proposition. Second, jurors can understand, appreciate, and critique the testimony of any expert—if the lawyers give them the proper tools. This is another version of empowering the jury.

These two principles may lead you not to call an expert as a witness in your case, even when the other side has assembled a formidable array of them. They should also lead you to spend the time and resources necessary to understand the experts' fields, as well as their backgrounds and prior testimony.

## HARD EXPERTISE AND SOFT EXPERTISE

Long ago, I began to think of two kinds of expert witnesses: "soft subject" and "hard subject." The distinction seemed useful given the broad latitude afforded lawyers by the Federal Rules of Evidence in selecting, directing, and examining experts.

A hard expert deals with what can be measured, drawn, photographed, recorded—qualities that we exercise within the left hemisphere of our brains. Examples include a ballistics expert, a pathologist, a fingerprint expert, and an accountant who testifies about technical accountancy issues.

A soft expert deals with intuitive matters of judgment, discretion, imagination—for which we use the right hemisphere of our brains. Soft experts include psychiatrists, theoretical economists, and "life value" experts. An accountant testifying about a public company's duties of disclosure to shareholders is a soft expert because such decisions involve a substantial use of discretion.

Many experts bring both hard and soft qualities to the courtroom. The psychiatrist is a physician who can tell us that a patient ingested a chemical substance that reacted in a certain way with what was already in the patient's body. That is hard science. When the doctor goes on to tell us that the patient took the substance from a compulsion that has its roots in childhood experiences, that is soft science.

The distinction is important for your choice of expert, your tactical decisions, and your appreciation of how jurors view experts. This last consideration is easily overlooked. In a complex antitrust case, the other side recruited a theoretical economist to review documents and depositions and to opine about collusion in the relevant market. There was a strong temptation to dismiss this sort of testimony as "conspiracy-ology" or, in lawyer cliché terms, "rank speculation." Indeed, a solid motion to exclude can be drafted for such a witness.

I caution against facile dismissal of such a soft expert. The negative or positive effect upon jurors of soft expertise is greatly enhanced by jurors' intuitive responses to the expert, the expert's field, and the expert's conclusions.

Soft science experts are accustomed to drawing inferences from impressions that often cannot be wholly documented. Although there are exceptions, they are likely to be far less prosaic and straightforward in their presentations than, say, a fingerprint analyst or chemical analyst. This tendency presents a challenge in selecting and presenting an expert, and it provides unique opportunities for the cross-examiner.

Many fields of soft science evoke strong juror feelings. These feelings vary depending on current public controversy, geography, and the demography of the jury. For example, media attacks in the wake of an unpopular jury verdict may push psychiatric expertise into disrepute. Some jurors react negatively to psychiatric testimony about alcoholism, perhaps because of their personal or family experiences, or their religious convictions.

One can see the effect of intuition—juror and expert—most strongly when looking at a soft expert's conclusions. Returning to the economist who saw collusion in the market, lawyers and jurors are likely to view her conclusions quite differently. Jurors in the area where the case was pending were disposed to believe that large corporations conspire against the public good and that such conspiracies may remain hidden for a long time. So, when a plausible-looking expert takes the stand and testifies that she has studied the case and finds collusion in the market, many jurors will find their prejudgments reinforced. "Aha," they will say inwardly, "I thought as much."

The same intuitive faculty might press other jurors to reject a soft expert. I have tried criminal cases in which the defendant had an alcohol problem so severe that psychiatric testimony was admissible. In such cases, many jurors are poised to say, "Oh, that is just headshrinker stuff!" This reaction is coupled with a sense that the defendant brought his troubles on himself or that psychiatrists are easily fooled by articulate patients.

The lesson is clear: When presenting or opposing soft expertise, you must honor juror intuition. In this and the next chapter, I discuss ways of tapping into juror attitudes that support you and dealing with hostile ones.

Soft science is also a good testing ground for rules of evidence and procedure. Analyze proposed expert testimony at four levels: materiality, relevancy, rules about experts, and demonstrative evidence.

## MATERIALITY

In Molzof v. United States, the Supreme Court held that a Federal Tort Claims Act medical malpractice plaintiff could recover damages for loss of enjoyment of life. The Court reversed a Seventh Circuit holding that such recovery is a form of statutorily prohibited "punitive damages." The case illustrates the importance of materiality determinations. If the issue of enjoyment of life is not properly in the case, no expert testimony—no matter how reliable—will be admissible on that issue. The testimony would not be "material" as that term is used in the law of evidence.

If the issue is properly in the case, testimony on it will be material but might not satisfy the other criteria listed below.

## RELEVANCY

The Federal Rules of Evidence and their state counterparts broadly authorize admission of relevant evidence that makes any matter in issue more or less probable than it would be without the evidence. Relevant evidence is generally admissible. However, it may be excluded if it wastes time, risks prejudice, or may confuse the jury. Some types of evidence, such as prior bad acts, are the subject of special rules.

Many lawyers mistakenly jump from materiality analysis directly to the rules governing experts. The relevancy rules are, as the guidebooks say, worth a detour. Even if an expert may be qualified under Federal Rule of Evidence 702, the testimony may nonetheless be ruled inadmissible under Rule 403 as too speculative, cumulative, prejudicial, or time-wasting. Particularly when a litigant offers up more than one expert, and where the claimed expertise or its basis presents a close question, the court will simply hold that Rules 702 and 703 seem to be satisfied but that there is too much risk of jury confusion.

In some complex cases, the number of experts designated and then deposed is shocking. Whatever tactical sense the proponent may make of barraging the jury with expert testimony, the trial judge can and usually will impose limits.

Expert testimony may be unduly prejudicial, particularly if accompanied by photos, charts, or other demonstrative evidence.

## RULES ABOUT EXPERTS

Under Federal Rule of Evidence 702, expert testimony is available to help the jury understand an art, science, or profession. The courts apply a four-part test to proffered expert opinion. As the Fifth Circuit explained in an en banc decision, *Christophersen v. Allied-Signal Corporation*, the questions are:

(1) whether the witness is qualified to express an expert opinion, Fed.R.Evid. 702;

(2) whether the facts upon which the expert relies are the same type as are relied upon by other experts in the field, Fed.R.Evid. 703;

(3) whether in reaching his conclusion the expert used a well-founded methodology [citing the venerable decision in *Frye v. United States*]; and

(4) assuming the expert's testimony has passed Rules 702 and 703, and the *Frye* test, whether under F.R.Evid. 403 the testimony's potential for unfair prejudice substantially outweighs its probative value.

Under Rule 703, the facts or data on which the expert reasonably relies need not be admissible in evidence. For example, an expert sociologist may testify about the results of interviews and studies; the basis for the opinion is a vast quantity of hearsay evidence from hundreds, perhaps thousands, of unknown declarants. These declarants may not even have personal knowledge on the issues that were surveyed. Yet the expert can give an opinion based on these studies. The liberality of Rule 703 will be limited, however, if the factual basis of the opinion is too flimsy, or where the expert is putting before the jurors evidence that is subject to question and yet cannot be effectively challenged on cross-examination—that is, where reliance is unreasonable. For example, a damages expert who claims to rely on projections and studies that are demonstrably too optimistic will either be compelled to rely on less speculative evidence or be excluded from testifying altogether.

Except when mental condition is in issue, it is not a ground of objection that the expert is giving an opinion on the "ultimate issue"; however, there is good authority that some ultimate issue testimony is unduly prejudicial and that the trial judge may preclude it. The proponent need no longer use the cumbersome hypothetical question to get the expert's opinion.

The federal courts of appeals, after a long season of liberality in construing the Federal Rules of Evidence, have begun to backtrack. In 1986, Fifth Circuit Judge Patrick Higginbotham wrote in an important opinion, "It is time to take hold of expert testimony in federal trials." He was writing about the plaintiff's use, in a wrongful death case, of an unqualified financial consultant whose opinion was based on inflated financial projections.

The *en banc* decision in *Christophersen* followed Judge Higginbotham's lead and announced new limits on the use of expert testimony, at least in toxic tort cases. *Christophersen* does not explicitly announce a new rule. The *en banc* majority affirmed the trial judge's refusal to admit in evidence a medical doctor's opinion that the decedent's small-cell colon cancer was caused by workplace exposure to toxic chemicals. The court of appeals authorized district judges to impose relatively high threshold requirements of specialized training in the relevant medical field, demonstrated reliability of the facts on which the expert relied, and strong support for the methodology applied. Having concluded that the doctor's testimony was inadmissible under Rules 702 and 703, the court did not reach the Rule 403 issue.

The dissenting judges ably argued that the majority had erected a higher barrier to admissibility than the Federal Rules permit and that the jury is able and should be permitted to decide the value of the doctor's opinion.

To these rules of evidence must be added the principles of applicable substantive law on burdens of persuasion. These rules may require that the expert be willing to opine to some degree of certainty on the validity of his conclusions: "reasonable medical certainty," "reasonable doubt," and so on.

*Christophersen* is only one element in the renewed battle over the latitude that should be given to expert testimony. The battle cries of opposing sides in this debate are "Keep junk science out of federal court!" and "Don't interfere with the jury's right to hear all relevant evidence!" I am not a partisan of either slogan. Most criticisms of particular experts seem to me resolvable by intelligent cross-examination, lawyer good sense, and modest judicial intervention—rather than by wholesale denial of admissibility.

## DEMONSTRATIVE EVIDENCE

I cannot imagine ever presenting an expert without using demonstrative evidence. I want the expert's message in more than one medium. I want tangible reminders of the message to use in the summation and previews of it for the opening statement.

I want the expert off her perch on the witness chair and down in the well of the court, talking directly to the jurors. If the expert has an intuitive message, I want eye contact and informality—to help the jury size up the message and the messenger. If the expert has an arcane specialty or suffers from the "expert's disease" of terminal arrogance, I want the interaction of expert and jurors to help break down the barrier between the jurors and the message.

For these reasons, planning the use of demonstrative evidence must begin while you are selecting the expert and continue through preparation and trial. You want a teacher, and one who is accessible and persuasive rather than lofty and didactic.

## CHOOSING A TESTIFYING
## OR SHADOW EXPERT

In choosing an expert, your dilemma is that the experienced courtroom performer can be attacked as a professional testifier, while the novice does not see how his professional judgment intersects with the law-defined claim or defense being supported or attacked.

I have argued both sides of this question and therefore have the solace of knowing that I have not been wrong more than half the time. To temper my fears, I now say that there is no answer; all depends on the expert you are dealing with. If the expert has demonstrable integrity, significant professional qualifications, and is willing to work under your direction toward an effective presentation, the level of experience is not so important.

By focusing upon qualifications and your own control over presentation of the case, you will learn to be suspicious of three things: the expert shop, the always-on-one-side expert, and the prepared dog-and-pony show. A given expert may exhibit more than one of these traits.

First, watch out for the expert who only testifies—and has not spent significant time practicing her profession outside the work necessary to prepare for litigation. There are dozens of opinion factories; if you are a member of any trial law organization, you are no doubt on their mailing lists. They claim every possible kind of admissible expertise: economic, engineering, chemical, medical, and so on. The fact that an expert comes from one of these shops is good fodder for cross-examination. More significantly, an expert closeted in such an environment may well have lost touch with the continuing research in her profession and with the academic peer review, symposia, teaching, and debate processes that sharpen theoretical formulations and expose their flaws.

You must also consider that the professional expert is motivated to define his expertise to maximize opportunities to testify in litigation. From thence, we get alleged branches of expert knowledge such as "accidentology," and "hedonic value of life." These may be legitimate branches of scientific or professional inquiry, but they have little relevance outside the litigation context. It is a double burden to present an expert who subsists only by litigation and who sponsors an expertise devised solely for litigation.

Second, the expert who always takes a particular side is more easily dismissed by the jury. The countervailing consideration is that such an expert will not let cross-examination change his opinion. You can adjust for these characteristics in your direct examination by letting the expert tell of the many cases he refuses to participate in because he cannot support the opinion asked for.

Third, beware the expert who has a prepared performance. Your investment pays dividends of difficulty. Your control of the presentation will either be diluted or achieved after time-wasting battles. At trial, the necessary rapport between you and the witness can evaporate. You lose credibility with the jurors. Jurors may be repelled by the witness's rigidity or by the barrier she seems to be erecting to two-way communication. Of the three symptoms listed, this is most likely to betoken an incurable malady. I wouldn't hire an expert who would not accept my guidance on how to run the litigation.

## SEARCH TECHNIQUES

At the end of your search, you may wind up with one of the experts from a company that has sent you its literature. I would not start there.

Litigation, in court and through arbitration and mediation services, is a means of settling a broad range of disputes in our culture. Even if you are not an experienced litigator, or practice in a town with few lawyers, you doubtless know many people who have been involved in lawsuits. If you care about building your practice, you have friends and associates in many professions in your community. Your college classmates went on to many callings. Lawyer friends have tried cases involving the same issue as your case.

You have, in sum, a ready-made collection of people who are, or know something about, experts who might be witnesses for you. Using this resource is more time-consuming than going to an "expert store" or "expert farm," but the results will be better. Once you have personally selected and prepared an expert, you can go back to that person again in your career.

From the following examples, you can gather all the techniques of expert finding you are likely to need. I twice used at trial and often consulted the late Dr. Bernard Diamond, who had taught courses on forensic medicine at the law school I attended. Another time I needed some advice on economic issues and turned to a professor I had heard speak at a program on Third World debt. For a bank fraud case, a colleague and I read all the economic literature we could find, and we then called the author whose work most impressed us as sensible and understandable. In a mental condition case in which the defendant's problems were complicated by alcohol and prescription drugs, I wanted a pharmacologist to add to the psychiatrist's testimony; a former dean of the University of Texas, San Antonio Medical School steered me to a dynamic witness. In a complex antitrust case, friends among the trial bar helped locate an economist with an impressive teaching and publication résumé who also worked with a research group that helped him be an effective expert witness. I have found an expert by reading testimony he presented in a congressional hearing. I needed an expert on explosives for a homicide case; at the suggestion of a friend, I turned to an expert witness consortium that advertises in bar publications. Lawyers in law firms where I have been an associate and partner have helped me as well.

## HOW TO PREPARE YOURSELF
## FOR THE SEARCH

In these pages, I caution against exhibiting arrogance when presenting or opposing an expert. Read deeply, but don't show off.

One joy of a diverse litigation practice is to be a nuclear science expert one week, an economics expert the next, and a pathologist the next. The hard question is the order of things. You cannot evaluate a potential claim or defense without reading and study. Sometimes legal research will be enough. In other cases, referral to a consulting physician will give you a report on which you can go forward.

You cannot, however, intelligently choose your expert until you have a coherent theory of the case—until a tentative story is written. You cannot write the story until you have read deeply enough to see how you are going to tell jurors about the matters on which the expert will testify.

At this stage, look for general reference works—college (or even high school) texts, the *Encyclopaedia Britannica*, magazine articles, and mass market books. You need at least this much help simply to talk meaningfully with potential experts.

For example, the bank fraud case I mentioned above involved compensating balance bank stock loans. These loans were common in states that prohibited branch banking and were part of the structure of correspondent bank relationships. To see the structure of the banking industry, I turned to Martin Mayer's book, *The Bankers*, a thoroughly researched and critical overview. Second, I learned that this type of loan had been the subject of congressional hearings. I have a dozen hearing transcripts; Congress hears from many experts whose prepared testimony is often laden with useful insights and citations to other authority. These experts often present partisan conclusions for which they argue as eloquently as they can. The rest of the file consists of a few relatively more scholarly articles.

Serial publications for almost every specialized field are stored in computer retrieval systems, either as abstracts or in full text. In our own field, the *Index to Legal Periodicals* no longer appears in print; one finds law journal articles on computer databases. Medical, economic, and other fields have similar resources. A growing number of providers store information about expert witnesses, which can be a source of information about the field of expertise as well as about particular experts.

## THE NONTESTIFYING EXPERT

In some cases, you should not present expert testimony, even when your opponent does. If you are the proponent of a claim on which expertise is helpful, you will almost always need an expert. If you are the opponent, you should always consider whether you need one.

When you cross-examine an expert, you should be empowering the jurors by equipping them with insights that lead to rejecting the expert and his conclusions. Having done that, you risk "redignifying" the expert and the expertise when you present your own witness who claims superior knowledge and, on the basis of that knowledge, reaches a different result. Many cases are top-heavy with experts these days, adding to case costs and "turning off" the jurors. Powerful cross-examination can do more than an opposing expert.

The theme of your cross, aided by your shadow expert, is that the "soft expertise" of the opponent's witness can be unravelled by common sense, the juror's superior ability to judge the facts, and by any treatises or other materials you are able to introduce under Federal Rule of Evidence 803(18).

Another approach is to make clear that your expert is only going to isolate a few major errors and mistaken assumptions in the plaintiff's expert's opinion. If one corrects these, one can see that the basic theory is flawed and that the opponent's view should be rejected. You can, of course, designate an opposing expert, see how the trial goes, and perhaps decide not to call her.

If you are going to do without a testifying expert, you must learn enough to cross-examine the other side's experts effectively. Search for a well-qualified expert. Retain the expert as your assistant, helping you provide professional legal services. Consultations are then shielded by the attorney-client and work product privileges. The purpose is not to learn so much that you can put on a show of knowledge on cross-examination to rival that of the testifying expert. Such a combination of arrogance and technical virtuosity makes the expert's calling and opinions more distant from the jurors, rather than arming them to demolish the expert's testimony. Rather, you will want to help in deconstructing the opposing experts and their expertise.

You can recruit a nontestifying expert from the ranks of bright graduate students or from friends in the right profession. This kind of expert need not have the communications skills you would expect of someone who was going to testify.

Working with the nontestifying expert can help you clarify your case presentation. You might start by trying to explain the opposing expert's views. Your first effort may be labored, hypertechnical, even condescending. Your nontestifying expert can help you put those views in terms that you understand well enough to communicate to others. Next, introduce the expert to the discovery materials.

He can go to work to find writings by the opposing expert and other relevant material for cross-examination. Thus armed, he can help you gain a good sense of how to dismantle the opposing expert's views through a well-structured cross-examination. You will probably have the expert on call for the trial, to help with the last minute details of cross-examination. He may have good suggestions about demonstrative evidence.

## PREPARING YOUR
## EXPERT TO TESTIFY

During a program on expert testimony, the lawyers and the experts traded ideas. The lawyers examined and cross-examined the experts, and a judge provided helpful comment. But the most impassioned statement of the day was from an expert who pleaded with the lawyers to treat their witnesses with consideration and dignity. The expert told stories of being asked at the last minute to rework presentations and of being ignored while cases were prepared and then being asked to drop everything to prepare to testify.

I sympathized because I had been guilty of treating experts shabbily—and had seen my case presentations suffer in consequence. The point was further driven home when I agreed to be an expert witness. A lawyer of my acquaintance called me and got my verbal agreement to testify after answering my questions about the facts and promising to send some materials for me to review. Then silence, for months. My faxed memos were not answered. Finally, a junior associate in the law firm that had retained me called and said my deposition had been scheduled. I protested that I had not been given the chance to learn enough about the case, that the short notice was not acceptable, and that I would withdraw.

A good expert must be prepared, as well as directed in ways that fit the sponsor's theory of the case. She must be given heavy doses of self-confidence and dire warnings on the pitfalls of arrogance.

The expert should attend trial team planning meetings and be invited to discuss how expert insight can help shape the case. The expert may have a suggestion about a new line of proof or legal argument. More than once, I can remember taking an expert through the tough questions that she must handle at trial, only to have her pause and say, "Well, I can answer that. But have you thought of [this or that alternative view]?" If expertise is to be convincing, it must be integrated with your trial plan. If you think of expertise in this way, you will treat the expert with proper regard.

## DIRECT EXAMINATION BEGINS: BIOGRAPHICAL INFORMATION

"Will you tell the jury your name?"

"What do you do for work?" The answer should be nontechnical and supportive. "I analyze the way big companies buy and sell things like crude oil. I write books and articles about that, and I teach about that at Massachusetts Institute of Technology." Or, "I work with people who are mentally ill, and with their families, to try and resolve problems and help them lead productive lives." "Have you made a list that shows what you did to prepare yourself to do this?" The answer might be: "I have a biographical statement that I have prepared." Your response is, "To save time, let me put that up on the overhead projector." You probably premarked this as an exhibit.

Using a highlighting pen, go over the biography, pausing at experiences or publications that are especially relevant. Spouting off the biography from memory or from notes makes almost any expert look arrogant. You can use the exhibit to make the telling more informal, in a question-and-answer format. Offer the biography in evidence so you can refer to it again in argument or later in the examination.

The biography should include the expert's prior litigation activity. There are four possible scenarios: experienced testifier with the same ideological bent, experienced switch-hitter, relative novice, and complete novice.

For the witness with experience all on one side: "It says here you have been a witness in a lot of cases. Let's look at the *Bronson* case. How did you decide you had an opinion to give in that case?" The expert goes through the process of decision in a few short sentences. "You listed here the cases where you were an expert witness. Have you been asked to be an expert, but declined?" "Are those cases listed here?" "How many times have you declined?" "Why?" You must defuse the image of a biased hired gun by having the witness refer to the technique of deciding and the fact of having rejected cases where the facts would not support a favorable opinion. If you can bring out instances of *pro bono* testimony, without fee, do so. "Can you tell us how many times you have been accepted by a court to testify as an expert?"

If the witness is a switch-hitter, let the jurors know early. "Here on page three of your biography, you have listed cases in which you have been a witness. Were these basically all on the same side?" This question may strike you as inartful. In a sense it is. Its purpose is to permit the witness to say, with conviction and without arrogance, "Not at all. In X, Y, and Z case I was an expert for the plaintiff. In A and B case, I testified for the defendant. My opinion is based on the individual facts that are presented to me."

The relative novice and complete novice have the advantage of not being professional witnesses. "Are you in the regular business of giving opinions in court cases?" "Not at all. My profession is. . . ." The witness can add, if appropriate, "In fact, this is the first time I have ever testified in court."

## QUALIFYING THE EXPERT

In most civil cases, qualification of experts will have been handled in the discovery and pretrial process, along with any limitations imposed on the expert's opinions. You will seldom need to "tender" the expert for a ruling on whether he may give an opinion. To review the standards with which this chapter began, the expert's testimony must meet three conditions: (1) that the testimony will "assist the trier of fact," (2) that the subject matter is a recognized body of expertise, and (3) that this expert is qualified to give an opinion.

The first and second decisions are made by the judge, and testimony about them may be taken outside the jurors' presence. I say "may" because often the expert's background discussion of a field of knowledge, and of his general conclusions, will be relevant both to the admissibility decision and to the jurors' use of the opinion. If I am sure that the expert will be able to testify, I want all to take place in the jurors' presence. If I am not sure, I opt to have testimony taken before the judge alone. If the judge rules for me, I will retrace the same steps in front of the jury.

Issue three calls for a threshold decision by the judge, but everything the expert says may be considered by the jurors in evaluating the testimony. Therefore, there is no basis for excluding them.

Once you think the testimony establishes these three points, you say something like, "I tender Dr. Wilson as an expert witness in this case, in the field of pathology, and on the issue of whether the ingestion of cigarette smoke contributed to the plaintiff's cancer. I have filed a brief memorandum of points and authorities with Your Honor." The opponent then has the right to take the witness on the "*voir dire*" on these issues. On issues one and two, the parties and the court are not limited to considering the expert's own testimony and may receive other written and oral evidence as well.

The court may also consider—under Federal Rule of Evidence 403—whether the expert's opinion, even if relevant and admissible, should be excluded as prejudicial, cumulative, or a waste of time.

In a civil case, if these issues have been explored in the discovery process, these issues will have been resolved by motion *in limine* and the judge's ruling reflected in the pretrial order. In a criminal case, the rules may require notice that certain kinds of expert testimony—such as evidence of mental condition—will be offered. The notice may lead to a pretrial skirmish on admissibility.

## INTRODUCING THE THEMES

Now the expert is qualified, and the judge has said the magic words: "The doctor may testify and give opinions as an expert." Move quickly to introduce your theme or themes. Remember that a soft expert requires more careful introduction than a hard one.

In your opening statement, you will probably have told the jury that there are hard questions presented for them to solve and that you will probably be calling witnesses whose life work is to help understand these questions. You will not have said that the expert is going to solve all the problems from a perspective of Olympian detachment. I say you will "probably" have promised an expert because you may have decided to cross-examine your opponent's expert and only then determine whether to call one of your own.

Your introduction of the expert will have shown that this is one of the people you promised to call. Your introduction of the theme must do two things: (1) it must fore-shadow the testimony that is to come, and (2) it must legitimize that testimony by relating it to the jurors' own intuition. Some jurors may be predisposed to accept the brand of soft science you are presenting; others may not.

In a criminal case, the defendant's mental condition was in issue. He was a chronic alcoholic. Because of his drinking, he let his business partners handle details. He worked on deals. He would often black out from drinking and forget what had gone on the night before. He had suffered measurable brain damage from alcohol.

We hoped the jurors would understand that he would not have understood the tax consequences of his actions. He was not living a lifestyle that was beyond the amount of income he reported. We argued that his partners in fact concealed from him how well the business was doing.

Psychiatric evidence is difficult for some jurors to accept. Evidence of alcoholism is doubly difficult because many people think the disease is self-inflicted. Others are deeply into denial of their own incipient or actual alcohol abuse. We worked on this problem by pairing hard and soft experts. The defendant's former wife also agreed to appear as a lay witness to describe the ravages of alcohol on the defendant and their marriage.

I selected our psychiatric witness first as a treating doctor. I did not think the defense would be credible unless the defendant acknowledged his problem enough to seek help for it. The doctor had never testified for a criminal defendant. He had testified in favor of suspending licenses of impaired doctors and had twice been appointed by courts to examine defendants in celebrated cases. He looked and sounded—and was—credible and qualified.

To introduce the themes of his testimony, I borrowed from a suggestion made by Chief Judge David Bazelon:

Q. Doctor, when someone like X here comes to you as a patient, do you find that their family has a hard time understanding why they are behaving as they do?

A. I would say that most people feel that way, about alcohol problems of others, and even about the alcohol problems in their own family.

Q. Do you ask the family to come in so you can discuss the condition that X is suffering from, and what can be done about it?

A. We do more than ask. We actively try to get them to come in.

Q. Do you sometimes find that family members are fearful, or skeptical, or even maybe a little hostile, about what you do, and about X himself?

A. Oh, yes. I think working with families is the most challenging part of what we do.

Q. Doctor A, I want you to imagine that the jurors and I are X's family and that we have come to ask you for an explanation of why he has been behaving as he has. Would you do that?

A. Sure, I'll try.

The next questions get the expert's opinion, the work done to come to an opinion, and how this condition manifests itself in behavior. With a psychiatrist, I always ask along the way, "Doctor, what you tell us about X is based a lot on what he told you, right?" "Do you have ways to check up on information the patient gives you?" The answers should include the physician's normal appreciation that any patient may be misinterpreting things for quite understandable reasons. If there will be witnesses in support of the expert's conclusions, remember to mention them. Because the patient's version is central to most treatment modes, your expert should be able to show that this is the kind of factual basis usually relied on by experts in the field.

With a soft science witness, you must introduce the themes of the testimony with a selection of topic sentences. In these, you must devise an introduction of theme that deals with the pitfalls of soft science as well as the particular conclusions being presented. With all experts, the root issue is, What do you know? With soft experts, you must also inquire, How can you possibly know this?

Let us take another example. You call a theoretical economist to testify that the participants in a given market are not behaving collusively. Testimony, pro and con, on this issue is a feature of many antitrust cases, subject to intense sparring on admissibility.

Start strong, with a clear summary statement of the expert's opinion. Then back up and find out the details.

Q.  Ms. Z, have you studied the Alaska crude oil market for the years 1970 through 1975?
A.  I have.
Q.  Did you look for evidence that the companies purchasing crude oil colluded with each other?
A.  I did, through thousands of documents, dozens of depositions, and a review of the economic data.
Q.  What is your opinion on that?
A.  In my opinion, there is simply no believable evidence that A, B, C, D, and E company colluded with each other or with anybody else.
Q.  Tell us how you can say that.

The next answer should give the key reasons for the opinion—five or so tests that you would expect to see met if there were collusion. If your expert is countering one already presented by your opponent, these five or so tests should carry the answer to that expert.

Once you have these forthright answers, your tone and manner should become more skeptical, inquiring, prodding. You are the jury's surrogate inquirer, and you share their doubts and their need/desire to interpret and judge the expert's conclusions.

## MAKING THE POINT

You will probably use an exhibit that contains the topic sentences that summarize each theme. Then you can go back and develop the themes in greater detail.

Remember, with soft expertise, you must counter not only skepticism about your factual position, but disbelief in this method of supporting it. How do we conquer disbelief? Two key methods are tapping into shared experiences and tying in to verifiable information.

From a criminal case, here is an example of using shared experiences. The witness is professor and chair of the pharmacology department of a major medical school.

Q. Now doctor, you say that the defendant could still function and appear fairly normal despite having drunk that much? Somehow that doesn't sound logical. Tell us how that could be.

A. [Turning to the jurors]. Oh, this is well documented in medical journals. You can drink so much that you are a sleepwalker. You are at the party and people think you are a little spaced out, but essentially all right. You carry on conversations. The next morning you wake up and you cannot remember much about the party or even how you drove home. Studies I've seen say this has happened at least once to about 30 percent of Americans. Maybe it has happened to someone on the jury. I sure know it has happened to me.

The answer was humane, fallible, and vivid. Several jurors nodded their heads in agreement. We had tapped in to one of their own experiences, personal or vicarious.

Could you do the same sort of thing with a theoretical economist? Yes. "One of the things that convinces me there was no collusion here is there was no mechanism to enforce a price-fixing scheme. When you get together with somebody to fix prices, you've got to have a way to make sure that your partners aren't taking advantage of you." The answer that taps shared experience begins "It makes sense that . . ." or "It doesn't make sense to say. . . ."

The second assault on disbelief is by verifiable information, by concretizing the expert's opinion in a demonstrable reality that exists in this lawsuit. In our tax case, the defendant's former wife provided that. So would a hard expert. The soft expert can self-verify by referring to procedures and tests used in coming to a conclusion and by consistent reference to hard evidence in the case. Remember Federal Rule of Evidence 703: "If of a type reasonably relied upon by experts in the particular field in forming opinions or inferences upon the subject, the facts or data [on which the opinion rests] need not be admissible in evidence."

You will ask, "How do you know [this or that]?" and the expert will tell the jurors about a test, an equation, a measuring device. Or the expert will direct the jurors—perhaps with visual aids—to depositions, documents, or tangible objects.

You want the jurors to be able to recreate the expert's results in the jury room. A juror who supports your position should be able, in discussion with another juror, to restate the tests and controls the expert used and the key evidence that supports the expert's conclusions.

## ARROGANCE

"Be careful what you say," Carl Sandburg wrote. "Use words that taste good, because you might have to eat them," somebody else said. As we have seen, arrogance is a fatal disease of witnesses. Experts seem to be more susceptible than most.

If you are the proponent of the issue for which the expert is called, and bear the burden of persuasion, your expert—and the other evidence—must withstand challenge and leave the jury convinced. Don't let this circumstance propel you to a siege mentality or let your expert adopt a stance of arrogant inflexibility. In your direct, anticipate some of

the cross. Your expert must willingly admit that there are
or could be opposing views—about the subject, and about
this case. In his job, as in almost everybody's, the highest
and best challenge is to make difficult choices among
alternatives; his testimony is stronger because he has considered the alternative formulations. One series of questions on direct must begin, "Did you consider alternative
ways of interpreting the facts?" Another series must acknowledge that the jurors are fact-finders and, in the usual
case, have some leeway. You might ask, for example:

Q. Suppose the jurors should look at the same weather
   report and radar data and conclude that the cloud
   cover was thicker than your analysis shows. How
   would that affect your conclusions?
A. I did do my very best to get it right about the cloud
   cover. But if somebody should try to claim that the
   clouds were thicker and lower, that would not affect
   the ultimate conclusion. The pilot would have had
   one less way of judging the approach. But that is
   one meaning of redundancy—he is supposed to be
   paying attention to all the systems that are there to
   inform him and guide him.

If your expert is being paid, which is usually the case,
track the hours spent, fees incurred, and the nature of the
work on direct examination, rather than leaving the inquiry
to the cross examiner. Warn your expert not to get into a
debate with the cross-examiner and to answer the questions as succinctly and directly as possible.

Your presentation of a soft expert, in sum, is an appeal
to intuition and reason. You and the expert will break
down the barrier between the witness stand and the jurors,
physically by the expert moving from the chair, visually by
demonstrative evidence, and figuratively by questions that
focus on how to figure out the right answer.

# Chapter Twelve

## Expert Witness: Soft Subjects—
## Cross-Examination

The theory of cross-examining a soft subject expert may be summed up: "An expert is someone who was not there when it happened but who for a fee will gladly imagine what it must have been like."

Cross-examining a soft subject expert is an exercise in jury empowerment. You want to give the jurors the tools by which they can deconstruct the expert and her conclusions. Because, by definition, soft subjects contain intuitive elements, jurors will be readier than in other situations to make critical judgments that go to the heart of the expert's testimony.

### "SOMEONE"

Who is this expert? Does she possess adequate qualifications? Are there others equally qualified? Are the expert's theories questionable? Debatable?

Most of us have heard "junk science" decried. Much of this rhetoric misidentifies the issues. Take almost any soft subject (and a few hard subjects) and find two opposing experts. Usually, the experts will arraign one another's conclusions from every conceivable perspective. They will start with lack of respect for the opposing expert's credentials and academic work, continue through rejection of the theoretical basis of the other's position, consider questions about the reliability of the methods used, and move on to a more case-specific analysis.

Almost all of these mutual criticisms are fair game for cross-examination, to help the jurors decide based on the clash of opinions. Only extreme instances of lack of qualifications or scientific foundation should call for excluding expert testimony altogether. However, as noted in the last chapter, judges have become bolder about exclusion—over objections that they are invading the jury's province.

With respect to some marginal soft expertise, concern for the jury's proper role points toward exclusion rather than admissibility. One clear example is the use of police witnesses in criminal cases to give expert opinion on narcotics transactions, crime world vocabulary, organized crime infiltration of business and labor, and other sociological issues. This expertise does not rest on impartial and verifiable research. To the contrary, some of these opinions are avowedly based on the hearsay of countless and unnamed informers the witness has encountered over the years. The basis for the opinion cannot, courts have begun to say, be effectively cross-examined. The jurors have no way to evaluate the opinion.

For the advocate who must cross-examine, these new judicial attitudes pose challenges and opportunities. Once, I would have advised waiting to cross-examine most experts until the direct examination was finished. Today, I more carefully consider the prospects of inflicting substantial damage on my opponent's case by taking the expert on the *voir dire* and moving to exclude the testimony.

Most federal trial judges construe the discovery rules as permitting depositions of experts who are designated as trial witnesses. This construction of the rules wastes inordinate time and money. Not only is the expert charging a fee for preparing and showing up, the party taking the deposition usually has an expert in the wings advising on deposition strategy. Where depositions of experts are permitted, the usual corollary is that the issue of qualifications must be resolved before trial by motions *in limine*. Where a party's case depends on an expert—as with many toxic torts—pretrial exclusion of an expert's testimony may pave the way for summary judgment.

When permitted to take an opposing expert's deposition, there are two goals. First, ask a few questions to make sure you really understand the expert's theory and the factual and theoretical research that underpins it. Second, try to lay the basis for a challenge to the expert's testimony. A challenge can involve a lack of qualifications, a theory not sufficiently recognized, testimony that is not helpful to the jury because it simply replicates what fact witnesses are saying, or testimony that is unduly prejudicial because it is inflammatory or conclusory.

Based on the deposition, you can file a motion *in limine* and fight the issue out before trial. You can also move at trial to exclude the testimony, an action based on the fuller record then available. If your earlier motion *in limine* has been denied, you should conduct a vigorous *voir dire* before renewing it. Renew it again after cross-examination. The new judicial temperament about experts makes it worth your while to support and preserve your objections.

If you decide to *voir dire* at trial, you take a risk because the odds are that the judge will permit the expert to testify: "Interesting points. They go to weight, not to admissibility." In order not to lose on *voir dire*—in the jurors' eyes—make your goals modest enough that you are almost certain to achieve them.

"May I take Dr. Wilson on *voir dire*, Your Honor? He may be qualified, but I think Your Honor should have a full record." Your *voir dire* will have one or more subject matters: qualifications and scientific acceptance, for example. You must have a solid question to end inquiry into each subject matter, and this question must require the expert to agree with you in some way that limits the impact of his expertise or his conclusions. Then approach the bench and make whatever motions you want to make, out of the jury's hearing.

These ending questions need not be earth-shaking; they just need to cover a potential defeat on the main issue of admissibility. Examples: "So, doctor, you have never worked in a state prison hospital?" "The theory you are telling us about has been challenged by economists at MIT?"

So much for how to end. Here are some thoughts on what to do before that. Let us consider, first, the expert's *qualifications* to testify and then the *subject matter* as a permissible subject of expert testimony.

## ARE YOU COMPETENT? ABOUT THIS SUBJECT?

Some experts have invented their subjects. For them, the questions of their qualifications and the reliability of their theory are bound together. For analysis, however, we must try to separate the issues, for the rules make qualification and reliability two hurdles for the proponent to cross. You can divide "qualification" in two: (1) competency and (2) competency for a particular issue, though the distinction erodes when you begin to cross-examine.

A business planner or financial consultant without extensive formal education, subject to no licensing requirements, and not tested in the alembic of academic discourse should face stiff opposition if called as an expert witness. In an air crash case in Louisiana, an economist projected that the decedent's income would have increased until his retirement at an 8 percent annual rate, undiscounted by the effect of interest rate fluctuations and the expiration of tax benefits that had added to cash flow in the years immediately before the decedent was killed. The Fifth Circuit held that the expert should not have been permitted to testify.

Such "economic" testimony can be demolished on cross-examination, but most judges will let you argue that it is not worth wasting the jury's time listening to it. First, identify the claimed expertise, in this case, income forecasts. Identify the relevant skills, and get a picture of the kind of person who could give a reliable opinion on that subject, e.g., an economist who is trained to watch trends and who in fact watches them. This person will teach the subject and will have published well-regarded work about it.

If the issue is forensic psychiatry, the ideal witness will surely have gone beyond general medical practice and even beyond general psychological, psychiatric, or counseling experience. The witness should have dealt with the kinds of disorders at issue and with people of the age and situation of this patient. Board certification in forensic psychiatry is a plus, though probably not essential to being recognized. The *en banc* Fifth Circuit said in a related context, however, that an M.D. degree "alone is not enough to qualify him to give an opinion on every conceivable medical question. . . . The trial judge rightly scrutinized lack of specialized experience and knowledge."

In choosing the ideal against which to cross-examine the opponent's witness, borrow heavily from the qualifications of a witness you have chosen to put on in your case. Your *voir dire* or cross-examination on qualifications takes this ideal and cross-examines against it. If the witness is too far from the ideal, the testimony is not admissible. Even if the testimony is ruled admissible, you will have set up your expert's qualifications as a model.

Be patient. The expert is ready to strut her stuff. She may become visibly impatient at your polite but determined questions directed at gaps in the résumé. Arraigning the witness against the ideal, your inquiry divides into (1) academic qualifications, (2) practical training, (3) state licensing (you'd be surprised how minimal the licensing requirements are for some professions), (4) experience, (5) specialization, (6) publications, (7) professional affiliations, and (8) relationship between expert witness work and other professional activity. Item 8 is designed for the expert who has no visible means of support, beyond preparing for and giving expert testimony. Such a person is always an advocate for some position, never pressing on the frontiers of a field solely for the love of knowledge.

Here is an edited sample of testimony from a research officer and economist at the Federal Reserve Bank, testifying in a bank fraud case:

Q. Is it proper for me to address you as Dr. Knight?

A. Yes, if you wish.

Q. Dr. Knight, I am Morton Susman, and I represent the Bank of the Southwest in this case.

A. Hi.

Q. We haven't met before, have we?

A. No.

Q. Now, I noticed that you got your Ph.D. in June of 1968?

A. Yes.

Q. And your Master's—when was that? What year was that?

A. 1965.

Q. And when did you get the B.A. degree?

A. 1963.

Q. Would you mind telling us your age?

A. Thirty-four, I believe.

Q. Well, then, you've got a lot crammed into the thirty-four years. Did you find some time in that period to work for a bank?

A. Yes. I have not spent, since I graduated from college, any time in a bank. However, my father has a small bank in western Nebraska, and I worked in that bank through high school and summers during college in various departments.

Q. Was that before you went to college?

A. That was before I went to college, all through high school, and it was also summers during the college vacations. When I needed money, I also worked during Christmas and Easter vacations.

Q. In working your dad's bank, did you make loans or pass on credit?

A. I did not do that.

Q. Actually, you have to be in the banking business for quite some time to get into that?

A. It is a specialized area.

Q. Yes, sir, because bankers would like to be sure they get their money back—

A. Of course.

Q. —if they loan it out? Is that right?

A. Correct.

Q. So it's a heavy responsibility, isn't it?

A. Yes.

This line of questioning is designed to undercut a claim that the expert knows anything about the decision to lend money and about management decisions on allocation of the bank's funds among different investment opportunities. The point is that such decisions require practical experience as well as formal training. The expert has written articles on this subject, and studied it in school and in his chosen profession, so it is unlikely that the testimony will be excluded. However, a motion to exclude is certainly in order, and the jurors have in the meantime heard some things that permit them to put the testimony in perspective.

The transcript is a partial sample. This style of inquiry lends itself to a review of all the elements listed above.

## HOW DID YOU GET HERE?

Up to now, we have been talking about qualities that the expert possessed before she was retained in the case. We move on to case-specific bias issues. For example, the best doctor-witness is a treating physician or therapist. The worst is somebody who read the file, talked to the lawyers, and has a surefire opinion.

In a civil case, one proper use of discovery is to retrace the expert's steps on the way to a conclusion. Defending an antitrust case, you might ask the plaintiff's economist: "Doctor, when did you agree to be an expert witness for the plaintiff?" "How did you let Dr. Amboy know that you were willing?" "You had made up your mind by then that there was collusion in this market, right?" On this last question, you will probably run into some resistance. Don't let the witness slide. At least, he has to admit having agreed to testify: "You had made up your mind enough to be able to call Dr. Amboy and volunteer to be on the case, right?"

Now focus on how much time the expert put in before making that phone call, what work he had done, and how the fee was being calculated. In tracing the work done, you are looking for a document trail and for conversations with counsel. Often big-gun experts are brought in late to bless the work of those who have gone before; they form "their" opinions based on predigested material absorbed from the experts who have been working the case.

Base your examination on the calendar. Ask, in order, for each time the expert spoke with counsel or counsel's representative. Identify all information provided at each stage, including oral presentations and documents. Then find out what opinions, conclusions, and impressions the expert communicated back to the lawyers. Were there any notes or other writings on this subject? Where are they now? What did they say? You are looking for the point at which the expert expressed an opinion; for your purposes, it looks best for your case if the expert expressed an opinion early, before deeply analyzing the facts, and was retained only after it was apparent that the opinion would be helpful to the person signing the checks.

Few witnesses, and fewer experts with any experience, will admit that they formed an opinion hastily and did so to earn a fee. Your patient examination builds the circumstantial evidence, to try and lay a basis on which to argue that inference.

If the expert reached a conclusion after a derisory amount of research and factual analysis, all the later study and document analysis is less significant than it would otherwise be. The expert was simply combing the evidence looking for material to support a conclusion already made.

The timeline of work, fees, and opinion—"How did you get here?"—lays the basis for challenging the expert's right to testify at all. An opinion formed by such a process is not the invocation of "scientific, technical or other specialized knowledge." It is vouching.

If the challenge is unsuccessful, the timeline cross-examination empowers the jurors to tread the same path and reach an opposite conclusion. "Let's go back for a minute. The week of June 24, you called Dr. Amboy and said you would be a witness?" "At that time, you had looked at this stack of paper right here?" "We have marked that Defendants 2502A, and it is in evidence. In addition, you had spoken to Dr. Amboy twice, and to Mr. Wilson a few times?" "The jurors can look at these documents, can they not?" "They can also look at these documents that I have shown you, Defendants 2502B?" "You had not looked at any of these documents, had you?" "The jurors can also figure out whether Dr. Amboy, and his assistant Mr. Wilson, have a good theory?" "Since the week of June 24, you have read many more documents?" "You have talked to Dr. Amboy many times?" "You have talked to these lawyers?" "And, you have billed five hundred more hours at $400 per hour?"

Having dwelt on how swiftly the expert formed his opinion, you take up the rest of the expert's preparation. Here is another brief excerpt from the bank fraud prosecution mentioned above:

Q. Now, sir, in preparation for your testimony in this case, did you study the bank examination reports for the Bank of the Southwest for '69, '70, '71, or '72?

A. No. I have never seen a bank examination report on the Bank of the Southwest.

Q. Did you study any bank examination reports of the First National Bank of Waco?

A. No. I've never seen those either.

Q. Did you study anything in this case other than [the prosecutor's] summary chart that you worked from?

A. I have studied nothing other than the various exhibits that were shown to me when I came here.

Q. And who showed them to you, sir?

A. The various lawyers for the prosecution.

Q. Okay. These gentlemen at the table here?

A. Yes.

Q. Did you ever ask to talk to me, or Mr. Tigar, or Mr. DeMoss, or any of these other gentlemen to get our side of it?

A. No.

In a recent antitrust case, the witness had consulted with his side's experts, read many depositions and deposition summaries, and waded through piles of documents. He was an eminent theoretical economist.

The case was about crude oil and the oil industry. Yet he had never spent time with people responsible for running integrated oil companies or even so-called independent oil companies. He had never been inside an oil refinery. He had not talked to the people responsible for running refineries and making the day-to-day decisions about how much and what kind of crude oil to process into what kinds of products and at what prices.

Our side had access to a theoretical economist who could match this witness's qualifications, and we had made sure our expert had taken the time for hands-on experience. In addition, we had a witness who was not a theoretical economist but whose expertise had been built up from making technical and business decisions in this industry. Cross-examination of the opposing expert about lack of practical wisdom set the stage for our case.

In a highly publicized Florida case, a man who claimed permanent injury won a large damage award with the aid of expert medical witnesses. Later it was proved that he was faking. Some concluded that the legal system was at fault for allowing the scam to happen. I wondered whether more thorough pretrial investigation of the plaintiff and the experts would not have blown the story apart on cross-examination.

Cross-examination is an art best practiced with all the tools available. Research into prior publications and computer searches are only a beginning. Even if you are permitted deposition discovery, it must be used as an adjunct to, and not a substitute for, independent research. You have to get up from your office chair—or hire somebody to do the footwork. If an expert witness is a college teacher, I want the reading list from her courses. Most college bookstores sell books of capsule biographies and teaching evaluations of professors; I want a copy. If the professor's lectures have been memorialized in canned notes, I want those as well. In the Florida case, I wonder if anybody thought to interview the plaintiff's neighbors.

Sometimes, you hit a home run. In a financial fraud prosecution, the government's principal expert had trouble preparing to testify. Maybe he and the prosecutor were short on time. So they wrote out all the questions and answers for the witness to memorize.

Q. Now, sir, one final question I have here. This was your questions and answers that [the prosecutor] prepared? Is that right, sir?

A. That's right.

Q. I noticed, in looking through this, that the questions are typed up, are they not?

A. Yes.

Q. And, on the other side, the answers are typed up, are they not?

A. Yes, sir.

Q. And I notice right up at the top your name is written in, in pen, is it not?

A. Yes, it is.

Q. How come they didn't type your name in like they typed all the others?

A. I wouldn't have any idea.

Q. Could it be that they didn't know you would be the expert until after you came down here?

A. No. I don't think that's true at all. They knew I was going to be the witness for these questions.

Q. Well, I notice the answers are typed in, too, aren't they?

A. Yes. Those are my answers on that particular page.

Q. Do you suppose that any expert they would have brought down would have the same answers?

A. Well, they certainly wouldn't have the same answers—

[The prosecutor interjects:]

Your Honor, the purpose that document was prepared was explained to the court. Counsel is using a line of questioning that is calculated to—

[The court interrupts:]

I told you to stand up; make your objection, and I'll rule on it.

[Defense counsel offers:]

I'll withdraw the question.

[The court:]

I'll overrule the objection.

[Defense counsel:]

I withdrew it, anyway.

The jurors enjoyed the spectacle. They acquitted the defendants.

## WILL IT ASSIST THE TRIER OF FACT?

The suggested line of questions is a bridge to the next subject. We turn from the expert's qualifications and reasoning process to the tests of the opinion itself. An opinion that the jurors can reach as easily themselves will not assist them. Nor will a statement that could as easily be made in the summation or by demonstrative evidence sponsored by a nonexpert. In addition to the expert witness evidence standard, evidence that is unfairly prejudicial or wastes time can be excluded under Federal Rule of Evidence 403.

Your cross-examination, however, has two goals. To be sure, you want to exclude the evidence if you can. You want in any case to show the jurors that the evidence does not in fact help them because the expert is claiming to perform a service they can more easily perform for themselves.

Reduce the soft science expert's conclusions to their simplest form. Shorn of the jargon, what is this person saying? The psychiatrist is saying that people under stress act strangely. The economist testifies in fancy language that documents, statements, depositions, and market analysis point toward collusion; the issue in the case is whether a bunch of people agreed to fix prices, and he has never met any of them.

Yes, you are turning your opponents' preparation against them. They have struggled mightily to put the evidence in comprehensible form. Your further reductionism brings it to the point where a juror can say, "I can figure that out. I don't need that guy."

Consider the example of an expert on eyewitness identification who presents a list of factors that make the identification unreliable. The challenge goes something like this:

Q. Doctor, you have a list of things that affect the reliability of eyewitness identification?
A. A list of topics to consider, yes.
Q. Your list includes the amount of time the witness had to look at the robber, the lighting, whether the witness was afraid, the race of the witness and the robber, and so on?
A. Yes.

Q. Doctor, assume I am not a Ph.D.—because I'm not—
and I just sat down and made a list of things that
affected how well I could see and remember
somebody. The lighting conditions could be on my
list, right?
A. Yes, of course.
Q. That makes sense, doesn't it?
A. Yes.
Q. And the amount of time I had to look at the person
who was robbing me?
A. Yes.

Reconstruct the list, or enough of it to make the point.
Then finish it off.

Q. So Doctor, the judge, the members of the jury, even I
can make a good list just by using our common sense?
A. You could make some kind of a list, yes.

Drive it home:

Q. Our list only lets us talk in generalities, right, about
the kinds of things that could affect an identification?
A. Yes, the list deals with topics, not specific events.
Q. The only way to know if somebody can really
identify a robber is to ask them to try, and then to
ask them some questions about their experience?
A. Well, to the extent they can interpret their experience.
Q. In a lawsuit like this one, the lawyers ask questions,
the witness answers, and then the jurors are going to
decide how to interpret what is said, right?

## IS IT RELIABLE?

Faust Rossi's brilliant chapters in *Expert Witnesses* will tell
you the law about expert reliability. Most jurisdictions still
hew to the test of *Frye v. United States*, which the Fifth
Circuit has summarized: "whether the methodology or reasoning the expert uses to connect the facts to his conclu-

sions is generally accepted within the relevant scientific community."

On this issue, you can introduce evidence for the judge alone, to make the reliability determination. This is a matter best addressed on motion for partial summary judgment or by pretrial motion *in limine*. True, the same evidence of scientific reliability, or lack of it, is probably admissible before the jury, but only if the opinion itself comes in. There is no sense in having the jury listen to evidence that is laden with difficulty and may turn out to be irrelevant.

This chapter is about cross-examination, however. You want to confront the expert with evidence that his opinion is unreliable. Your consulting expert should have assembled materials that fit the requirements of Federal Rule of Evidence 803(18):

> To the extent called to the attention of an expert witness upon cross-examination, or relied upon by the expert witness in direct examination, statements contained in published treatises, periodicals, or pamphlets on a subject of history, medicine, or other science or art, established as a reliable authority by the testimony or admission of the witness or by other expert testimony or by judicial notice. If admitted, the statements may be read into evidence but may not be received as exhibits.

In addition, the witness you are cross-examining may have read the depositions of your expert and be aware that the latter has a completely different basic theory. If you have deposed the witness, you establish the authority of some works on which you will cross-examine at trial.

Armed with these impeachment tools, you can safely ask questions like:

Q. Doctor, you have told us that examining the prefrontal lobe of somebody's brain gives us valuable clues to their antisocial behavior?

A. Yes, I have.

Q. Do you know that there are medical doctors and professors who think that idea is bunk?

A. I know there is some disagreement.

Have your stack of learned treatises and prior depositions at hand, as a visible expression of the cross-examination you are about to do. Pick up the first one. Ask the witness to acknowledge its authority. If he will not do so, have available the material on which you will seek judicial notice. Confront the witness with the adverse opinion. This process continues as long as there is adverse material available to you.

Sometimes, if you are not going to call an expert of your own, you must debunk the expert's opinion without reference to other authority. I cross-examined an expert on the hedonic value of life. The expert disavowed special training in philosophy or religion. He was an economist by trade, though he had not completed a doctorate. He developed his theory from reading economic literature.

In short, he was saying that had the decedent lived he would have enjoyed life—and that this enjoyment could be quantified. How does one enjoy life? This expert's calculations were primarily based on the goods and services that the decedent would have bought in order to enjoy life.

The cross-examination focused first on that list. Then I asked whether people make choices among things to enjoy. These choices are limited by what we can afford. Some people can afford more choices than others. For instance, an expert who gets paid for working on a big case can afford to take a nice vacation in the Caribbean, and somebody else has to make do with a long weekend at the campground.

Where does somebody get the money to make these choices? Working people get the money in wages. So the hedonic value is nothing more than a calculation based on how somebody might spend the money he would earn. If that's true, the entire theory duplicates the amounts listed under potential earnings, discounted to present value.

## "WHO WAS NOT THERE"

Almost by definition, the expert was not present at the crucial event—did not see the shooting, attend the allegedly conspiratorial meeting, or watch the patient ingest a controlled substance. The expert is expressing an opinion based on facts found from investigation or furnished by others. The rule permits reliance even upon inadmissible evidence if it is of a type *reasonably* relied upon by experts in her field in forming their opinions.

Admissible or inadmissible, observed or provided, patent or inferred—the expert's facts are simply the working assumptions of someone who was "not there." And the jurors are final judges of the facts.

*In limine*, on *voir dire*, and in cross-examination, you must be alert to identify facts and data that are an impermissible basis for the expert's opinion because they are not reasonably relied upon. Some testimonial experts have become such high-volume hacks that they don't do their own homework, preferring to rely upon summaries furnished by litigation support staff. Expertise means specialization in some science or art outside the courtroom that is then brought to the jury. "Testifying about something" is not a form of independently admissible expertise. If no proper doctor in a medical office would rely on a litigation support person's summary of a patient's condition to make a diagnosis and treatment decision, then a testifying doctor should also be disqualified from doing so.

Be sure that in deposition, *voir dire,* or cross-examination, you follow the trail of the expert's preparation. Make a list of the expert's assumptions—those that she must make to express an opinion and those that are necessary to make the opinion relevant. This is a logical extension of the "How did you get here?" inquiry. Let's take it further.

An economist was testifying about collusion. The plaintiffs had, during discovery, furnished a list of those they claimed were conspirators to fix prices. I read the names on the list and asked after each name whether the expert had ever met that person. He answered "no" to each name.

Q. Now, Doctor, you know that a corporation cannot conspire, can it?
A. Well, it is an inanimate object.
Q. A corporation cannot do anything except through the people who work for it, right?
A. That is right.
Q. So the question is going to be whether some real human beings conspired with each other, isn't that right?
A. Yes.
Q. And who will answer that question in this case?
A. The jury.
Q. The jurors here are going to hear these people you have never met, and hear what they said under oath, right?
A. I assume so.
Q. And if they deny that they did anything wrong, the jurors are going to decide if they are telling the truth?
A. I suppose so.
Q. You don't claim to be an expert on who is telling the truth and who is not, do you?
A. No.
Q. In the courtroom, that decision is for the jurors, right?
A. Sure.

A physician treats symptoms. Some are obvious, like a broken leg. At other times, the physician bases an opinion only on what the patient and perhaps others have said happened. Maybe the patient was hit with a two-by-four; the head wound is consistent with that. The wound is just as consistent with falling and hitting her head on a banister railing.

A patient develops cancer. The doctor must theorize about causes. But, in assessing probabilities, the doctor must rely heavily on the patient and her family for a truthful account of the many potential carcinogens to which the patient was exposed.

Soft subject psychiatrists and psychologists have even more difficulty because their diagnoses are based to an even greater extent on what their patients tell them. The doctor will assure you that he is trained to sift truth from imagination, but he must admit that is an imperfect process. Pick up a psychiatrist's report and go through it identifying every statement based on what the patient or a family member said. You will see what I mean.

As you take an expert through the questionable factual assumptions, pause after each group of items and ask, "Who will decide this question?"

A theoretical economist makes models. The models are accompanied by phrases like "in competition" and "at the margin." These phrases represent key factual assumptions. There is no such thing as "competition" in the sense theoretical economists use the term. "At the margin" is another weasel-word that describes predicted behavior divorced from the myriad pressures and forces that actually affect economic decision makers. The process of deconstruction is two-stepped. First, ask a series of questions like, "There is no such thing as perfect competition, is there?" "So when you talk about what you would expect to see 'in competition,' that is just a model you build to study, and it could not exist in the real world?"

Second, when the expert goes on to say what somebody "would have done at the margin to maximize return," you must make her concede that real world decisions are greatly more complicated than the model suggests. The model may be based on all elements of the factory running at capacity, on infinitely available transportation facilities, on infinitely elastic demand for products—or any number of things that in the real world of running a business do not all come true, and certainly not at the same time. Make the expert acknowledge the assumptions, which you must state in plain language and not in economic jargon, and focus on the ones that your fact witnesses can demolish.

Conclude by making her dignify your fact witnesses and by conceding the value of real world experience, as shown in the bank fraud example given above. Economic experts are fond of saying that they prefer to validate the decisions managers make; if such a concession is available in your case, extract it. In any case, you can ask, "Doctor, you and I have just agreed that there are a lot of practical factual matters that are very important to how real people make these decisions in the real world. Somebody who makes their living by going to work every day and running this factory could answer those factual questions for us, couldn't they?"

In this process, try to develop analogies that make your point. In one case, an economist took memoranda in which people in a company had talked about value, and using the economist's definition of value, spun a theory about the authors' objectives and intentions. Value can mean different things to different people—and even to the same person at different times. "Doctor, do you see this belt buckle I am wearing? I don't know what it cost, but say my mother paid $50 for it, so she could give it to me as a birthday present. What was the value of that buckle to the artisan who made it and sold it?" You would then track the value of raw materials, the wholesale value, the retail price, what the buckle might be worth now, and the fact that to me it is priceless because I would not sell it for any amount of money. It is all right for us to use all or any of these ideas of value, and only by asking more questions or by careful attention to context would we know which use was meant. The best way, of course, is to ask the person who used the word what she meant. An economist reading a memo ten years later is probably not a good witness on that.

## "BUT WHO FOR A FEE"

Many studies tell us that jurors think bought-and-paid experts are suspect. Verdict reports also say that some professional experts are very effective and persuasive. We recall the cross-examination of James McNeill Whistler about a painting for which he charged two hundred guineas, and completed in two days:

Q. Oh, two days! The labor of two days, then, is that for which you ask two hundred guineas!

A. No;—I ask it for the knowledge of a lifetime.

The court reporter recorded applause at this point.

It is not the fee itself that counts, although some fees may be large enough to shock the jurors without respect to the amount of work done. No, it is the amount when considered in connection with the expert's qualifications and what he was asked to do. In final argument, you want to tie the amount of the fee to some demonstrable defect in the expert's opinion.

A psychiatrist who is retained to examine the patient and prepare testimony, and whose hourly rate works out to double or triple the going rate for top treating psychiatrists, is suspect. The suspicion grows if the psychiatrist consistently supports one side of an issue.

Many theoretical economists build huge models of data and then run series of equations until they develop a theory of liability and damages. The fees mount swiftly. Tracking the fee and its basis on cross-examination could yield fodder for a theory that the experts were given a virtually unlimited budget to keep at it until they came up with a plausible sounding theory supported by a lot of fancy equations.

In final argument, I have borrowed from an old *New Yorker* cartoon to characterize that kind of economist number-crunching. The cartoon showed the sign at the entrance of a small town:

| WELCOME TO SMITHVILLE | |
|---|---|
| Founded | 1678 |
| Population | 5328 |
| Elevation | 675 |
| TOTAL | 7681 |

## "WILL GLADLY IMAGINE WHAT IT MUST HAVE BEEN LIKE"

In a criminal trial, a noted law professor—let's call him Smith—was an expert witness. The prosecution had called him because he is an expert on injunctions. A judge was being tried for taking a bribe to influence a preliminary injunction hearing. One contention in defense was that the judge ruled as he did because the law gave him no choice.

On direct examination, Professor Smith described the process of balancing hardships in ruling on preliminary injunctions. Defense counsel had found cases holding that in certain situations there should be no balancing, and that the question was therefore cut-and-dried. Counsel wanted to confront Smith with this authority.

Defense counsel's attack on Smith's expertise failed because he failed to understand something that Gertrude Stein understood, even as she lay dying. Ms. Stein's longtime friend Alice B. Toklas asked, "Gertrude, what is the answer?" Ms. Stein intoned, "What is the question?" Counsel outsmarted himself because he wanted the jury to believe that he was one-up on the law professor and that the rule was not as the professor had portrayed it. In putting the contest on those terms, the cross-examiner risked too much, particularly with a savvy witness who just happened to know the line of authority the examiner was talking about and had written about it in his latest book.

Instead of showing off, the cross-examiner needed to define the question. He did not need to convince the jury that Professor Smith was completely wrong. His client's position was adequately served if Professor Smith conceded that a *reasonable judge might think* he was not supposed to balance hardships, or even that some case—albeit aberrant—could make a judge think so. This lesser concession does not make the issue a contest between the lawyer and the witness; it is easier to give and therefore to obtain. If the witness will not give it, the opposing expert will have an easier position to attack.

Moreover, jurors are mystified and even offended by a cross-examination which seems designed to strut the lawyer's claimed knowledge and which, for that purpose, becomes mired in technical lore.

How should Smith have been cross-examined? I admit that I have the advantages of knowing Smith and his work, and of talking to him about the issue.

Q. Professor Smith, you know the XYZ Transport case, don't you?
A. Yes, I do.
Q. It was decided by the appellate court right here in this state, right?
A. That's correct.
Q. Do you want to look at a copy of it, or can you remember it well enough?

You don't care what the answer is. Smith looks arrogant if he waves away your proffer of a copy, and you gain a point or two if he takes the case and is seen to be reading it in the presence of the jurors.

Q. Now, I am not going to ask you if you agree or disagree with that case.
A. All right.
Q. We are not here to find out what you think the law ought to be, are we?

A. No, I suppose not.

Q. The court in that case says, "Don't balance the hardships on these kind of injunctions"?

A. Yes, it does.

Q. Some other courts have said different, right?

A. Decidedly so.

Q. In your book, you say there is "confusion" among appellate judges in this area, right?

A. I said that, yes.

Q. Looking at XYZ Transport, and knowing there is confusion among appellate judges, wouldn't it be possible for a busy trial court judge reasonably to believe that he should not look to alleged hardship when irreparable injury was present?

This last question is risky. But you have the XYZ case, you have Smith's book, and therefore you have control. You have the ingredients for a searing rebuttal from your expert. Let's assume for the moment Smith said, "No, I don't think a reasonable judge could be mistaken about that." Take his book and show him some cases that come to the conclusion he labels unreasonable. Take him through the "other expert" cross discussed below.

If he will answer "yes," memorialize that answer. For example, walk to the large pad of drawing paper with a felt marker. Ask, "Professor, I want to get this right, 'A reasonable trial judge could believe that the law required him not to consider hardship, and to grant a preliminary injunction in this kind of case if irreparable injury was shown.' Is that right?"

When you get him to agree on a statement, write in big letters. Tear it off. Ask Smith to sign it. Put a sticker on it and offer it. If it is not admitted, save it, and use it in the summation.

Generalizing from this discussion, your cross-examination should focus on the minimum needed to achieve your goal. You must reduce the inquiry at the end to a set of principles that you can state clearly and to which the expert will agree. If possible, you should put these principles into a form that can be used again with other witnesses or in the closing argument. Even if the concessions you achieve are only given orally, you can get those portions of the transcript typed up and put on transparencies for an overhead projector. I particularly insist on this approach when cross-examining an expert whose side has the burden of persuasion. Your job is done if your opponents fail to meet their burden.

Suppose the expert simply will not yield substantive concessions. Her opinion on the merits is unshakable. She cannot imagine thinking otherwise. In the previous section, we have seen how to attack that witness by going back over her factual assumptions, as to which the jury is concededly the final arbiter.

You have to decide whether to shut down and wait for your case or do an "other expert" cross. I lean toward the latter alternative, particularly if I am going to call that other expert. I think that an expert who doggedly sticks to her position against all evidence and refuses to concede the possibility of a reasonably supported opposing view tends to look bad.

Of course, this judgment is case-specific. Cases in which your opponent's experts are impregnably right on a key issue probably should be settled and not tried.

## THE "OTHER EXPERT" CROSS

A soft subject expert who refuses to admit the possibility that her theory, method, and conclusions can be criticized by someone as well qualified as she appears arrogant.

Each of the following sentences states a theme for cross-examination.

1. There are different theoretical paradigms for most soft subjects.

2. There are well-qualified people who support any of several basic theories.
3. There are books and articles that support and oppose the different theories.
4. Even among those who have the same theoretical perspective, two qualified observers might honestly disagree.

Each of these themes can be developed with little or no risk, even with an expert who will not concede anything to the position you are taking in litigation.

Here are some sample questions. "Doctor, you are not a Freudian, are you?" You might get back, "Well, all of us have been influenced by the work of Sigmund Freud." To which the reply must be, "Doctor, you do not describe yourself as a Freudian, do you?" If she says, "No," fine. If she says, "Yes," you can say, "All right. You are not a Gestalt therapist, are you?" In your preparation, you have identified some major schools of thought about psychotherapy. You want the witness to admit that there are therapists out there who identify with some of these schools. Even a witness who declines to classify herself will concede that there are therapists who do self-classify.

The next step is to ask, "Would it be right to say there are these different schools of thought about psychotherapy?" Depending on your litigation position, you may want to bring in writers such as Dr. Thomas Szasz who doubt the validity of most psychiatric theory. Have the witness agree that such views are expressed by respectable physicians.

Now you take the witness through publications by people who adopt the different theories. Establish that people with different theoretical approaches who saw the same patient might come up with different explanations for that patient's behavior. Or at least they would have different ideas on how to treat that patient. In fact, two people who have the same theoretical outlook might come to different conclusions.

How do you know you can get something along this line? If the witness begins to balk, go back to process. If the witness is a reputable therapist, her training and her practice include "rounds" in clinical facilities and conferences with supervisors, at which diagnosis and treatment are debated. The very purpose of these sessions is to uncover disagreements among professionals and to resolve them. If your witness is not reputable or well-qualified enough to have participated in such events, that is itself a telling admission.

As Judge Higginbotham suggested in the *Eymard* case, discussed above, this sort of peer group argument is not unique to therapeutic professions. Every discipline has some form of it. When you have brought this out, you can ask, "In these conferences about patients, who has the last word? I mean, who decides which one of you therapists is right?" It doesn't matter what the answer is. The next question is, "In this case, who is going to decide whether you or another therapist has made the right diagnosis of Mr. Wilson?" The answer is, "The jury."

This line of inquiry can be dispositive. For example, in a legal or medical malpractice case, the expert's concession that reasonable people could disagree as to either the standard of care or its observance in this case powerfully supports a motion for directed verdict.

You may be able to interrogate your opponent's expert about your expert's views, even if you do not call your expert to testify. Because of liberal discovery rules, all experts will probably have been deposed. The expert you are cross-examining may well have read your expert's deposition. If you can establish, in deposition or by other research, that your opponent's expert has a good opinion of yours, you might ask, "You know Dr. James's work, don't you?" "He is a recognized expert, isn't he?" If the witness will admit having read your expert's deposition, you can confront her with it, as with any other material consulted in preparing her opinion.

This sort of comparative examination can be played another way. In a criminal case, discovery told us that the government had consulted a particular expert, call him Dr. Day. The government's first expert witness confirmed that Dr. Day was in the courthouse helping with the prosecution. We asked that witness and every other one whether Dr. Day would testify. We asked them all whether Dr. Day was an expert. We were ready for Dr. Day. The government took the bait, and Dr. Day's cross-examination destroyed their case.

# Chapter Thirteen

## *Expert Witness: Hard Subjects—*
## *Choosing and Presenting*
## *Your Expert*

On a recent evening, I hosted a dinner party for some lawyers and a noted trial consultant. We started discussing who jurors are most likely to believe. Without prompting, everybody agreed on a high school science teacher. Not just any teacher, but an exciting and challenging teacher who made the subject come alive and seem important.

Jurors today, like our population today, are better educated than some years ago. While the media's capsulized presentation of events has influenced styles of listening, jurors are still willing to follow a coherent story through to the end. The opening statement can give an overview, but you obviously will not win unless you prove what you claim.

Add to this the recognition that not every juror is paying attention at every moment. Even with twelve, or even six, people all concentrating on the same witness or exhibit, their impressions of what the witness said or the exhibit meant will differ.

These observations define your search for and presentation of the hard subject expert. You do not want simply to explain something, for the explanation itself can be misunderstood. You want to take the event apart and show how it happened. Along the way, you and your expert must concede that the facts and assumptions on which an opinion is based may be challenged—you and the expert claim wisdom, not perfection. Put another way, if you don't concede the imponderable, you weaken the indisputable.

Suppose you had a case involving a construction site accident. A worker has been seriously injured. You claim that the scaffolding was defective. The employer denies that claim and asserts that the worker was behaving improperly on the scaffold, slipped and fell, and missed the safety net underneath because he had been standing in the wrong place.

You can understand this accident in two ways. You could ask engineers and physicists to give you a report on the forces involved, and how they were most likely resolved at that time and place. If you took this approach, you would be more likely to pay for a computer-generated graphic recreation of the event.

The alternative—and in my view, better—approach is to search for people who know how to teach and who have practical skills and insights that they can make accessible to the jurors. So, a high school physics teacher might be the best person to teach about the forces involved. And a high school woodshop teacher with experience in construction might be able to help recreate the "reality" of the workplace. They would surely use visual aids, but these would consist of models and diagrams that the jurors could imagine themselves constructing.

In sum, you are looking for the witnesses who are most credible to jurors, and you are looking for presentation techniques that empower and involve jurors. You are suspicious of witnesses and techniques that distance themselves from the experiences and lives of the people who will be deciding the case.

## THE SEARCH

Although someone who teaches for a living is your best choice, she need not wear the title "teacher." Many people's jobs involve explaining their conclusions to others. Inside a corporation, an actuary draws up numbers about potential changes to a benefit plan, and he must then describe and evaluate the options for management. The management people have no actuarial expertise; the actuary is teaching—about technique and how it leads to given results on the basis of assumed facts. That is what an expert does. Mechanics, engineers, accountants—any of these may be a teacher for your purposes. If your client is a business entity, look to its resources for an expert who really knows the business. One of the most effective experts with whom I have worked was someone who had spent thirty years working in many responsible jobs in the oil industry. He was not an executive in a suit; he was someone who combined engineering training and hands-on experience.

A teacher is accustomed to putting information into a logical order—a story, if you will. A teacher maintains eye contact with the learners and adjusts the presentation to ensure that everybody is keeping up. A teacher learns not to take for granted the learners' prior knowledge and yet manages not to be condescending; a teacher knows where to pitch the information. A teacher knows how to move around in front of the class. A teacher knows how to use mnemonic devices—or demonstrative evidence—to spark interest and help learners remember.

Your expert must also have the right motivation, as seen by the jurors. Someone who teaches for a living is regarded with respect because teaching is a form of public service. If your witness is not a public servant in this way, she should have some other demonstrable commitment to the public good, such as *pro bono* work.

When I interview an expert, I do not ask her to read and prepare a lot about the case. I choose a subject about which the expert and I know something, and start asking questions. I say, "I'm sorry, I don't understand that. Can you explain?" I challenge, "I don't see how that can be. It doesn't make sense." I try to vary the facts, "Well, if it were a sixty-five-year-old man and not a sixty-year-old man, would that make a difference? Why?"

Is the expert maintaining eye contact with me? Is the expert staying cool and unthreatened? Is the expert not condescending to me, despite my best efforts to be worthy of condescension? Are we having a good time talking about something in which I am interested and that she is making interesting?

And, most of all, is the expert really listening to my questions and trying to make sense of them rather than trying to put them in a preformed matrix to produce a canned answer? You want to be sure that the expert will operate on your terms on direct examination. More important, you want the expert to answer the cross-examiner's questions as asked, not as the expert mentally reformulates them.

## DO YOU NEED AN EXPERT?

If you are the proponent of a position that involves scientific or technical material, a testifying expert will usually help you. A good expert presentation is like an extra summation because you and the expert—and your demonstrative evidence—take the most intricate part of the case and make a clear statement about it.

There is a well-known test that illustrates how people perceive or fail to. The examiner puts a sentence on an overhead projector screen and asks people to count the number of times a certain letter appears in the sentence. The responses vary widely. People are far less able to perform that perceptual task than they think they are. Almost everybody will get the right answer if you draw a red circle around each letter you want people to count. Now they are counting red circles. That's easier.

The lesson of this test, which is used by trial consultant Hale Starr, applies strongly to hard subject expertise. You are not concerned only with explaining and teaching. You must make sure that every juror is receiving the message you are trying to send. You do that by the persuasive, "teaching" way you present the expert.

If you are opposing a hard subject position, you face a more complicated choice whether to call an expert to testify. Calling a counterexpert invests your opponent's position with dignity; you are saying that it is troubling enough to require a detailed response. Not calling a counterexpert risks leaving the jury with no alternative except "all or nothing."

To return to a topic introduced in Chapter Eleven, this point is clearest when you consider damages testimony. In Pennzoil v. Texaco, the lawsuit over Texaco's alleged interference with Pennzoil's contract to buy Getty Oil, Pennzoil presented a witness on damages, Thomas Barrow. In *voir dire*, Pennzoil counsel Irv Terrell set the stage for Barrow's appearance:

> Now, the man who will testify about this generally and who is Pennzoil's primary expert is a man who does not work for Pennzoil.
>
> He is a man who Pennzoil believes is a man with great experience, great skill in the oil business. He's an oil man. He's not from Wall Street. His name is Thomas Barrow.
>
> Mr. Barrow, until June of this year, was vice-chairman of Standard Oil Company of Ohio, also known as Sohio. Prior to becoming vice-chairman of Sohio, Mr. Barrow, for years, was the chairman of Kennecott Copper Company, the largest privately owned copper company in the world.
>
> Prior to that time, for about twenty-five years, Mr. Barrow was with Exxon . . . and had spent, I believe five or six years on the board of directors of Exxon, and I'm talking about the parent company, Exxon Corporation.
>
> . . .
>
> Mr. Barrow has studied, made a great study of the Getty reserves. He had some personal knowledge of them before he began this study. He has been made

available to Texaco. They have taken his deposition on two separate occasions.

Mr. Barrow will testify that this measure of Pennzoil's loss of bargain, this replacement cost model is an appropriate way under the circumstances to measure Pennzoil's loss. He will testify to this $7.53 billion number.

There's one other fact I need to tell you about Mr. Barrow. Mr. Barrow is not doing this for money. Mr. Barrow is not paid a cent. Mr. Barrow is not friends with Mr. Liedtke. Mr. Barrow is not friends with Mr. Kerr. He knows who they are. He has no personal relationship with either one of them, and you may judge for yourself why Mr. Barrow is testifying in this case.

All I want to ask you now is, Do any of you know Tom Barrow?

Barrow was as good a witness as the advance publicity promised. He presented a model of lost opportunity that did indeed add up to about $8 billion. The jury agreed.

Texaco's cross-examination of Barrow focused a great deal on Barrow's alleged bias—with little effect. Texaco did not call a damages witness of its own.

The dramatic verdict in *Pennzoil v. Texaco* has quickened the debate over calling experts to battle experts. I do not believe it was essential that Texaco call its own damages expert. However, they then assumed the burden of completely negating Barrow's damages model or of convincing the jury on liability. Having done neither, the jurors had no stopping place short of $8 billion compensatory damages once they made the liability decision.

If you call an opposing damages expert, however, you risk the appearance that you have conceded liability. Your trial lawyer instinct tells you to stay focused on the "main event" and not to be diverted by a sideshow on damages. Faced with this kind of choice, your client will get very nervous. Repeat players in the system, such as corporate clients, will remind you that litigators always get pumped up about the chances of success and then sometimes lose big.

Barrow could have been confronted with several alternative damage theories, all supported by experts and publications in the field, and he would have had to concede these had some validity. He is an honest person.

Here, then, is how I parse the choice. If you can build an alternative model, and dignify it by cross-examining the opposing expert, or if you can show the opponent's theory is baseless, cross-examination alone can do the work. If the expert's conclusions can be attacked on fundamentals such as qualifications or a crazy theory, then an opposing expert will be helpful.

If you call an opposing expert, you must warn the jury in the opening statement, and invoke the "thirteenth stroke" theory. Many lawyers take credit for this metaphor; however, it was used by A. P. Herbert in one of the fictitious judicial opinions that grace his book *Uncommon Law*. The case is *Rex v. Haddock:* the defendant was charged with several offenses for having, on a bet, jumped into the Thames from the Hammersmith Bridge:

> But in addition to these particular answers, all of which in my judgment have substance, the appellant made the general answer that this was a free country and a man can do what he likes if he does nobody any harm. And with that observation the appellant's case takes on an entirely new aspect. If I may use an expression which I have used many times before in this Court, it is like the thirteenth stroke of a crazy clock, which not only is itself discredited but casts a shade of doubt over all previous assertions. For it would be idle to deny that a man capable of that remark would be capable of the grossest forms of licence and disorder. It cannot be too clearly understood that this is *not* a free country, and it will be an evil day for the legal profession when it is.

Your theory: The proponent's expert is not simply wrong; he is wrong in a way that casts doubt on the proponent's entire case. Someone who would make the kinds of claims the proponent's expert made is so reckless and extravagant as not to be believed. Why, even accepting the proponent's own theory, the damages would be at most 5 percent of what the proponent claims. The proponent's expert testimony is therefore like the thirteenth stroke of the clock.

In opening statement, you might say:

"From the time you came in, even in the first questions these other lawyers asked, there has been talk about money—the money they are going to ask you to write down at the end of the case and say we should pay the plaintiff. What is the evidence going to be? We are going to show, with witness after witness and with all these documents that you will have in the jury room, that the plaintiffs don't have a case, that they brought this lawsuit to break a fair deal they had with us. If they don't have a case, then we don't owe them any money.

"You have heard a little bit about an expert witness they are going to call, a Ph.D. economist, Dr. Larsen, who is going to present some figures. Now I will be allowed to cross-examine him. And he is going to admit to you that if the plaintiffs don't prove their case—don't prove to you that Mansfield Oil conspired—then we could not possibly owe the plaintiffs any money.

"After Dr. Larsen has admitted that to all of us, I will cross-examine him some more, because he will have charts and diagrams about barrels of oil and quantities of money. And we will show you that Dr. Larsen's evidence is not reliable and that it suffers from the same basic error as the liability testimony of the other expert, Dr. Winston.

"Dr. Larsen will even tell you that there is a respected economist in this field that Dr. Larsen studied with, Dr. Margaret Oakley. When it comes our turn to put on evidence, we are going to call Dr. Oakley and let her grade

Dr. Larsen's paper for us. We are not doing this to quibble about $10 million versus $50 million. The evidence will show that the right number is *zero*. Dr. Oakley is going to show that the plaintiff's side has no support in any evidence."

You can so confidently predict Dr. Larsen's concessions because you have taken his deposition. When you cross-examine him, make him admit that the jury will decide liability. Sprinkle your questions with the prefatory phrase, "Doctor, even if we assume liability, and even if we assume your basic numbers. . . ."

This approach can work because it can rob the other side of credibility with the jurors. You want the jurors to ask, "If they would exaggerate that much about that issue, what else are they trying to hide?"

Follow through on the metaphor when you call your expert. That expert's conclusions should be grouped into two parts. First, she will tell us what happens even if you accept the other side's theory but use proper data and analysis. Then use a transition: "Doctor, you have told us that these numbers are based on the assumption that the plaintiffs collusion theory makes sense. Does it make sense?" The expert says, "No, it doesn't make any sense." Asked to explain, she can begin by saying that one clue is that the numbers used by the other side's expert are so far-fetched that you have to question the underlying theory.

If the issues of damages and liability are so distinct that you cannot find an expert who can deal with both issues, you will have to settle for putting up a damages analysis and making clear that you do not concede liability. This expedient will seldom be necessary in commercial and antitrust litigation because your liability expert will have enough training to analyze the numbers as well. Given the Federal Rule of Evidence 703 provision that permits an expert to rely on the work of others, "number crunchers" can provide the data on which the combined no liability–no damages expert relies.

If you must present a stand-alone damages expert, you can nonetheless tie the testimony back to liability issues:

Q. Have you made a study of the way that Model 1600 corn shellers are designed?

A. No. That is not my field.

Q. You have read Dr. Winston's [the opposing damages expert's] report?

A. Yes.

Q. Is he an expert on corn sheller design?

A. No, he is an expert on lost income projections, just as I am.

Q. Do you agree or disagree with him?

A. I disagree.

Q. Tell us in a summary way why you disagree.

A. I have two basic reasons. First, he does not make clear the most important thing that an expert needs to emphasize: Calculations of lost income from an event are completely artificial and made up out of thin air, unless and until the jury finds that the plaintiff has proved—not just alleged, but proved— that the design was defective, and that the defect proximately caused the injuries that the expert uses to make the calculations. In this case, there are at least two reasons to question such an assumption. First, there is the design dispute, and second there is the question of other causes of Mr. Olson's injury. . . .

## PRESENTATION

When you present a hard expert, you should be able to validate his methodology without much trouble. The potential problems lie in assumptions made before applying the method. A gas chromatograph indisputably tells you what was in the sample, provided you are operating the machine properly. If the sample is corrupted, the reading is wrong. This could happen in the lab or in the field. If the sample was not gathered from the place and at the time assumed by the expert, the conclusion is irrelevant. The expert who claims too much for the conclusion, or who fails to admit the fallibility of assumptions, dramatically loses face and in the process draws into question even the precise measurements he is presenting.

A further observation. You empower jurors by letting them come to the expert's conclusion along the same path the expert took. To do that, you need demonstrative evidence because most hard expertise is opaque when described in mere words. *MEGO*, the acronym goes: *M*ine *E*yes *G*laze *O*ver. The expert will not recreate the laboratory process in the courtroom, for the reasons discussed in Chapter Six. The demonstrative evidence will be a replica, perhaps a computer or video re-creation.

Once you have introduced the expert and qualified her, begin with the ultimate issue: "Doctor Wilson, this is Government Exhibit 503. It is a check. Here it is on the overhead projector screen. Did Richard Koster sign that check?" She says confidently, "No." "Doctor, I want to ask you first, how you go about coming to that conclusion as an expert. Can you do that?" She says, "Yes," because she knows to answer only the question asked. You continue, "Then, Doctor, can you take us all through the steps you took to prove that Mr. Koster did not sign this particular check?" Again, she says, "Yes."

You return to background information. Document examination expertise lends itself to graphics that show the characteristics of handwriting. One can show what happens when somebody tries to imitate handwriting, how artificial the result appears. It may be relevant to talk about tracing signatures.

Handwriting experts often use a Tasco brand pocket magnifier with a light, where the telltale signs of forgery are obvious or where a particular typewriter leaves obvious signs. I once convinced a judge to stop proceedings and let the jurors use the Tasco magnifier to look at some handwriting, to see how the differences appeared when you magnified them. I had the text magnified on a chart so a juror could know "what you're supposed to see" upon looking through the magnifier. If you had a magnifier and a sample exhibit for each juror, the same exercise would go more quickly. You want the expert up off the witness chair and teaching now, working with charts or a separate copy for each juror.

In this kind of presentation, charts may be far better than more sophisticated images because they are more clearly an extension of the expert's presentation. They are a way to draw jurors into the interaction with your expert. Do not tarry overlong on technique. The judge grows visibly impatient. The jurors know that this is only the preliminary to the main event. They become restive.

The main event: The expert tells us how she found the truth in this case. Begin with candor about the method. "Were you there when that check was signed?" "No," she says. "How can you know that Mr. Koster didn't sign it?"

The expert tells the science of handwriting samples—the particular "knowns" for this exercise. We have already heard about "knowns." We ask again, "Can somebody fake their handwriting when they are being asked to give a 'known' or an 'exemplar'?" The expert is candid about fakery but tells us what was done in this case: She is using the same exemplar used by the other side, and she has also collected handwriting specimens from a period before the litigation, the authenticity of which cannot reasonably be questioned.

Now, we turn to the "questioned" document. If you truly are "questioning" the document, call it that. If not, call it what you claim it is—a check, a deed, a letter—and ask your expert to do so as well.

Again the charts come out, and we see the differences that are decisive. The expert is guiding us toward the conclusion. There should be one exhibit that summarizes the entire story. It should be in the form of a chart or overhead projector transparency. It can be made up of elements of other exhibits, including frames from video or computer evidence. It should be something you can use in summation and, if possible, admissible in evidence.

Put this item up. "Doctor, have you shared with us the essential things that lead you to find that somebody signed Mr. Koster's name to this so-called check?" "Yes," she says. "Does this chart summarize what you find?" "Yes," she says. You ask one more question; she explains briefly. You pass the witness—and probably leave the chart up for your opponent to take down.

This example contains all the elements of any hard witness presentation: Who I am, how I figure things out, and how you and I can figure out what happened in this case.

# Chapter Fourteen

## *Expert Witness: Hard Subjects—Cross-Examination*

In Chapter One, I rejected any rigid distinction between facts and values, and I argued for a holistic view of perception and understanding. It is possible to make rational choices among competing values. Jurors—which is to say people—do it all the time in their daily lives. In the fields of soft expertise, they will do so whether you want them to or not. Therefore, you must empower jurors with the means to make rational choices that support the story your expert is helping to tell.

Now we must apply this insight to cross-examining the hard expert. The knowledge—or expertise—of such an expert is difficult to confound or contradict unless you can have it ruled out under the *Frye* test as lacking scientific validity. More usually, your task will be to empower jurors to reject the expert's *conclusion*, even if they respect him and his field of knowledge.

Preparation is the key. This cliché, though valid, has led many lawyers astray. They have drunk deep at the spring of the expert's science and, besotted with their new-found knowledge, have sung and danced their way through a cross-examination that does one of two wrong things.

Perhaps the cross fails because the lawyer-as-novice-expert cannot keep up with the "real" expert on the stand. The lawyer is—to borrow from Samuel Johnson—like a dog dancing on its hind legs. It is not done well, but the wonder is supposed to be that it is done at all. I have read transcripts of trials in which the lawyer tried to be a greater expert than the witness and failed. Worse yet, I have read and heard lawyers who have advised trying such tactics— without warning of the danger.

Or the lawyer may succeed at all this "no-I-am-not-a-doctor-but-I-play-one-on-television" whizbang and leave the jurors in his dust. The display of erudition has distanced both the lawyer *and* the expert from the jurors, and the two of them have made the cross-examination into a spectator sport. Fans can root for their side, so the lawyer can seem to win in such a match. But this kind of victory can evaporate in the jury room because the lawyer's fans do not come away with solid arguments to convince the other jurors.

True, the second kind of cross can be saved by a solid, picture-oriented closing argument or by having one's own expert analyze the other side's conclusions and set out detailed responses. But such palliatives should be unnecessary.

The issues unique to cross-examining hard experts are relatively few.

### IS IT A SPECIALTY?

Every form of hard expertise becomes judicially accepted at some point through the adversary process. When it does, *stare decisis* controls its use in future cases. Until that point, you must litigate scientific validity under whatever version of the *Frye* test or its antidotes holds sway in your jurisdiction. You litigate the issue through the motion *in limine* and *voir dire* techniques discussed in earlier chapters.

### MAKE THE EXPERT'S
### CONCLUSIONS IRRELEVANT

The fingerprint expert is as reliable an expert as you can find. No two people's fingerprints are alike. Sometimes the expert has only a partial print to work with and must qualify the opinion. I deal with that case later in this chapter, when I discuss making the expert's conclusion doubtful. I am talking now about the full, indubitable fingerprint, with twelve or more points of coincidence to your client's known print. I could as well be talking about a typewriting sample, a tire tread, or a tool mark. You get nowhere by doubting that this expert can reliably match the "unknown" sample to the known exemplar. You can cross-examine that expert only by empowering the jury to reject her factual premise.

For example, an expert testifies that an envelope carries the defendant's fingerprints. The expert received the envelope from the police or the FBI and has treated it with a solution of ninhydrin or some other chemical substance that makes latent fingerprints appear. This is the envelope, let us suppose, in which the letter bomb arrived. Your client will deny sending the bomb, but the defendant's credibility is always impaired by his obvious interest in the outcome. Here is a sample series of questions.

Q. Agent, there is no doubt in the world that Mr. Moss touched that envelope at *some time,* is there?

Q. That envelope is made from ordinary bond paper, isn't it?

Q. How did you learn how to make the fingermarks on a piece of paper like that become visible?

The expert is going to give you an explanation, of some sort, of how she learned. The questions from here on will vary depending on the answers you get. You need the following equipment for this experiment, the list of which can be adapted for cross-examining other kinds of hard experts: sample paper with fingerprints on it, treated and untreated; ninhydrin solution or other latent fingerprint revealer as prescribed by your expert; and some pictures of treated paper showing latent fingerprints.

Q. Agent, here is a book that has been sitting in my house for a few years. Could you spray this with your solution and make fingerprints appear?

Q. In fact, we might see fingerprints that have been on there for years?

Q. Did you do that kind of exercise in your courses?

The agent was probably asked during her course work at the FBI academy to bring a book from her home and do a fingerprint analysis of it as an exercise. You don't have to choose that example. Your own expert may suggest one. You may want to have the agent develop some prints on a sample piece of paper. You might consider using a piece of paper that somebody connected with the government has touched. Maybe when you were in their office one day, you asked to borrow a piece of paper from somebody's memo pad, and you now describe it. The agent admits that if that is the paper you borrowed, some of your opponents' fingerprints could well be on it. It is all right to have an opposing expert perform a simple experiment of this kind because the risk of failure is low, and the consequences of it not working are minimal. In any case, her failure is not truly attributable to you.

Continuing:

Q. Agent, if many people handled this piece of paper, each of them might leave a full or partial fingerprint, right?

Q. And, in the case of partial fingerprints, you often do not get enough in order to be able to say who left that print, right?

Q. You told us you need a certain number of points of identity to make a match, right?

Q. How many was that?

Using the facts of your case, pin down the access to this envelope and how many people would have been able to touch it during the relevant time. If, for example, frame-up is your theory of the case, ask about that possibility.

Q. The fact that there are no two fingerprints alike is pretty well known, isn't it?
Q. Do you read detective fiction?
Q. In paperback novels and on television and in movies, the villain often wears gloves, right?
Q. If I wear rubber gloves when I handle this piece of paper, I am not going to leave a fingerprint, am I?

This type of cross-examination goes back to the basic principle of tangible evidence: An object has no more relevance than that attached to it by a credible testifier with personal knowledge. The expert's conclusion is indisputable but irrelevant if the object she tests has nothing to do with the case.

The fatal bullet may have been fired from that gun; this means nothing unless the evidence places the gun in your client's hands. The trajectory of an entrance and exit wound may cut against a self-defense theory but only if you assume the decedent was standing in a certain way and that the gun was aimed in a certain way; angles are relative, and you get quite a different picture by keeping the angle constant and hypothetically moving the figures around.

There are specialized publications and experts that can help with this kind of alternative crime scene reconstruction. Calculating, and then showing, the angles can become so complicated that you will need a series of charts and diagrams, or a set of model figures, so that the jurors can see exactly how to critique your opponent's expert.

Another example: The deceased indisputably died from lung cancer, but is it because he smoked two packs of cigarettes a day, worked near a toxic substance, or breathed unhealthy air?

This is the classic "So what?" cross-examination. It works. Do not assume, however, that because the expert must be telling the truth about the fingerprint—or the tire track, or whatever—that she is "neutral" on the case as a whole. The expert is an adversary; do not ask a question that assumes otherwise. Be prepared with a "Do you believe in America?" line of questions, as discussed in Chapter Nine, if the expert makes a gratuitous remark.

## MAKE THE EXPERT'S
## CONCLUSION DOUBTFUL

Sometimes the hard expert is compelled to choose among alternative explanations for a result, and there is a fair argument over which alternative is correct. In that case, the expert's conclusion may not be attackable as irrelevant; you must play the probabilities. Remember, whenever possible, take the issue back to something the jurors must decide. Putting learned treatises or the views of other experts into play may be good tactics, but they are secondary lines of defense; these techniques are discussed in Chapter Nine and its Source Notes.

For example, an expert looked at data about the reentry into Earth's atmosphere of a satellite containing radioactive material. He looked at background radiation levels in the area where the satellite returned to earth and concluded that it had disintegrated. He looked at engineering specifications and manufacturing records and concluded that the satellite's core system had been improperly manufactured, so that disintegration was a likely possibility under the stress of reentry and speedy trajectory through the atmosphere.

Every one of his measurements was right. Radiation measurements in the relevant area had shown increases. Manufacturing records had not been properly kept and did not show with certainty that an important manufacturing process was properly performed: the plaintiff would indeed argue persuasively that the absence of a notation in a regularly kept record can be evidence that a certain event did not occur.

This expert's conclusion is an instructive blend. The background radiation issue will require an opposing expert to say that variations are normal and that these variations do not establish that radioactive material from a disintegrating satellite was present. You may impeach with treatises and opposing views. Your purpose is to show that even if the satellite was improperly manufactured, it might not have disintegrated and caused an increase in background radiation levels.

This is a classic issue because the expert is talking about departures from "normal." "Normal" is good cross-examination fodder because it is the middle of a range of data, calculated as mode, median, or mean. The data from which "normal" is calculated can be shown as a curve, the ends of which may show very disparate but nonetheless "normal" phenomena. This observation applies to many kinds of calculated values, including market value. In our hypothetical case, one would find dozens of recorded instances of surges in background radiation not attributable to any external or wrongful cause.

To make the point in another context, consider a market value case. An expert can testify about values but must usually rely on a database that includes values that include divergent numbers. Moreover, value in markets is usually a sum of transactions between willing buyers and willing sellers; immanent within a value calculation are many idiosyncratic personal judgments. An expert must not only acknowledge this but admit that the value a person attaches to an item—as distinct from a perception of market price or exchange value—is a valid determinant of the price at which she will part with it.

In a bank fraud case, the government charged the defendant with conspiring to convert bank funds. The defendant bought majority control of a bank in Waco, Texas. He financed the purchase by borrowing from a large Houston bank, which loaned him the funds at 3 percent interest. As soon as he got control of the Waco bank, the defendant caused the Waco bank to establish a noninterest-bearing demand deposit account in the Houston bank in the exact amount of his loan. At that time, banks did not pay interest on demand deposits.

The government said it was not normal to have so large a demand deposit balance because it was well in excess of the amount necessary to induce the Houston bank to perform correspondent services for the Waco bank. The excess "value" of the demand deposit, over and above the amount necessary to fund correspondent bank services, was said to represent a theft of the Waco bank's assets.

It sounds a bit complicated, and it was. The bottom line is this, for all the nonbankers out there: It was important for the government to prove that the services the Houston bank did for the Waco bank were "worth" $x$ dollars and no more. That is a value question. The government called a Ph.D. from a Federal Reserve Bank.

Unfortunately for the government, the Ph.D. had a colleague who had written an article about valuing services banks perform for customers. The article supported the Ph.D.'s basic point, which was that a "norm" for services pegged them at a certain level. However, the author had also said that banks set their fees for services on a number of bases, all of which were reasonable and permissible as a matter of management's judgment. Here are two keys. First, the Waco bank was well-run, so we could invoke management judgment. Second, a statistical study of banks showed variations of as much as 2,000 percent among banks in the same market area in the pricing of some services, for example, processing checks, handling account inquiries, and so on.

The witness had to agree that these variations were a normal part of competition and that the main thing was that the correspondent relationship be beneficial to both sides, and perceived as such by their managements. I chose a series of services that large banks perform for smaller ones, and as to each one showed the range of charges the larger banks "normally" made. We also talked about the intangible values of a correspondent relationship. All of this was based on having read everything written and spoken by this witness that was available to us. The style of examination was to have the witness acknowledge favorable material in his writings and then see whether he would be drawn out on subjects where he seemed to be helping us. Other parts of the examination dealt with the witness's relative lack of practical experience.

Here are some excerpts from the cross-examination:

Q. Dr. Knight, you are the author, are you not, of a series of three articles on correspondent banking?

A. I am.

. . .

Q. I'm going to show you what's been marked as Defendant's Exhibit 9, Dr. Knight. Are these some computations that you did, sir?

A. Yes.

Q. All right. And these show, do they not, these figures, the various amounts that are charged by banks in your area for performing different services, isn't that right?

A. Yes. Actually, it is a national survey, and it covers all Federal Reserve Districts.

Q. Oh, it does? So it's fair to say, isn't it, sir, that the charges that are listed as for each item that the bank charges for are subject to wide fluctuation?

A. Oh, that is correct.

Q. We've got some fluctuations in here that run into up over 1,000, 2,000 percent, don't we, between the high and the low?

A. I don't think they're quite that large, but they're pretty large.

Q. Don't think they're quite that large. Well, what about this difference between 212.16 and 2,320.4 in that one? Is that about 1,000 percent?

A. Okay, yes.

Q. And I didn't have a chance to read all these numbers, but there's one, anyway?

A. Yes. That's certainly 1,000 percent.

Q. As a matter of fact, sir, in your article on correspondent banking that you wrote you had a little hypothetical about some group of bankers getting together and deciding what their bank should charge for their services, isn't that right?

A. [Nodding.]
[The court:]
You'll have to speak up, sir.

A. Yes, sir.

Q. And the first fellow that talked in your hypothetical said, well, we've got a lot of extra time on our computer, so let's try to get these people in here and we won't charge them very much, isn't that right?

A. That's right.

Q. And then the second fellow that spoke up was another accountant, and he said, well, let's try to recover some of the costs of running our whole operation—

A. That's right.

Q. —or clearing operation,

A. Variable operation.

Q. The third fellow that spoke up, he was the chairman of the board and he said, no, let's charge him for everything including the polish on the front door. Isn't that right?

A. That's correct.

Q. In other words, these figures here, they are kind of arbitrarily chosen, in a sense, aren't they, by the bank that's charging for services, isn't that right?

A. They are arbitrary to a certain extent in that there are a number of different ways to approach this.

. . .

Q. Now . . . on the earnings allowance. That's another thing that banks kind of make up on their own, isn't it?

A. Well, there's wide variation . . . It can vary depending on the particular management philosophy of the bank.

Q. As a matter of fact, the last time you talked to some bankers about this subject out there in California— wasn't it?

A. Yes.

Q. —you said that it ranged from 3 percent up to 8.3 percent, didn't you?

A. That's correct.

Q. All right. And that was true, wasn't it?

A. Very wide range, yes.

Q. Sure. And the Bank of the Southwest, when they chose their figure, . . . do you know how they did it?

A. I don't know how they did it, no.

Q. You never talked to them over there about that?

A. No, not at the time that this—for the time period that this analysis pertains to.

Q. And, as a matter of fact, Doctor, you don't know how they figure their account analysis charges, do you?

A. Today?

Q. Yes.

A. No.

Q. Or as of the time you're talking about?

A. No.

Q. Oh, one more. As a matter of fact, don't bankers expect to make a profit on interbank balances?

A. Yes, of course. That's what they're in the business for.

. . .

Q. And are you aware, sir, that a lot of aspects of the correspondent banking relationship can't be reduced to dollars and cents?

A. Yes.

Q. As a matter of fact, there are many services that a correspondent bank performs for the smaller respondent bank that can't be quantified, isn't that right?

A. Can't be easily quantified, I would agree with that.

Q. And, in point of fact, very few correspondent banks quantify many important services?

A. That's correct.

Q. So those services wouldn't appear on the account analysis, would they?

A. That's correct.

Q. That would include such things as account referrals, isn't that right?

A. Account referrals, loan participations, credit checks. The account analysis consists of standard activity-type services that are readily quantifiable.

Q. Oh, just the ones that are readily quantifiable?

A. In general.

. . .

Q. Now, as a matter of fact, correspondent banks often perform a lot of services for the customers of their respondents that are just designed to keep the customers happy, isn't that so?

A. That's quite true, yes.

Q. You found one case, didn't you, where the correspondent bank went out, negotiated the purchase of an alligator for the customer of the respondent bank? Isn't that right?

A. That's correct. Well, it was an important alligator.

Q. Is that right? Well, we deny the allegations and despise the alligators in here.

The cross-examination of a value witness identifies the elements of his decision and makes him admit that these elements are subject to variation in the "natural" world, defined as "a world uninfluenced by your client's conduct." All the while, the techniques you use help the jury to perform the same calculations themselves.

Returning to our satellite hypothetical, we consider the expert's views on construction of the satellite. You want to establish that this expert's conclusion on the ultimate issue, an improperly made satellite that came apart, is less probable than the contrary conclusion. You cast doubt by showing a sensible alternative hypothesis and empowering the jury to adopt it. You are probably going to help by putting on an expert of your own, but you want more scope for jury argument than the battle of experts with equal qualifications.

In our hypothetical case, a witness who knows the manufacturing process first-hand would be a contradictory expert. In addition, witnesses would testify that they properly built and assembled the satellite. The expert we are cross-examining will say that the satellite could not have been properly built and that the manufacturing processes could not have been properly carried out. He goes on to say that a properly built satellite would not have disintegrated. The precise configuration of this evidence will depend on the legal standard being applied—negligence or strict liability, or some hybrid such as *res ipsa loquitur.*

On these facts, here is one approach to cross-examination:

Q. Doctor, how far was this satellite from where we are sitting right now when it entered the Earth's atmosphere?

A. Well, about 4,000 miles, give or take.

Q. We are in Houston, so that would be about as far as from here to Reykjavik, Iceland?

A. Right.

Q. Now, doctor, if there was an intersection collision in Reykjavik, Iceland, just offhand, who would be the better witness to call if we wanted to know what was going on—somebody who was at the intersection, or somebody who was sitting in Houston?

A. Well, the person in Iceland.

Q. Doctor, this satellite was manufactured in the San Francisco Bay area, in April 1985. What was the closest you ever got to it when it was being made?

A. Well, I am not sure. I never saw it being made, and never visited the factory, if that's what you were asking.

Q. I wasn't asking that. I asked how close you were. Do you remember?

A. Not really.

Q. I'll take your answer—you weren't there when it was being made?

A. Right.

We are not at this stage taking on the expert's conclusion, that an improperly built satellite might endure certain kinds of stresses that would blow it apart. We are instead moving the locus of relevance to the factory, from which witnesses will come to talk about how the actual object was made. We are returning the focus to matters within the jury's ken.

## LIARS AND VERY BADLY MISTAKEN PEOPLE

Once in a while, you run into an expert who is lying for pay, who has faked the results. Or else you may find a good faith expert who has been misled by those who fed him information.

If you suspect fakery, your first task is to seek sufficient discovery to prove it. Next, you are going to need an expert of your own. Do not be afraid to believe your client who says that a certain expert conclusion is impossible. Do not be taken in by the asserted certainty of the expert's judgment. Although faked expert conclusions are not as frequent as celebrated exposés suggest—nor as clients think—they occur often enough to make the search worth doing.

Remember that the scientific method requires that test results be repeatable. That is, no clinical or experimental study is accepted as valid unless its conclusions can be replicated by someone using the same techniques and samples. You can find many experts who will tell you this, particularly in the hard subjects. In soft subjects, conclusions are more impressionistic and intuitive, and may not be verifiable through repetition in the same way. If your expert cannot get the same results as the other side, then there is a risk of fakery.

The risk of fakery increases if the expert has done destructive testing or if the samples have been destroyed for some other reason. It will have been possible in most cases to test without so far destroying the object being tested that another expert is unable to replicate the experiment. And destruction of samples, at least when the expert knows litigation is planned or underway, is fodder for cross-examination and a jury instruction.

Have your expert find for you a set of recognized testing standards for the particular field, as well as some more general material. On cross-examination, use this material to establish either that the expert has departed from standards she agrees with or is unwilling to abide by standards that everybody else agrees with.

The expert whose results are false may be testifying truthfully. The mistake may have arisen from the misconduct of others. A sample may have been doctored, or even substituted. A report on which the testifying expert relies may have been faked. We have all read about this sort of thing, in and out of litigation.

The law gives you weapons against the honest but seriously mistaken expert, but they are notoriously ineffective. The system plays probabilities and establishes authenticity rules based on the chances for error. A chain of custody of a tested sample may be proven by a series of initials and dates, and you will not break the chain without some proof of wrongdoing with which to begin.

In some fields, there are special protections. For example, the electronic surveillance provisions of 18 U.S.C. §§ 2510-20 contain requirements for sealing and custody of original recordings. Violating these requirements may result in suppression of the recordings for use as evidence.

Most reputable laboratories have procedures for handling materials being tested, but, again, compliance with these is usually certified by a series of cryptic entries in a logbook.

You are entitled to cross-examine on the express and implied bias of those in charge of taking samples, making recordings, and doing tests. Without some proof that the bias resulted in them behaving in a certain provable way, the cross-examination will not produce dramatic results. The cross-examination, to be effective, must fit other parts of the story the evidence tells. To cross-examine effectively on bias, first discover. What oral and written directions and information did the expert receive? Was he told the "right" result? Was he impressed with the importance of a particular result? Was there time pressure? Was there a choice of test procedures? Who made the choice? Would a procedure other than that used yield greater reliability or a better chance for an opposing expert to check the results?

I usually begin this kind of cross-examination with a hunt for all the relevant documents and memoranda. In a civil case, I do the hunt in discovery. In a criminal case, discovery and Jencks Act production are usually inadequate; you will have to do the hunt in the early stages of cross-examination.

Take nothing on faith. I recall a case in which the defendant's fingerprint was allegedly on a fragment of wrapper from an exploded stick of dynamite. There could be no question that on that paper was an image of the defendant's fingerprint. The paper was the same color and type used to wrap dynamite. The obvious inference was that the defendant handled the dynamite stick before it was detonated.

We took the expert carefully over his technique for developing the latent fingerprint. He said he developed it with a water solution of a certain chemical. With a little research, we found that the dynamite wrapper for that brand was waxed. He told the jury that the paper he tested was not waxed. Had it been, he would have used an alcohol solution. We then subpoenaed paper samples from the dynamite manufacturer and found a fingerprint expert of our own.

We put together enough evidence to argue that the fingerprint was either faked or that somehow the defendant had come into contact with some unwaxed paper that resembled dynamite wrapper enough to pass inspection.

When you conduct this elaborate an inquiry, you leave a paper trail. If you find nothing wrong, your opponent may be able to claim that even the most diligent investigation has not shaken the expert's conclusions. Initial inquiry, to determine whether a full-scale investigation is warranted, should be done discreetly, by an investigator, and not by formal discovery.

## "NO QUESTIONS"?

There will be a case in which the hard expert testimony is so compelling that you have no answers. Or perhaps you have a factual irrelevancy point, but the expert has put on such a polished show that you don't want to cross-examine at length. You want to wait until your own expert takes the stand.

If you have warned the jury that they are going to hear two sides of the issue from two different experts, you may be able safely to say, "No questions." Or you might ask one question designed to set up your expert's views. If the opposing expert is an experienced testifier and counter-puncher, and you doubt your ability to control her responses, this course will commend itself. The experienced testifier will be waiting for a line of inquiry that permits repeating the direct, perhaps with an extra argumentative spin.

# Chapter Fifteen

## *Closing Thoughts: Dignity—Yours and the Witness's*

In the lore and literature of advocacy, there are many vignettes of bravery and dignity. Lord Brougham defended Queen Caroline in the House of Lords—her peers—against a charge of adultery, and defended his own conduct thus:

> I once before took leave to remind Your Lordships— which was unnecessary, but there are many whom it may be needful to remind—that an advocate by the sacred duty which he owes his client knows, in the discharge of that office, but one person in the world, that client and none other. To save that client by all expedient means, to protect that client at all hazards and all costs to all others, and among others to himself, is the highest and most unquestioned of his duties. And he must not regard the alarm, the suffering, the torment, the destruction which he may bring upon any other. Nay, separating the duties of a patriot from those of an advocate, and casting them if need be to the wind, he must go on reckless of the consequences, if his part it should unhappily be to involve his country in confusion for his client's protection.

There are few cases today that call up so stark an appeal to an advocate's duty. Lawyers in criminal cases come closest on a regular basis, for each criminal trial draws all over again the most important line the state can draw: between its power and the defendant presumed innocent.

Your client is entitled to your undivided loyalty and to your warm zeal in defense of her rights. You, in turn, are entitled zealously to maintain the defense even against the hostility of judges and the contumely of your opponents. The celebrated English advocate Erskine was defending a criminal libel case in 1783. The jurors returned a verdict of "guilty of publishing only," which amounted to their refusal to find the defendant guilty as charged, for they refused to find that the contents bore a libelous interpretation.

Mr. Justice Buller interrogated the jurors, who affirmed that they refused to decide if the pamphlet was a libel or not. Buller became agitated. Erskine insisted that the word "only" be recorded. Buller became angrier still:

Buller: Sir, I will not be interrupted.

Erskine: I stand here as an advocate for a brother citizen, and I desire that the word "only" may be recorded.

Buller: Sit down, sir, or I shall be obliged to proceed in another manner.

Erskine: Your lordship may proceed in what manner you think fit: I know my duty as well as your lordship knows yours. I shall not alter my conduct.

We celebrate the lawyers who stayed on their feet and spoke truth to power. The judges who heckled them are largely forgotten.

From this bit of legal lore comes a lesson for me and you, today, in our trials. Much has been written about "Rambo" litigation tactics and the professed need for civility among advocates. Courts and bar associations have adopted creeds and codes for lawyers to sign and obey.

At the same time, some clients urge their lawyers to adopt the junkyard dog tactics of which they have read— and that they see on television. Lawyers compete with each other for publicity. Some law firms boast of how aggressive they are, and of how obstructionist in discovery and motions battles.

Shielded by the harmless error rule, or by limits on federal *habeas corpus* review, prosecutors seem freer these days to step over the line between hard-hitting advocacy and inflammatory appeal to atavism.

To be a trial lawyer, you should read the speeches and study the lives of great advocates—Erskine, Andrew Hamilton, Darrow. You should carefully study the rules of professional responsibility, paying special attention to those dealing with litigation. Ignore other voices and claims.

You must answer the question the creature asked Alice, "Who are you?" The burden of this closing chapter is to show that the answer to that question moves you toward being an effective advocate. Moreover, from true rules of effective advocacy comes a commitment to dignified, ethical, and professional conduct. From this, I conclude that the dignified advocate who has a sense of self is persuasive. Rambo litigation tactics are impermissible; lawyers should not engage in them because they are wrong; judges should censure them and, by doing so, will motivate more lawyers to eschew them. Altruism and enforcement aside, such tactics harm you and your client.

## AN ANECDOTE ABOUT DIGNITY

A year or so ago, I sat with a plaintiff's lawyer who consistently wins large verdicts. I had successfully represented him on a charge of contempt, and we were musing about lawyers and judges. I had just celebrated my fiftieth birthday, and he was approaching his. In talking of his trial, we noted the number of times that I had been tempted as a lawyer, and he as a witness, to vent anger. We had both resisted the temptation. As a result, I tried the case hard, cross-examined diligently, and argued with conviction. I wanted the trier of fact and the onlookers—and the court of appeals, if it came to that—to know that I was committed to my client's cause and to be confident in that knowledge because I radiated a quiet and unshakable dignity.

I am not saying I reached that goal. But my friend-client and I remarked that as younger lawyers we had a hard time keeping in our seats. We were always up and worrying about something. We objected. We made sidebar remarks. We moved a lot. Maybe we thought it was advancing age that kept us in our seats, but we had both noticed having adopted a similar style. We stay in our chairs. When we get up, it usually takes a while to unfold ourselves and get to our feet. But we don't do that very often; the result is that when we do get up, jurors, the judge, and our opponents know that something important is going to happen.

Dignity has two sides: It ignores petty annoyances, but it does not tolerate unfairness. Dignity knows the most dangerous form of righteousness is self-righteousness. Dignity says, "I know who I am, and I am seeking justice at your hands." Dignity knows there is no snare set by the fiends for the mind of man more dangerous than the illusion that our enemies are also the enemies of God.

## WHO ARE YOU?
## THE JURORS ANSWER

Informed students of trials will tell you that jurors have expectations about lawyers. These expectations are not flattering. Many jurors think criminal defense lawyers are sleazy, although most are willing to believe that they should observe and protect the defendant's legal rights. Jurors think defense lawyers in civil cases are, well, like they usually are: white, male, bland, wearing nice suits, and with a fairly neutral air. Beyond that, some trial consultants say, jurors who watch television expect most "law firm" lawyers to be slimmed down from frequent trips to an expensive health club and tan from frequent vacations or regular trips to the spa. Jurors know plaintiff's lawyers are getting a contingent fee, but they also identify more strongly with plaintiffs than with defendants in most civil litigation. This is especially so if the plaintiff is cast as an underdog against a powerful individual or corporation.

Despite these attitudes, sophisticated testing shows that the great majority of jurors asked to separate wishes from duty can do so—and hold the scales even.

What do these perceptions tell us about our own behavior? They tell me that if I show up and play to a juror stereotype, I forfeit my claim to have the jurors follow me on a voyage to discover the facts and the law of this case, involving as it does a unique claim for justice by a person or entity deserving of respect.

We have all seen how powerful stereotypes influence our response to people telling us things. The particular stereotypes we rely on may vary, but we all have them. With your family members, you are geared up to have a certain attitude to what your spouse, parent, child, worthless brother-in-law, or some other relative tells you—based on a set of perceptions built up over time. Republicans, Democrats, blacks, whites, people who whine—you get set to interpret the message based on the stereotype.

In this book, we have emphasized how to use positive stereotypes, for example, in selecting expert witnesses. For you, as a trial lawyer, it is important to see how you appear to others, so that you can act against type enough to focus on your message rather than yourself.

If your practice takes you to different places, you will perform this study over and over, for juror attitudes differ. My usual informal manner and sort of Southwestern look evoke different reactions in New York, Houston, Denver, and San Francisco. In each community, I need to listen to the radio, watch television, read the newspapers, and hang out in social gathering places to study the kinds of communication styles people use.

When you think about stereotypes, you are dealing with a form of prejudice. You must be brutally candid. If you are a woman, does your manner play into conservative ideas about "shrill, hag-like" conduct or "tearful whining"? Defending a corporation, do you play to type by harrumphing your way through the case in a superior manner?

It used to be easier to gain litigation experience by trying a number of smaller cases, to work toward a dignified and centered image of yourself. Today, you have to get the same training in mock trial courses, by reading about advocates and advocacy, and—when the case budget permits—by working with a good trial consultant.

In this context, Rambo litigation is another form of stereotypical behavior, in which lawyers let their conduct get in the way of their message. Jurors are spectators. Watching lawyers behaving petulantly, hostilely, even viciously, usually turns them off. Usually, the lawyer who answers that sort of conduct with personal dignity and a renewed attention to the facts will prevail.

If you can predict that such tactics will be used, you can begin to address them in the opening statement. You tell the story of the evidence, and then you empower the jurors by telling them that treading the path to truth will require a special commitment and effort.

You act against stereotype by making sure you are telling "*the* story," and not "another one of *those* stories." Your themes must of course be powerful and resonant, but only by weaving them into a unique fabric can you rightly claim the jurors' full attention.

Jurors are more observant than many give them credit for—and both more tolerant and more judgmental than many assume. My friend Joe McLeod, a great trial lawyer who lives in North Carolina, told me a story of a trial he did when he was somewhat younger. His opponent was an older lawyer who was not doing a good job, but Joe thought to curry favor with the jury by complimenting his opponent in summation. After the verdict, a juror—a young woman—came up to him in court as he was packing up to leave.

"Mr. McLeod, can I talk to you?"

"Sure," Joe said. "I always like to hear from members of the jury."

"Well, we thought you did a good job, but there was one thing. Mr. McLeod, that humility stuff is not your bag."

Joe learned from that encounter and proclaims the lesson that jurors know how to spot game-playing, and they resent it.

Trial consultant Hale Starr tells of a test series of mock opening statements done to make a point to lawyers who thought that charm and its associated qualities triumph over trustworthiness. The issue was not framed quite that way, but the lesson that was taught was exactly that. Contrary to all expectations except Starr's, the lawyer who did best was the least flashy. He was prepared, sincere, and no-nonsense. He had the qualities we associate with our favorite teacher in high school—perhaps a teacher of science, which has some technical things that have to be mastered, just as a lawsuit usually does.

## WITNESSES AND DIGNITY

Your witnesses look to you for guidance and strength. You want to insist that they be treated with dignity by your opponent and the judge. I do not think you can protect your witness if you are, figuratively, rolling around on the floor and trading punches with your adversary.

You restrain your adversary by setting an example that the jurors and maybe the judge will enforce by punishing your adversary's downward departures. You maintain your claim on the judge's intervention by yourself meeting certain standards.

Perhaps most important, witnesses who see the lawyer doing things that signal "out of control" are going to get in trouble. They may become fearful and timid, so their point doesn't get across. They may decide to join the fray and become recklessly combative. How, then, will you protect them?

## LEVELS OF FORMALITY—
## SOME CAUTIONARY WORDS

None of this says that you must abandon vigorous advocacy, the vigor of Brougham, Erskine, and Darrow. Trials take place in a context—social, geographical, ideological, personal. Some courtrooms are naturally less formal than others, so dignity means something different.

David Berg, a Houston trial lawyer, once testified about the stylistic differences between state and federal court in Houston, Harris County, Texas. In state court, there is an informal air. You are more likely to see lawyers putting their feet on the tables, and in some courtrooms smoking may be permitted. In federal court, there is a more austere atmosphere.

It would be a mistake, however, to let the informality of the court lure you into informality that belies your commitment to your professionalism and your client. It would be a mistake to let informality become a license for your opponent to adopt Rambo tactics—and a worse mistake for you to follow suit.

In federal court, you have to ask yourself whether the atmosphere is too much a product of the judge's robe fever. If it is, your dignity must emphasize strength—the strength of your presentation and of your message.

### SEVEN DEADLY SINS

"You mustn't let it make you conceited," says a character in Christopher Fry's play *The Lady's Not for Burning*. "Pride is one of the deadly sins."

"It's better to go for the lively ones," intones the hero, Thomas Mendip.

For ease of reference, here are the sins jurors find it hard to forgive:

1. Falsehood to yourself. Don't be what you are not. Learn from others, but do not just imitate their ways. Take

insights, but make them yours. The analogy between trial lawyering and theater can help, but it is only an analogy.

2. Falsehood to the jury. No explanation necessary.

3. Condescension to jurors. Empower the jury.

4. Condescension to people jurors identify with. Don't be a bully, to witnesses, court personnel, or your colleagues.

5. Sharp practice and trickery, to the court and your opponents. Strike hard blows, not foul ones.

6. Wasting jurors' time. Five experts instead of one, heedless, needless repetition—violating the principle of parsimony. They resent your wasting their time, in a society increasingly conscious of time. You also do yourself in by repetition because two presentations of the same issue make it likely that there will be some contradiction, however minor, between the two.

7. Unpreparedness. Inexperience can be excused. Not being a performer can actually help you. But not knowing your case will do you in.

## CONCLUDING WORDS

Studies of our profession, and especially of the litigators, tell us conflicting stories. Many voices have decried the "litigation explosion" and have said there are far too many lawyers filing far too many lawsuits.

When you look at who is filing all this litigation, you find that people without substantial means do not have anything like equal access to justice in the courts. It is probably true that too much litigation is being filed; one study reported that more than half the time, lawyers did not even call up the other side and try to settle the case before filing suit. Most cases settle, and a lot of those could have been settled before filing. Some litigation is filed to create unwarranted costs for the opponent.

It can be demonstrated, however, that except where public assistance, fee-shifting, or the contingent fee work to make lawyers available, ordinary people with ordinary claims are left out.

So, in my view, a lot of the litigation we are seeing is the wrong kind. When we combine that with the fact that much litigation is conducted inefficiently, without attention to goals, we can see an important contradiction. Sure, many young lawyers self-identify as litigators. Almost all of them are involved in what is called litigation. Yet the kinds of litigation they do, and the kinds of tasks they are assigned in that litigation, hardly fulfill their own image of what trials and trial lawyers are about.

The result: Young litigators become cynical, or they go along with skewed views of the litigation process, or they change jobs within the profession, or leave the profession altogether.

I hold a unitary, holistic, view of the profession and the professional. Your commitment to the defense of rights, your view of litigation as storytelling within a certain principled framework, and your insistence on your and your client's and witnesses' dignity are all of a piece.

Surely you will not approach the ideal in every case. I am, however, arrogant enough to say this: If your work situation does not permit you to develop trial strategies that fulfill your professional standards and goals, you may want to look for another job.

If you cannot, in a particular case, develop a story that will appeal to jurors' sense of justice, that case should probably be settled unless your opponent leaves you no choice but to try it. You operate within personal as well as ethical constraints that counsel against going to trial on "smoke and mirrors."

I remember hearing comedian Don Adams aping a lawyer's opening: "Members of the jury, my opponent has told you that he will prove my client is a thief and a liar. That's easy for him to say. He has evidence. Me, I have to rely on guile and trickery."

Of course, great lawyers have prevailed against odds by finding a story where others said there wasn't one. In criminal cases particularly, there is often no choice but to go to trial, treading the honorable path of putting the state to its proof. In criminal cases, there is a tradition of jury independence that makes the story more important even than some narrow and technical view of legal obligation.

If you find your practice is making you litigate case after case in which there is not really a story to be told, that is a signal about you and the profession. Maybe you need to recharge. Maybe you need to practice in a different setting, where cases are chosen by different standards.

The more I read, study, teach, and exercise our profession, the more convinced I am that access to justice by adversary trial of grievances is a basic element of any fair system of governance. I find this faith reinforced as I talk to people who are fashioning and refashioning systems of justice in other countries. If, in a particular country, or among particular people, justice is demonstrably not being done by this means, that is not a criticism of the tools of our profession but of the manner in which they are being used, or the way in which the tools are rationed.

So keep on learning. Don't confuse losing a case here and there with the utter failure of yourself or the bankruptcy of your situation. As Mark Twain reminded us in "Pudd'nhead Wilson's New Calendar":

> We should be careful to get out of an experience only the wisdom that is in it—and stop there; lest we be like the cat that sits down on a hot stove lid. She will never sit down on a hot stove lid again—and that is well; but she will never sit down on a cold one any more.

# Source Notes

These notes are cross-referenced to the page to which the source material relates.

Works cited frequently are presented in abbreviated form, and these abbreviations are:

- THE LITIGATION MANUAL: A PRIMER FOR TRIAL LAWYERS, SECOND EDITION (1989) [LITIGATION MANUAL 2D]. This is a collection of articles that first appeared in the ABA Section of Litigation magazine LITIGATION. It is an invaluable reference on all phases of trial preparation and trial.

- EXPERT WITNESSES (1991) (Faust Rossi, ed.) [EXPERT WITNESSES]. This book was published by the Section of Litigation and contains chapters by many contributors. Professor Rossi's long introductory section ably summarizes the legal principles governing use of expert testimony. The remaining sections offer practical insights into particular kinds of expertise and strategies for preparation and examination of experts.

- STEPHEN SALTZBURG & MICHAEL MARTIN, FEDERAL RULES OF EVIDENCE MANUAL (5th ed. 1990) [EVIDENCE MANUAL]. Michael Martin has joined Professor Saltzburg for the latest edition. This two-volume work presents the text of the Federal Rules along with their legislative history, including the Advisory Committee Notes. The textual material consists mainly of able discussions of case law. I almost invariably reach for this treatise first when beginning research on an evidence issue. Often I will find the case citations I need without having to go further.

- FRANCIS WELLMAN, THE ART OF CROSS-EXAMINATION (Collier, ed. 1962) [WELLMAN]. This classic book contains transcripts of exemplary cross-examinations, some of them classics. The social attitudes of Mr. Wellman, and of some of the lawyers whose work is portrayed, are reactionary, but the book is worth reading. A paperback edition is available.

Although I have modified my ideas on trial advocacy over the years, some major themes have remained constant. In these notes, I refer to some of my prior work, limited almost entirely to articles that are available in law libraries. Those articles and their abbreviated cites are:

- The Lawyer Who Broke the Retaining Wall (under the pen name Edward Michaels), 18 LITIGATION 27 (Fall 1991) [*Retaining Wall*]

- *Cross-Examination of Expert Witnesses*, in EXPERT WITNESSES (1991) (Faust Rossi, ed.) [*Cross of Experts*]

- *The Expert Who Walked Off Angry* (under the pen name Edward Michaels), 17 LITIGATION 27 (Summer 1991) [*Angry Expert*]

- *The Prosecutor Whose Sword Was Taken Away* (under the pen name Edward Michaels), 17 LITIGATION 6 (Winter 1991) [*Prosecutor Sword*]

- *One Man's Freedom, One Man's Faith*, 16 LITIGATION 1 (Spring 1990) [*One Man's Faith*]

- *Voices Heard in Jury Argument: Litigation and the Law School Curriculum*, 9 REV. LITIG. 177 (1990) [*Voices*]

- Book Review, *Federal Habeas Corpus Practice & Procedure*, 90 COLUM. L. REV. 255 (1990) [*Death Penalty Review*]

- *Jury Argument: You, the Facts, and the Law*, 14 LITIGATION 19 (Spring 1988) [*Jury Argument*]

- *The Warrior Bards* (I wrote this play with Kevin McCarthy) (1989) [*Warrior Bards*]

- *The Trial of John Peter Zenger* (1985) (another play) [*Zenger*]

- *Talk-Show Advocacy*, 12 LITIGATION 61 (Fall 1985) [*Talk-Show Advocacy*]

- *The Foreign Sovereign Immunities Act and the Pursued Refugee: Lessons from Letelier v. Chile*, 1982 Mich. Y.B. Int'l Legal Stud. 421 [*Pursued Refugee*].

## PREFACE

xi  **"the great advocates":** The quotation is from *Talk-Show Advocacy* at 62.

xi  **"Mark Twain tells":** The story, *Science vs. Luck*, written in 1870, is in The Complete Short Stories of Mark Twain 64 (C. Neider, ed. 1957).

xii  **"The American jury":** *See Voices.*

xv  **"Expert Witnesses":** The book is cited above.

## ACKNOWLEDGMENTS

xvii  **"Edward Bennett Williams":** A longer tribute to Ed is *One Man's Faith*. Biographies include Evan Thomas, The Man to See (1991). *See also* P. Schwab, *Interview with Edward Bennett Williams*, Litigation Manual 2d 1178.

## CHAPTER ONE

1  **"Hanley counseled":** R. F. Hanley, *Brush Up Your Aristotle*, 12 Litigation 39 (Winter 1986).

1  **"Aristotle . . . Quintilian":** *Rhetoric*, 26 Encyclopaedia Brittanica 803 (15th ed. 1990); *Quintilian*, 9 *id.* 863.

1  **"rhetoric, it is said":** In addition to material cited above, see generally R. Barilli, Rhetoric (G. Menozzi, trans. 1989) (originally published as La Retorica (1983)), a survey from ancient to modern times. Barilli cites many of the leading works and authors.

2  **"drama is a principal means":** *See* G. Thomson, Aeschylus & Athens (2d ed. 1945), a classic study of the didactic role of drama and the reflection in dramatic literature of themes of social change.

3  **"provocative modern literature":** See the material cited below at pages 14–17.

4     **"Zenger":** *Zenger.*

4     **"Juror personal knowledge":** Juror decisions based on personal knowledge rather than on evidence are last reported in the mid-1500s. The question whether jurors were ever "witnesses" in the formal sense is debatable. *Compare* J. F. STEPHEN, 1 A HISTORY OF THE CRIMINAL LAW OF ENGLAND 301–02 (1883) *with* T. F. T. PLUCKNETT, A CONCISE HISTORY OF THE COMMON LAW 126–29 (5th ed. 1956). Surely, the character of village life in England meant that jurors had personal knowledge of the facts, and this knowledge appears to be one basis of the vicinage requirement.

4     **"disqualifying classes of witnesses":** The history of witness disqualification rules is narrated in McCORMICK, EVIDENCE §§ 62–68 (1st ed. 1954). P. Westen, *The Compulsory Process Clause*, 73 MICH. L. REV. 71 (1974), contains useful history. *See also* Washington v. Texas, 388 U.S. 14 (1967) (invalidates Texas accomplice disqualification rule).

5     **"The American Jury":** Harry Kalven & Hans Zeisel, The American Jury (1966). Under a grant from the Ford Foundation, Kalven and Zeisel directed a research project that studied about 3500 criminal jury verdicts. In every instance where the trial judge would have decided the case differently, they asked the judge to give reasons. They were able to build an impressive model to explain why and how jurors and judges see cases differently. For most offenses, jurors tended to be more lenient than judges, because jurors were more open to "human" factors. I have tried to use the insights of the Kalven-Zeisel study in discussing lawyer storytelling, and the testimony of witnesses.

6     **"theoretical works":** *See, e.g.,* W. KOHLER, GESTALT PSYCHOLOGY (1959). Introductory material can be found in *Psychology*, 26 ENCYCLOPAEDIA BRITTANICA 322 (15th ed. 1990), and *Human Perception*, 25 *id.* 474. *See also* BARRY STEVENS, DON'T PUSH THE RIVER (IT FLOWS BY ITSELF) (1970), a highly personal account of Gestalt theory, dealing with both perception and personal empowerment.

7     **"diplomat in exile":** *See Pursued Refugee.* The *Letelier* case was eventually settled with a payment to the survivors in the amount of the judgment.

11 **"exhibit rulings . . . before trial":** Federal Rule of Civil Procedure 16 empowers the trial judge to make evidentiary rulings before trial and requires the parties to file lists of exhibits and witnesses. For practical help with pretrial evidence rulings, see Edna Selan Epstein, *Motions in Limine—A Primer*, LITIGATION MANUAL 2D 685; Stephen A. Saltzburg, *Tactics of the Motion in Limine*, *id.* at 692.

13 **"Cicero":** The argument was *Pro Murena.*

14–17 **"Jack Balkin":** The quoted example is taken from Jack Balkin, *The Rhetoric of Responsibility*, 76 VA. L. REV. 197 (1990). The *Daniels* case is reported at 42 So. 2d 395 (Miss. 1949). Modern legal scholarship on rhetoric focuses on the relative indeterminacy of legal rules. This work can help the trial lawyer understand the process in which we engage. In addition to Balkin's cited work, see *Symposium, Beyond Critique: Law, Culture, and the Politics of Form*, 69 TEX. L. REV. 1595 (1991).

18 **"Facts are mutable":** *Death Penalty Review* at 256. On the notion of a theory of the case, see *Prosecutor Sword.*

22 **"Stevie Smith":** The quoted lines are from her poem "Childe Rolandine," COLLECTED POEMS 331 (J. McGibbon, ed. 1976), about an artist who "went to work as a secretary-typist." Thanks to Professor Carolyn Heilbrun (aka Amanda Cross) for steering me to it.

24–25 **"Brecht":** "A Worker Reads History," SELECTED POEMS 109 (Hays, trans. 1947).

25 **"cultivated ignorance":** The issue of different voices, cultures, and genders has, in my opinion, been most eloquently raised by Professor Mari Matsuda. She does not write about trial lawyering, although the Yale article cited below is an account of a case in which she was counsel. Rather, she understands the need to listen to voices of victims, jurors, and witnesses. The term "victim" can here refer to anyone who feels wronged and seeks redress in the judicial system, for every case is a plea for justice. Indeed, a well-tried case will see a plea for justice from both sides. Professor Matsuda's work includes *Voices of America: Accent, Antidiscrimination and a Jurisprudence for the Last Reconstruction*, 100 YALE L.J. 1329 (1991);

*Public Response to Racist Speech: Considering the Victim's Story*, 87 Mich. L. Rev. 2320 (1989); and *When the First Quail Calls: Multiple Consciousness as Jurisprudential Method*, 11 Women's Rights Law Rep. 7 (1988). I have written on these issues in *Retaining Wall.*

27 **" 'theory of the case' instruction":** United States v. Cullen, 454 F.2d 386, 390 (7th Cir. 1971); United States v. Vole, 435 F.2d 774 (7th Cir. 1971); Strauss v. United States, 376 F.2d 416 (5th Cir. 1967); Pattern Jury Instructions, Criminal Cases 52 (1990 edition), published by West and authored by a committee of the Fifth Circuit District Judges Association.

28 **"Dan O'Connell":** *Warrior Bards.*


CHAPTER TWO

29 **"Why Direct Examination":** *See generally* J. Patrick Hazel, *Direct Examination*, Litigation Manual 2d 506. I have also benefited greatly from Tony Axam & Robert Altman, *The Picture Theory of Trial Advocacy*, 12 Litigation 8 (Winter 1986), and from the insights of Jim McElhaney, Trial Notebook 233–54 (2d ed. 1987). Many of the techniques discussed in this chapter will be useful in taking depositions or in preparing your witnesses for them.

29 **"personal knowledge":** Federal Rule of Evidence 602 requires that you establish, by the witness's testimony or otherwise, that the witness has personal knowledge. The personal knowledge requirement also applies to all statements offered under Rules 801, 803, and 804. 1 Evidence Manual 529–30.

31 **"Preparing the Friendly Witness":** As you prepare witnesses to testify, remember that writings you make or use may be producible to your opponent, in criminal and civil cases. *See generally* 1 Evidence Manual 703–14. In Nobles v. United States, 422 U.S. 225 (1975), the Supreme Court upheld production to the prosecution of defense witness statements taken by an investigator employed by defense counsel. On the facts of that case, there was no work product or lawyer-client privilege issue. The *Nobles* result

is codified in Federal Rule of Criminal Procedure 26.2. Prosecution witness statements are producible under the Jencks Act, 18 U.S.C. § 3500.


## CHAPTER THREE

49    **"vouch for":** The common-law rule is expressly abandoned by Federal Rule of Evidence 607. *See* 1 EVIDENCE MANUAL 566–72.

49    **"agents of your client":** *See* 2 EVIDENCE MANUAL 146–47, 194–211.

60    **"ethical rules":** On joint representation, see generally United States v. Cunningham, 672 F.2d 1064 (2d Cir. 1982) (attorney not disqualified by prior representation in light of minor nature of alleged conflicting representation; as to other attorney, hearing required to determine if he was party to crucial conversation so that he "should be" a witness); United States v. Garcia, 517 F.2d 272 (5th Cir. 1975) (waiver of conflict possible after full hearing); United States v. McKeon, 738 F.2d 26 (2d Cir. 1984) (attorney disqualified because of making statement as agent of client that made it likely attorney should be witness); J. Sutton, *The Testifying Advocate*, 41 TEX. L. REV. 477–85 (1963). On the general issue of the entity's counsel conducting interviews that are then protected by the lawyer-client privilege, see 1 EVIDENCE MANUAL 430–36.

68    **"refresh recollection":** *See generally* M. Freedman, *Counseling the Client: Refreshing Recollection or Prompting Perjury?*, LITIGATION MANUAL 2D 490, and the discussion in EVIDENCE MANUAL of Federal Rules of Evidence 612 (writing used to refresh memory) and 803(5) (past recollection recorded).

72    **"The Journalist":** On the newsgatherer's privilege for sources, see 1 EVIDENCE MANUAL 426, 492–97.


## CHAPTER FOUR

73    **"Difficult Direct":** Do not overlook that some testimony may be so unreliable that it should not be received at all.

Testimony that has been subjected to undue suggestion is excluded on a variety of rationales. On eyewitness testimony, lineups, photo arrays, and kindred issues, see generally W. LaFave & J. Israel, Criminal Procedure §§ 7.1–7.5 (1985). Hypnotically refreshed evidence is dealt with in Judge Alvin B. Rubin's learned opinion in United States v. Valdez, 722 F.2d 1196 (5th Cir. 1984). Threshold competency issues are resolved under Federal Rule of Evidence 601.

74    **"Foreign Language Testimony":** *See* J. Solovy & R. Byman, *Foreign Witnesses—Alien Concepts*, 1992 Fed. Litig. Guide Rep. 35.

79    **"Child Witness":** On the use of leading questions to develop the testimony of a child witness, see 1 Evidence Manual 697. *See also* L. Ring, *Cross-Examining the Sympathetic Witness*, Litigation Manual 2d 608.

85    **"Character Witness":** The evidence law issues are canvased in 1 Evidence Manual 602–29.

## CHAPTER FIVE

90    **"Does the Client Testify?":** My thoughts on transfer of credibility and jurors following the law—including the instruction to make an adverse inference because the defendant does not testify—are set out more fully in *Jury Argument.*

94    **"Preparing the Client":** On the ethical issues involved, see M. Freedman, *Counseling the Client: Refreshing Recollection or Prompting Perjury?*, Litigation Manual 2d 490.

## CHAPTER SIX

109    **"Wigmore reminded":** The quotation is from 3 J. Wigmore, Evidence § 790 (3d ed. 1940). For a more complete treatment of themes in this chapter, I recommend Gregory Joseph, Modern Visual Evidence, published by Law Journal Seminars Press and updated regularly. There are several chapters on demonstrative evidence in Litigation Manual

2D. Deanne Siemer's chapter in EXPERT WITNESSES is entitled *Demonstrative Evidence and Expert Witnesses.*

110   **"Basic Principles":** The evidence law issues on the five principles are set out in EVIDENCE MANUAL in the discussion of each of the cited Federal Rules of Evidence.

112   **"computer-based demonstrative evidence":** On computers and litigation, there are several helpful articles in WINNING WITH COMPUTERS: TRIAL PRACTICE IN THE 21ST CENTURY ( J. Tredennick, ed. 1991), published by the ABA Section of Law Practice Management. *See also* M. Keating, *Computer Evidence*, LITIGATION MANUAL 2D 754.

129   **"Someone, in a forlorn battle":** M. Tigar, *Foreword*, 84 HARV. L. REV. 1, 5–6 (1970).

133   **"examination is a composite":** The transcript, based on several cases in which I was counsel, is taken from my short story *Prosecutor Sword.*

## CHAPTER SEVEN

145   **"hostile witness":** The interrelationship of Federal Rules of Evidence 607, 611(c), and 801(d)(1)(A) is discussed, with good case citations, in 1 EVIDENCE MANUAL 566–68, 592–95, 696–97, from which I learned of the cases and Advisory Committee material mentioned in this chapter.

146   **"Eleventh Circuit has said":** The Eleventh Circuit case is Haney v. Mizell Memorial Hospital, 744 F.2d 1467 (11th Cir. 1984).

146   **"Seventh Circuit law":** The dog case is Ellis v. City of Chicago, 667 F.2d 606 (7th Cir. 1981).

147   **"Jerry Solovy and Robert Byman":** J. Solovy & R. Byman, *The Adverse Witness: Don't Call Me, I'll Call You*, 1990 FED. LITIG. GUIDE REP. 251. *Compare* G. Spence, *Questioning the Adverse Witness*, LITIGATION MANUAL 2D 577.

## CHAPTER EIGHT

155   **"legal engine":** 5 J. WIGMORE, EVIDENCE § 1367, at 32 (Chadbourn rev. 1974).

155 **"Supreme Court":** Leading cases on cross-examination include Coy v. Iowa, 108 S. Ct. 2798 (1988) (screen between defendant and child-witness violated confrontation right); Delaware v. Van Arsdall, 475 U.S. 673 (1986) (constitutional error to forbid inquiry into witness's bias and motive to falsify); Davis v. Alaska, 415 U.S. 308 (1974) (discovery and disclosure of witness's juvenile record for impeachment); Giglio v. United States, 405 U.S. 150 (1972) (disclosure of rewards to government witness). A leading lineup case is Manson v. Braithwaite, 432 U.S. 98 (1977).

157 **"Edward Bennett Williams":** The view I take in this chapter owes much to my mentor, Edward Bennett Williams, a brilliant cross-examiner. Ed was of the "control" school. Terry MacCarthy has caused me to rethink my theory of cross-examination. My tribute to Ed, and the Jacobsen cross-examination excerpt, are in *One Man's Faith*.

158 **"Ten Commandments":** I. Younger, *Cicero on Cross-Examination*, LITIGATION MANUAL 2D 532.

164 **"Irish advocate":** The story is retold in *Warrior Bards.*

166 **"videotapes and audiotapes":** For fuller discussion of tape recorded evidence, see my article *Crime on Camera*, 9 LITIGATION 24 (Fall 1982).

169 **"quarrel openly":** The point about a witness being situationally adverse may be obvious. Dr. Bernard Diamond has explored this issue in the context of expert testimony in his article *The Fallacy of the Impartial Expert*, 3 ARCHIVES CRIM. PSYCHODYNAMICS 221 (1959).


CHAPTER NINE

187 **"recant the prior statements":** The quoted material on cross-examination of informers is from *Prosecutor Sword.*

188 **"Character Witnesses":** The permissible scope of character witness cross-examination is broad. *See* 1 EVIDENCE MANUAL 613–29.

## CHAPTER ELEVEN

205 **"two basic principles":** Sources for this chapter include
EXPERT WITNESSES and materials cited therein, as well as the
chapters on experts by Peter Ostroff, Robert F. Hanley,
Faust Rossi, Pierre Leval, James McElhaney, and John L.
Jeffers in LITIGATION MANUAL 2D. Juror attitudes toward ex-
perts are reported in a superb empirical study, A. Cham-
pagne, D. Shuman, & E. Whitaker, *Expert Witnesses in the
Courts: An Empirical Examination*, 76 JUDICATURE 5 (June–
July 1992).

208 **"Molzof v. United States":** 112 S. Ct. 711 (1992).

209 **"Christophersen v. Allied Signal Corp.":** 939 F.2d 1106
(5th Cir. 1991) (en banc). *Christophersen* is part of a
growing body of federal case law holding that the expansive language of Federal Rule of Evidence 702 is not a
license to invade the jury's function or to pollute the truth-
determining process with pseudo-science. For example, in
a line of cases typified by United States v. Brown, 776 F.2d
397 (2d Cir. 1985), *cert. denied,* 475 U.S. 1141 (1986), the
Second Circuit had upheld use of a police officer "expert"
to talk about the role of the players in a drug deal. *See also*
United States v. Daly, 842 F.2d 1380 (2d Cir.), *cert. denied,*
109 S. Ct. 66 (1988) (FBI agent testimony admissible on
definitions of terms used on tapes and general information
on organized crime; little overlap between this evidence
and allegations of indictment, hence minimal impact on
confrontation rights). However, the warnings in those
cases against overuse of experts went unheeded by prosecutors and trial judges, leading to the reversal in United
States v. Castillo, 924 F.2d 1227 (2d Cir. 1991) (reversing
narcotics conviction because purported expert testimony
not helpful to jury, trespassed on jury's role, and violated
cautionary statements in earlier cases; admission violated
Federal Rule of Evidence 702; if admissible under that rule,
Federal Rule of Evidence 403 would be required) (New-
man, J.). *Castillo* echoed the concerns of other circuits. *See,
e.g.,* United States v. Doe, 903 F.2d 16 (D.C. Cir. 1990)
(police detective called as expert testified that "Jamaicans"

had taken over drug trade in District of Columbia; evidence irrelevant and prejudicial because it tended to connect defendants to unlawful activity based solely on their ancestry and not acts they were proven to have committed). Other cases evidencing the trend include Daubert v. Merrell Dow Pharmaceuticals, Inc., 951 F.2d 1128 (9th Cir. 1991) (unless expert testimony conforms to procedures accepted by recognized authorities in the field, it is inadmissible); Peters v. Five Star Marine Serv., 898 F.2d 448 (5th Cir. 1990) (trial judge did not err in excluding proffered expert testimony of sea captain on dangers of trying to offload cargo in heavy seas; this is not a matter on which expert testimony would be helpful). See also the Second Circuit's rejection of the vouching witness called in Andrews v. Metro N. Commuter R.R., 882 F.2d 705 (2d Cir. 1989). In that case, a "forensic engineer" replayed Erie v. Tompkins and made it come out the other way. He found that the trespasser acted properly and that the train engineer did not. However, as this court held, he did not have proper qualifications, made up his own rules, and did not qualify as an expert. Andrews notes that if a witness is not properly qualified as an expert, the opinions could not be received under Federal Rule of Evidence 701 either; the court evaluated admissibility under that rule as well and found the testimony wanting. Rule 701 is sometimes a fallback position for receipt of opinion evidence. On related issues, the cases are many that reject lay opinion not based on personal knowledge. *See, e.g.,* United States v. Rea, 958 F.2d 1206 (2d Cir. 1992) (error, though harmless, to admit opinion of lay witness that defendant "had to know" that invoices were sent for purpose of evading taxes; such opinion not "helpful" under Federal Rule of Evidence 701); Coca-Cola Co. v. Overland, Inc., 692 F.2d 1250 (9th Cir. 1982) (affidavits of bartenders and waitpersons that they believe customers ordering "Coke" mean "a cola drink" inadmissible under Federal Rule of Evidence 701 as lacking personal knowledge sufficient to form such an opinion); Swajian v. General Motors Corp., 916 F.2d 31 (1st Cir. 1990) (lay opinion on crash improperly admitted; under Federal Rule of Evidence 701, lay opinion must be based on personal knowledge, have a rational connection to the facts on which it is based, and be helpful to understanding the issues); United States v. Calhoun, 544 F.2d 291 (6th Cir. 1976) (error to permit probation officer to give lay opinion that defendant was person shown in bank robbery photographs; officer did not have expertise superior to that of the jury). In criminal cases, there may be confrontation clause issues because the rules give the expert latitude to rely on facts reasonably relied on by like experts, though not admissible in evidence—and therefore, by definition, not subject to cross-examination, let alone to the personal knowledge requirement. In United States v. Ruffin, 575 F.2d 346 (2d Cir. 1978), the court held that although an FBI agent with a J.D. and substantial property law experience was an expert for some purposes, his opinion on certain property title issues was impermissible because it was improperly based on hearsay. *See also* United States v. Calhoun, 544 F.2d 291 (6th Cir. 1976) (defendant could not effectively cross-examine identifying probation officer without revealing damaging and otherwise inadmissible information; cross-examination, the "antidote" to broad admissibility under the Federal Rules of Evidence, could not do its job; exclusion required in any case under Federal Rule of Evidence 403 for this reason). Courts have also excluded expert testimony based on unreliable data, under Rule 403 as well as Rule 703. *See, e.g.*, Advent Systems Ltd. v. Unisys Corp., 925 F.2d 670 (3d Cir. 1991) (plaintiff's damages expert used factual basis not proven to be reliable nor found to be "data experts in the field find reliable"; testimony based on outdated figures, unsupported assumptions, and "wildly optimistic" projections); Shu-Tao Lin v. McDonnell Douglas Corp., 574 F. Supp. 1407 (S.D.N.Y. 1983), *rev'd in part*, 742 F.2d 45 (2d Cir. 1984) (expert testimony rejected where factual basis not adequate to support particular expert conclusions; expert testimony also internally inconsistent). *See* 2 EVI-DENCE MANUAL 79–80 (an expert's opinion must be based only on data reasonably relied on by those in the profession; for example, it would be improper under most circumstances for an expert to rely on selected documents without interviewing their authors, and without distinction as to which authors knew what they were talking about and which did not).

210    **"Higginbotham":** The case is *In re* Air Crash Disaster (Eymard), 795 F.2d 1230 (5th Cir. 1986).

## CHAPTER TWELVE

231    **"The theory of cross-examining":** For convenience, most of the references relevant to this chapter are collected in the notes to Chapter Eleven.

237    **"How Did You Get Here?":** Federal Rule of Evidence 705 provides that the direct examiner need not elicit the underlying facts or data supporting the expert's opinion "unless the court requires otherwise." However, "the expert may in any event be required to disclose the underlying facts or data on cross-examination." 2 EVIDENCE MANUAL 118–19 argues that "may" means "shall," subject to control under Rules 403 and 611(a) (court control over interrogation to prevent waste of time). If an expert may have based a conclusion on unreliable data, the court may order advance disclosure of basis. *Id.* at 119.

251    **"James McNeill Whistler":** This exchange is quoted in WELLMAN at 45.

255    **"The 'Other Expert' Cross":** In Aetna Casualty & Sur. Co. v. Guynes, 713 F.2d 1187 (5th Cir. 1983), the court upheld use of a nontestifying expert's report to impeach a testifying expert, noting that the nontestifying expert could have been called as a rebuttal witness. *See also* Bobb v. Modern Prods., Inc., 648 F.2d 1051 (5th Cir. 1981), and Bryan v. John Bean Div., 566 F.2d 541 (5th Cir. 1978), which find error in using a nontestifying expert's opinion to impeach a testifying expert, but solely on the ground that the impeachment material had not been relied upon by the testifying expert. A few preliminary questions can establish whether the expert you are cross-examining has read the deposition of, or other discovery material by or about, an opposing expert.

## CHAPTER THIRTEEN

259 **"hard subject expert":** For convenience, most of the references relevant to this chapter are collected in the notes to Chapter Eleven.

263 **"Pennzoil v. Texaco":** For insight on the use of exhibits and testimony in the Pennzoil/Texaco litigation, see the book written by juror JAMES SHANNON, TEXACO AND THE $10 BILLION JURY (1988).

## CHAPTER FOURTEEN

271 **"cross-examining the hard expert":** For convenience, most of the references relevant to this chapter are collected in the notes to Chapter Eleven.

284 **"Badly Mistaken People":** United States v. Salerno, 937 F.2d 797 (2d Cir. 1991), *reversed on other grounds*, 112 S. Ct. 2503 (1992), *reversal of convictions reinstated on remand*, ___ F.2d ___ (2d Cir. 1992), holds it error to have cut off cross-examination on and evidence of FBI bias against the defendant; the bias might have resulted in unfair selectivity of overheard conversations being recorded by covert electronic surveillance.

## CHAPTER FIFTEEN

290 **"Buller . . . Erskine":** This exchange is quoted in J. F. STEPHEN, 1 A HISTORY OF THE CRIMINAL LAW OF ENGLAND 331 (1883).

299 **"Pudd'nhead Wilson's New Calendar":** Twain's wisdom was quoted in Snell v. Tunnell, 920 F.2d 673, 675 (10th Cir. 1990).